Cracking the Code

A Divine Intervention

Including:

An introduction to the Wounded Butterflies
– Overcoming Adversity™ program

The Ten Steps to Vibrational Alignment

Michael Smith

First published by Busybird Publishing 2025

Copyright © 2025 Michael Smith

ISBN:
Paperback: 978-1-923216-90-7
Hardcover: 978-1-923216-86-0
Ebook: 978-1-923216-87-7

This work is copyright. Apart from any use permitted under the *Copyright Act 1968*, no part of this publication may be reproduced, stored in a retrieval system or transmitted in any form or by any means, electronic, mechanical, photocopying, recording or otherwise, without the prior written permission of Michael Smith.

The information in this book is based on the author's experiences and opinions. The author and publisher disclaim responsibility for any adverse consequences, which may result from use of the information contained herein. Permission to use any external content has been sought by the author. Any breaches will be rectified in further editions of the book.

Cover Image: Michael Smith

Cover design: Michael Smith

Layout and typesetting: Busybird Publishing

Busybird Publishing
2/118 Para Road
Montmorency, Victoria
Australia 3094
www.busybird.com.au

'Once the divine love is felt that is all that is needed, when the vibration is received, source will set the wheels in motion to accomplish everything that is universally desired.'

– IAM

Contents

Chapter 1
IN THE BEGINNING — 1

Chapter 2
GETTING CONNECTED – EVERYTHING YOU COULD EVER WANT — 19

Chapter 3
A NEW BEGINNING — 37

Chapter 4
SHARING MY CONNECTION — 52

Chapter 5
FEELS LIKE EASE — 78

Chapter 6
CONNECTED SOULS — 95

Chapter 7
QUIETING THE MIND – DISCOVERING MEDITATION — 113

Chapter 8
RECOGNISING THE SIGNS — 136

Chapter 9
WOUNDED BUTTERFLIES – OVERCOMING ADVERSITY™ — 160

Chapter 10
ANOTHER CONNECTED BEING — 188

Chapter 11
A NEW HOPE — 209

Chapter 12
THE TEN STEPS TO VIBRATIONAL ALIGNMENT — 231

This book is dedicated to anyone who is still searching for the light, please know that you are the light.

This book contains instances of child abuse, drug use, self-harm and suicide.

If you feel triggered, please reach out to Lifeline on
13 11 14

Chapter 1

IN THE BEGINNING

We are all energetic beings,

We are a spirit in a body,

Not a body with a spirit,

Our body, our shell, has an expiry date,

But our spirit is infinite, our spirit lives on,

Vibrational Alignment is the complete alignment
of our three universal centres,

Our Body, our Mind and our Spirit,

Once this is achieved, we become true vibrational beings,

We become connected beings,

This is my journey to Vibrational Alignment

As it stands right now, I have been on the verge of dying three times in this life so far.

I make this statement because of my belief that in our moment of transitioning, when your surroundings start to shift and the visual reality of what you consider normal starts to change, you have begun your transcending journey. Once the spiritual beings appear and when your subconsciousness witnesses your entire life being played back to you as if in a movie reel. It is at this moment that you have now begun your transition into the afterlife. Even if there is still some part of you remaining in the physical world.

Many people refer to these experiences as near-death events and, in my life, I have survived three of these such events. As well as several other moments that could have become disastrous – really fast.

I was born in a small hospital at the foothills of the Dandenong Ranges in Victoria, Australia. I was the first child born to a young married couple. As with many children, during my first few years of life, my home was a comfortable place. We had a couple of pets, a cat and a dog, and plenty of social experiences, birthday parties, mother groups and the like.

After a significant event occurred encompassing our young family unit, this pleasant family environment started to change over the following years.

Alcohol became a 'thing' at home, bringing with it all that it does: many arguments, a sharp changing of moods and violence. This then led to terrible events unfolding within my home resulting in traumatic physical and emotional abuse.

In addition to what I endured in my own home, there was also sexual abuse inflicted on me as a child, perpetrated by an individual outside of my immediate family over a number of years.

Walking on eggshells

When my father was at home, particularly if it was a Friday night, Saturday or Sunday and alcohol was around, my mother, brothers and I would carefully attempt to navigate our waking hours so as not to trigger anything that would tip my father into a rage. We knew only too well how uncontrollably violent he could become the more he drank.

At least during the last few years of my childhood while my parents were still together, my father would stay out drinking most weeknights after work. He would often come home in the late hours of the night, long after my brothers and I were already tucked away in bed asleep – or so my parents thought.

When he would eventually arrive home drunk, loud arguments would ensure, more often than not. Following the yelling and screaming would be the violence, the punching of holes in walls and doors. And on many occasions, my father would slip into my bed and sleep to try and hide his late arrival and drunkenness.

The unique scent of his chosen brand of beer is still stained into the deepest memories of my mind, so much so that even today I cannot stand the smell. Considering that in the darkness of night as a young child sleeping in bed, that was all I could smell. At least, when he was drunk and sleeping in my bed, he would hug me to sleep.

On the weekend if he was home and drinking, he and any drinking companion would consume large amounts of beer. Yet, there was a recurring pattern that unfolded every time. After the first few cans, there would be laughter and silly games, then after a few more drinks, the games would become a little more painful. For instance, he would pretend to shake our hands but crunch our knuckles together until we winced with pain. Finally, when more cans were consumed, we would have either Dr Jekyll or Mr Hyde to deal with. Who would we be living with for the next few hours?

Dare we do something to trigger his drunken aggression, like imitate him or someone drinking with him, because then all hell would break loose. One evening, when I was only ten years old, my father was drinking with Ivan. Ivan was the husband of Kathy. They were a couple who were family friends with my parents. Ivan was a big strong Croatian man, an intimidating character to any child, who was well over six foot tall and a seriously heavy drinker. To top it off, when Ivan drank, he swore profusely. While Ivan and my father sat in the living room surrounding the TV, my younger brothers and I sat with them, absorbing their behaviours and their words like little sponges.

As usual, my two younger brothers went off to bed first, leaving me sitting out with my father and Ivan. Not long had passed when I stood up to go to bed, before Ivan turned to me in front of my father and yelled, 'Hey, Michael, *fuck off!*' followed by a gesture of 'up yours' with his middle finger. (What a beautiful message to deliver a ten-year-old child on his way to bed!) In reply, I said to him, 'Hey, Ivan,' and rather than swear or raise my middle finger (which I knew was rude and totally unacceptable), I raised my ring finger. Innocently, I thought that by doing this, I had just joined in on their fun and laughter without doing the wrong thing… but, boy, was I wrong!

Almost immediately my father launched himself up out of his chair, grabbing me and gripping my ring finger, wrenching it backwards profusely. Furious, he dragged me into the bathroom, beset on inflicting a violent punishment. All the while ignoring me as I pleaded with him. 'Please, please I haven't done anything wrong. I didn't use my middle finger, it was my ring finger. Pleeeease…' I cried out in fear.

By this time, my finger had been bent so far backwards that it was in excruciating pain. Even though I was unsure as to what was about to follow, I knew that whatever was coming was going to hurt. The punishment started with soap on my toothbrush that he shoved into my mouth, back and forward, forcefully ensuring the experience was in no way pleasant. Then, I suppose he must have thought a few hits would set me straight. The hits were easier to take by now, since I had learnt to somehow find comfort in pain. If I smiled in my mind, somehow the pain didn't hurt as much. There had been many occasions in the past to learn this technique. My father often said, 'If you don't stop crying, you will get more of this,' and so I had to teach myself a way to not show him that I was upset, since for some reason, my crying and distress enraged him further.

With my pleas for compassion and understanding left unheard, this violent and confusing night eventually finished with me crying myself to sleep, just like many other evenings.

Having someone who is meant to care for you flip into a violent monster would be mentally and emotionally hard for any child to try to comprehend. This ingrained fear of not knowing what might come next affected me for many years, even as a teenager long after he was gone.

At least towards the end of their marriage, when I was eleven years old, he stopped coming home on weekends. With just Mum at home, we knew we were safe. We knew we'd be okay.

Family visits are fun, right?

From the ages of eight to eleven, two to three times a year, my immediate family would visit my father's sister Susan and her teenage children. We would have catch-up barbecues and dinners where the adults would socialise and converse together, while my brothers and I would be wowed into my cousin Daniel's room. Daniel was about seven years older than me, so he had toys that we didn't have yet, like a music player, CDs and other cool stuff.

The first time it happened, I was eight years old. He put his hands down my pants and forced himself onto me, then he forced me to reciprocate and touch him as well. Daniel clearly had his own issues and was using me for his self-gratification. As a child, I was confused and unsure as to what was even happening.

Every tri-annual visit after that first evening, he would force himself onto me, and force me to do things to him. Even on an annual vacation with my extended family, my parents unfortunately agreed to bring him along since they were not aware. A period of relaxing and spending quality time together with my family was quickly ruined as he continued his molesting rampage.

For many years I resented both my parents, and all the other adults who were around at the time who had not connected the dots, or who had no situational awareness to identify what was actually occurring. I regularly questioned, how could they let this happen? Not once but multiple times over three years! In grade three, I wrote a short story titled *The House of Horrors*, mirroring what was happening to me in real life, but no red flags we raised. At least today, I would hope that questions would be asked by the adults around the child if they were handed such a piece of writing. I would also hope that the child would be given the chance to tell the teacher what the book was about and to explain the pictures drawn.

As a child, I didn't know whether or not I was at fault for what had happened. Not willing to take the risk of getting into trouble from my father, which surely meant a beating, I didn't speak up to either of my parents until late in my teenage years. For years I hid my pain and shame out of fear that somehow, I had caused this abuse to happen.

From the moment of my first significant beating at the tender age of five, up until age eleven, I lived in a constant state of fear around my father. Then once I reached grade six, on Father's Day of all days, he decided he would not be returning home. An annual day for families normally filled with celebration, love and laughter was now a reminder to my brothers and me of how little we meant to him – at least that's how we interpreted it as children. In the years after, the annual build-up to Father's Day was a constant trigger of how we felt on that day.

Even on this final day of my parents' relationship, my mother, who was carrying her own emotional baggage, including the feeling of failure for not being able to hold her marriage together, unintentionally gave the power to my father one last time. Giving him the choice to leave – 'Choose your family or your social life' – was the final ultimatum that he was presented. Although she had suffered her own pain and trauma throughout their relationship, she was still prepared to give him another chance, in the hope that he would somehow change. In reality, this relationship should have ended long before. But now finally, the end had arrived, and my father had left.

As the realisation set in that her marriage was over, her tears flowed. On top of this, Mum was also saddened about having to deliver such life-changing news to her young children. This was the news that their father would not be coming home anymore and that he'd chosen his social life over his family. Unintentionally, this teary response by Mum, along with our juvenile interpretation of the situation, planted the seeds of abandonment and worthlessness in our young minds.

By now, the life events that I endured as a child had damaged me, crippling my soul, spirit and mind. By the tender age of eleven, already ingrained within me was the generational physical and emotional abuse suffered from my father, along with the trauma from the sexual abuse inflicted by my cousin. I'd also learnt witnessed behaviours including alcoholism and the art of using violence and fear to control those around you. The mental confusion I suffered was as extreme as the physical damage. Though there was definite love and warmth within my home, it was bundled with significant trauma too.

Deep down, I believe that my father did love and care for my brothers and me, but I believe he was just too damaged, too broken and too unprepared from his own earlier life experiences to be any other parent than what he was.

So, I was eleven when my father left, and my mother was raising three boys on her own. It was around this time that I began to refer to the two of them as the 'yin and yang' of parents. My mum was everything you could ask for in a mother and more – always loving, caring, nurturing – whereas my father for many years was the complete opposite.

It was also around this age that I had my first experience with some real-life angels. Special people who had come into my life. After what I'd endured between the ages of five to eleven, this was a welcomed blessing.

These real-life angels were the parents of my best friend Rick, Sue and Steve. Sue and Steve had no familial connection to me and owed me no favours, but they welcomed me into their family home with open arms and without wanting anything from me. They were beautiful people who to this day and forever will have a special place in my heart.

As I grew into my teen years, I quickly became rebellious. Alongside my low self-esteem was the influence I absorbed by socialising with the older crowd. This came with the introduction to drugs and alcohol, to self-harm, and to girls… there were a lot of girls, a lot of physical relationships. With such a messed-up idea of what love was, I was forever searching. My virginity was lost at age twelve, and I was constantly exploring and searching for some form of physical connection. The older I grew, the less I cared for school and the more I became the bad boy. This included drugs, bandanas, gangs and chaos.

Spiritual awakening

As sure as night follows day, with drugs and alcohol come bad choices. The first particular event, which I would now describe as a spiritual awakening, came when I was seventeen. After living hard, partying every day, burning the candle at both ends, smashing my body and my mind, one night at a house party I experienced a minor heart attack.

After indulging in some of the drugs that I was holding, I began to feel unwell. I decided to make my way to the bathroom since something just did not feel right. By the time I opened the bathroom door, I was coughing, and by the second or third cough, blood was coming out of my mouth. Concerned and distressed, I knelt down on the floor trying to steady myself, where I could feel my heartbeat intensify to a level that I had never experienced before.

I attempted to stand up and get to the living room so an ambulance could be called. I can only describe what happened next by comparing it to the 1990s movie *Ghost* when the evil people die. It was as if the feeling of life had been completely sucked out of the entire space I was in. If there was life in wall paint, then that life vanished. Exacerbating my experience was the fact that my entire surroundings had become extremely dark. Even though the lights were still on, the darkness had arrived. As I stumbled my way to the kitchen area, I quickly noticed that my interpretation of the visual reality that I could see in front of me was playing out in slow motion. Witnessing this interpretation was a surreal life experience.

Immediately, my girlfriend at the time, who was hosting the party, called an ambulance and I was laid down on the floor in the living room while everyone anxiously waited for the paramedics to arrive.

The paramedics entered the house in an inquisitive manner and a relaxed frame of mind. They sat down on the couch and proceeded to talk with me about the events of the evening as I laid on the floor. 'Why don't you tell us what's been going on here tonight?' one of them asked. They seemed more interested in trying to understand whether this was an overly dramatic teenager or something more serious. Confused and alarmed, all I could reply was, 'I think I'm having a heart attack!'

While outstretched on the floor, one of the paramedics held his hand over my chest and as he felt my rapid heartbeat, the entire mood changed. In a flash, the professionals swiftly moved into rescue mode. They connected my body to their heart-monitoring equipment, placed me on a patient trolley and moved me out to the ambulance. Before I knew it, we'd arrived at the local hospital, and I was admitted straight into emergency.

By this stage, the slow-motion effect I was experiencing had dissipated and my visual reality was once again operating at a normal pace. Yet the darkness that had consumed my surroundings was still in effect and instead of seeing the bright lights and white décor of the hospital, my surroundings were still so black. A nurse approached me, attempting to put the drip needle into my vein but repeatedly missed, causing my blood to squirt out everywhere. It was in this moment that I questioned, 'Is this real?' as I was convinced that I was dying or already dead.

As I laid shaking on the bed the alarm for the heart machine went off. About five nurses and a doctor rushed over to me and began working around me. 'Don't worry; this is all normal,' they tried to reassure me. I glanced at the machine measuring my heartbeat and pulse, witnessing that my heart was now racing over 250 beats a minute. This was all happening while my body was convulsing on the bed in some sort of distressed shock. Then I was out. Blackness.

Hours later when I eventually opened my eyes, everything seemed so gentle and calm. The element of life had returned to my surroundings bringing back the brightness and colour. There was no more darkness and fear. As extreme as the experience had been it was finally over. My mother was at the end of my bed with her hand gently rested on my foot and I could tell that she was relieved that I'd returned.

The events of that evening had such a profound effect on me that for the next year and a half, I went 'cold turkey' – no cigarettes, no alcohol and no drugs. That one experience and the journey into the darkness made me alter my life choices… well, at least for a while.

As with life though, sometimes, some things just seem to come back around and with my soul still in chains and my spirit still emotionally battered and bruised, self-medicating became my way of coping again. Things started off as they always do – just one time, just one drink, just one taste – with the make-believe understanding that I had everything under control, I could handle this, I was bulletproof. I would constantly reinforce this message, convincing myself I had control, right up until the usage eventually transitioned into a full-blown addiction.

Over the next years, I served in the defence force and moved in and out of sales jobs. It was also during this time I was lucky once again to meet some more life angels. Special people who came into my life. Four men who each played a significant role in my life as either a close friend, a trusted confidant or a mature guide. They each came into my world at different times, and they all saw something special in me, something worth connecting with. I will forever be grateful for knowing them and I will always cherish their friendships and guidance.

In my early thirties, I managed to beat my addiction for a number of years; at least that's what I thought. This period of my life coincided with me meeting an incredibly special person. We forged a life together, experiencing some wonderfully special memories. The dark period started around my mid-thirties when drugs reared their ugly head again. After a few years of being sober, I fooled myself into believing that I could tempt fate once again and control the beast that is 'Drugs'.

I started by using them as a reward for working hard. At this stage I was running a company, working in a separate partnership and operating a small business as well. I would be clean for months at a time, sometimes four or five, and then I would disappear for three to four days, get a private room somewhere and write myself off completely. In the years that followed, the disappearing frequencies became more regular. The good work I'd done – helping others, donating my time, assisting in creating some very special projects – none of that mattered. I was still a broken soul, suffering with the pain wrapped around my spirit.

It was around this time of my life that I disclosed to one of my closest friends that I thought I would be done at forty. I was convinced that after all that I'd consumed and after all that I had put my body through, including an addiction to amphetamines for many years that cost me hundreds of dollars a day, my body would start packing itself in and break down. This all came to a head in late January 2018, after the ending of my long-term relationship. This day would be the beginning of my second spiritual awakening.

The day in question had begun with me helping my ex-partner move into her new place in the morning. An emotionally challenging event in itself, since this was not the future that I had foreseen for the two of us. After a challenging morning, I eventually made my way to my brother Seamus's home, where I spent that afternoon and evening with him and his three sons. This was such a magical experience; everything was perfect. During the evening, we all went out together to a local house party not far from his place and at the end of the night, we returned to his home where I stayed with him and my three nephews.

The following day after, we enjoyed breakfast together. I made my way home, where I found myself alone in my house for the first time in nine years.

Like a perfect storm, all my meetings for the coming Monday had either deferred or rescheduled until later in the week. So, I now had an open Monday – or, thinking as a functioning addict does, a clear thirty-six hours to artificially feel better. In my depressed state of mind, a window of opportunity had opened and as fate would have it, I made a conscious decision to get some drugs. This would make me feel better, I convinced myself. 'It's been ages,' I said. Plus, I reassured myself, I would only have a little bit… just a little taste.

As it would be, that fateful choice led to a chain of events and by Tuesday morning, I found myself in an extremely fragile position where my mental health had been pushed to its limits. Feeling fragile, alone and depressed, I was suffocating with an immense feeling of worthlessness. I tried to push through the fear that I was feeling and made a phone call for help at six am. During this call, I misinterpreted the response to my request for help and what was being said to me. Whichever way the person meant for their words to come across, I heard it as a laugh and a comment, that to me reinforced my worthlessness.

That misinterpretation of words sadly triggered something inside me that set the wheels in motion. Amplifying the belief that if I was such a joke and so worthless, then I might as well just end my life. If all I have done means nothing, then I may as well just go. Steadfast to the idea that it was my time to leave, I proceeded to try to take my life with a large pair of scissors.

I won't share with you the gory details of how I did this, but this was a gruesome experience and a bloody mess. Realising I was close to death, as I lay on the ground reside to the fact that I was slowly dying, I knew that I needed to write a note or a letter of some description. I needed people to know that I was thinking of them and that I loved them if I were to leave.

With my body running out of life, my finger my only pen and my blood the only ink, I began to scrawl a 'love' letter.

'I love you Wa, Mum, Jose, Seamus, Mat, Kristie, Jake, Sean, Joel, Dad, Jackie, Frank, Cathy…' I wrote as many names as I could remember. I wanted everyone to know that if they never saw me again, I was thinking of them all as I was leaving this life.

Unlike my previous near-death experience, though, this time was different. This time the light was bright, and there were two special little beings sitting on the fence with their heads in their hands just watching me and waiting. Each time I looked in the reflection of my window, I could see these two beings shining back at me. Yet when I looked directly at the fence as I sat in my garden bleeding out, they disappeared.

Not wanting them to witness the horror of what I was doing to myself, I continued to move around my backyard in an attempt to get out of their view and remove myself from their line of sight.

At the time, I did not know who or what they were. After sharing this experience later, it was highlighted by someone close to me as to who they might have been.

This is what they looked like.

The damage to my body was extensive. My forearms were opened, I had stabbed myself deep into my chest twice, my throat had been sliced open, I had stabbed the scissors through my throat, and I had sustained a significant abdominal wound.

By the time I was found, I was slumped down against a wall with the scissors handles still protruding from my throat. The scissor blades had touched my spine, shorting out my nervous system and temporarily paralysing me. The only active responses I was able to offer were blinking and breathing.

Yet my mind was still completely active, and my vision was fine. It was around this time that I actually felt like I might survive. The two little angels had departed, and the emergency services had now arrived. My wounds, though, had been exposed extensively to the elements and I'd sustained significant blood loss too. As adults, we have between five to six litres of blood in our bodies at any one time. I had lost four and a half of those. My body was just hanging on.

I was rushed to hospital as a critical emergency. One of the paramedics in the ambulance radioed ahead to the hospital, 'Get everything ready, we have a live one here!' On the hospital bed, camera flashes were going off all around me as they photographed my extensive injuries. There was a lot of commotion as these special people rushed to try to save my life. I received a blood transfusion and a large amount of antibiotics to try to kill off any infection.

Drifting in and out of consciousness, I was transported into the MRI room. Lying strapped to the patient tray, the machine started spinning when I noticed myself beginning to rise upwards. As I rose closer and closer to the internal edge of the MRI machine, I could see tiny words printed on the inside of the spinning surface. These words were a catalogue of every sentence and word that I'd ever spoken, typed or texted. Listed in front of me were all the conversations and interactions that I'd ever partaken in and experienced, a complete library of communications from my life. This was truly an end-of-life experience. Overcome with amazement as to what I was witnessing, the light went out in me.

After the surgery was completed, the doctors and medical staff informed my family that they had done all they could, but they could not guarantee that I would survive. My wounds were so severe, and because they had been exposed to the natural elements for a significant amount of time, the risk of infection was drastically increased. The doctors advised them to prepare themselves and to be ready to say their goodbyes.

As I was transported out of the operation room, I was in and out of consciousness. At some stage, I was wheeled past my extended family where I managed to open my eyes for them. Seeing my eyes open, they all verbally encouraged me to pull through. I would spend the next twelve weeks in hospital, where I learned to use my left hand again. I did my rehabilitation exercises in my hospital bed. Unbelievably, the paralysation had been short-term, and the scissors had missed all my vital organs and parts.

Although I would be physically altered now for the rest of my life.

It was in hospital that I received my first message of inspiration after my end-of-life experience. Whilst laid up in my bed, a gentleman was moved into the space next to me. We started talking with each other and he shared with me about his condition. He had been diagnosed with brain cancer a few years back and at the time, the doctors had given him around six months to live. Yet, miraculously, the surgeons had been able to successfully remove his cancer, gifting him a year and a half more than what they'd predicted. But now, the cancer had returned and he was back in hospital once again for more surgery on his brain. He shared that, for him, he was undertaking this operation with the hope of extending his life, even if this was only going to be for one more year.

As he spoke, his words flicked a switch in my mind. The message was loud and clear. 'Come on, Michael! Here is a guy who is trying everything to get an extra year of life, any extra time he can have and here you are with a fit, healthy body and brain, and you were trying to leave this earth? What for? You need to focus on getting better and start living the life that you were meant to!'

Receiving this first message by no means meant that my recovery journey was complete. This was only the beginning. Nevertheless, this was the first of many signs that I received to push forward, heal, recover and prosper.

After my stay in hospital was complete, I was transported home to begin my long haul down the road to recovery. This would not just be physical healing, as mental and spiritual healing would also be required since I knew I now had to finally deal with and overcome some significant mental demons too.

Just trying to understand what had happened that day was a huge challenge to work through. Questions such as how did those thoughts even come into my brain? How did those thoughts transpire into the actions that I inflected onto myself? Along with the reality of needing to accept what was now the new me.

There were many teary emotional nights and other nights where I just could not speak. Numb, I could not even gather a thought as to why, what or how this had all unfolded. For the next six months, my recovery at home was hard. My mind remained stunned for a significant amount of time as I tried to process what had occurred.

On top of this mental battle, I had multiple tubes protruding from underneath my clothing, attached to the medical paraphernalia my body needed while healing. Most days I managed to put a mask on to disguise what was happening underneath, so much so that those around me, unless part of my inner circle, were none the wiser and had no idea that anything had happened to me at all.

But it was in the quietness of the evenings and during the stillness of night that I found I was most susceptible to the sadness. Since there were no pleasant distractions to take my focus.

During this period of time, I must have been so hard to be around, just an emotional wreck. Not feeling sorry for myself but just emotionally sad at how the events had unfolded and the aftermath of it all.

I did have some support, though: a beautiful woman, who helped me with my day-to-day tasks as I tried to operate under the guise of 'business as usual'. After about six months, that help had to come to an end. The special person who'd been helping me had her own life to get on with, and in the days before she decided to leave, I was finally starting to feel human once again. My mind was no longer numb, and my creativity juices were starting to flow once again.

The night that she announced to me she was leaving, I cannot say that I didn't fall apart, because I did. After the events of 2018, I was physically changed and once again, she was leaving. How would I survive? Who would accept me for who I was now?

Although this time, while I was alone, I did things differently. Instead of inflicting more damage on to myself, I had to try to learn to become comfortable with the new me. I had to discover how to control my thoughts and regain control of my overall life experience. I took comfort in filling my eyes and ears with laughter and comedy in an attempt to try to lift my spirits when they'd fallen down. But it was on the first weekend alone in my home that the consequences of my choices and the gravity of my actions really sunk in.

Previously in the months before, there would have been noise and movement in my home on a relaxing Sunday morning, but this time it was just me and the silence. An overwhelming sense of sadness entered my body. The reality of my situation was kicking in, but to my surprise, the universe threw me a bone. I received a random phone call out of the blue from someone whom I did not regularly talk with and it completely broke my train of thought. This was my first such introduction to a 'circuit breaker', a powerful tool that would play a very important role in controlling negative thoughts.

Once my phone call ended, I headed to the shower. As I stood under the water, sure enough the sadness began trying to creep back in. Yet it was in this moment that I received another powerful message loud and clear:

Controlling negative thoughts

The words I received were this: 'You can let this feeling of sadness overwhelm and control you emotionally for the next two years, or for the next year, or for the next six months, or the next two weeks or for the next few days – or you can park this today! Not to forget about what it is but to put it to the side and focus on controlling the only thing that you can control, and that is how you choose to feel, and you can choose to feel good!'

This was an extremely powerful message.

Instantly from that moment forward, I agreed to let go of the uncontrollable negative emotion that was influencing how I was feeling. I was now beginning to take back control. I was back in the driver's seat, trying to not allow the circumstances of life to completely dictate how I felt.

A new level of awareness was developing inside me, and these powerful messages were now providing me with new tools to use as I continued to grow.

Reflecting on the choice that my support person made to leave, I think that it was in fact the best choice that she could have made for both her and myself. Her choice helped me to get better faster. I was forced to do all the basic tasks around my home. I was forced to get up and keep on going, since I only had myself to rely on. My family had offered to help but I did not want to burden them, nor did I want this from them. I had to heal myself. I had to get back to being the person that I was always meant to be.

Over the next twelve months, I started to become more comfortable with my new self. I started to be okay with the new me. I was learning to accept without regret everything that had occurred. Though, from a spiritual perspective, unbeknown to me, I was still broken inside. Tangled with the trauma of my past, my soul was still metaphorically chained, and I now had the physical scars on my body as a consistent reminder of what had unfolded. Also, none of my emotional baggage had been dealt with yet, but this would soon change.

I am not like you – still broken on the inside.

As part of the alterations to the physical make-up of my body, there were now some ongoing changes to life that I had to become accustomed to. Those changes and challenges were often hard to deal with and accept, and like many addicts or people who have battled with mental health, self-medicating seemed like the only way in which I thought I could get through the day. I guess on the surface, apart from the visible scars, I may have looked fine, but beneath the surface, I was still tangled.

Late in the following year, I once again found comfort in self-medicating. It was not like I was trying to repeat the earlier events from 2018, but my after-hours activities were not healthy. Once again, I had begun to poison my body in an attempt to forget about my past.

This time around it was cocaine, copious amounts of cocaine. Two, three, four grams a day. Yet, unlike other cocaine addicts who destroy their nostrils, I was using it intravenously. Sending the chemical straight into my bloodstream. Blowing my mind away.

The consequences of my actions once again came to a head in early 2020 when on a particular evening in late February, I'd taken my body to the end of the line. After administering a hit, I collapsed in my home, smashing my head as I fell to the ground. Helplessly laying on the ground as my heartbeat slowed, my breathing became laboured, slow and succinct. After a little while, when I felt that my breathing had returned to somewhat normal and my heart rate increased, I picked myself up off the floor and made my way through my house to another room. Lost in the moment, I collapsed once again.

This time as I dropped to the floor, my breaths became spasmodic, and my heartbeat was slowing down to almost a complete stop. *Doooooooom, dooooooooom* was the elongated sound coming from my chest. I knew at this point I was on the way out. With my arms spread out beside me, I suddenly heard two voices talking with each other. I couldn't see them, just their eyes but I heard one say, 'This is it!' To which the other replied, 'No, no! We like him too much.'

Then after hearing those words, I can only describe what happened next like being hit with a heavenly defibrillator. Two huge bursts of energy hit me right in my chest, *BOOM, BOOM!* Lifting my chest off the ground with each blast. This was like nothing I'd ever felt before. Lying on my back with my arms outstretched to the side, I was filled with this electric energy, like a lightning bolt hitting a tree or a car battery being jump-started.

After some time had passed, I regained my strength and managed to make my way to my bedroom where I would finally fall asleep.

Over the coming months, my life started to unfold and eventually bought me forward to where I am today.

This is my story.

---

* I am forever grateful for the love, support and care that I received on that day in 2018 and during my time in hospital from everyone involved. I know that there is a special place in heaven for all of those who dedicated their life's work to helping other people, when help is needed. I believe their offering of help does not go unnoticed.

Chapter 2

GETTING CONNECTED – EVERYTHING YOU COULD EVER WANT

Tuning in my antenna

So now here we are! Welcome to the real-life story of my transformational journey to Vibrational Alignment. A journey that unfolded after I freed my spirit and unchained my soul. Uncovering my relationship with all that is, bonding with the energy of the universe, the energy that creates worlds.

In this book, I am going to share a lot of information with you. This will include my unique journey to date, the individual steps that were revealed to me and the outcome of walking this path, along with the unlocking of my spiritual door, the universal realisations that continue to evolve, the manifestations that became reality and the many experiences that were documented as they unfolded.

The first thing to consider and appreciate is, as physical beings, we are a spirit with a body, not a body with a spirit. This means that our spirit is our controlling entity, the main life force within us. Our human body or shell, if you will, has a time limit for its existence; however, our energetic spirit's life is infinite.

What do I mean by this? Well, I believe when our individual life experience comes to an end and we have reached our final day, our spirit, our internal life force, leaves our body and transcends into the next stage of our existence. From here, we all return to our original spirit form as we reunite with the universal oneness. Death is not the end; it is just the beginning of the next phase.

As an energetic being having a physical life experience, we all have the potential to live as vibrational beings if we desire. As a vibrational being, your body can communicate with you in ways that not many have experienced. People may have felt this vibrational connection during specific moments in their lives, but not in a manner that allows for interpretation or guidance. Yet we can all achieve this consistent level of connection if we wish.

Consider this as I try to explain the concept of vibration. Scientific research shows our physical body is made of up to sixty per cent water, our brain and heart are composed of seventy-three per cent water and our lungs are about eighty-three per cent water. Our skin contains sixty-four per cent water, our muscles and kidneys are seventy-nine per cent, even our bones are thirty-one per cent water.

Water is a vibrational element.

When you drop a stone in a puddle, you see the rippling effect occur as the water vibrates.

The same effect will occur when your three universal centres – your body, mind and spirit – are in a moment of pure alignment, your body will vibrate much like the water. You will feel like you have been connected to the stream of pure positive energy. This positive energy is received as a euphoric feeling, which carries the energetic sensation throughout your entire body. Your skin cells become alive; they become amplified. Your vision sharpens; lights become brighter. Your mind becomes clear, and any feelings of pain disappear.

The vibrational effect felt throughout your entire body can even feel like you have been touched by a much higher power, a force that we cannot see but we can feel. As I have experienced many times now, you are able to feel the energy as it enters your body, turning your body's receptors on so they become vibrationally alive. This experience is like nothing I've ever naturally felt before.

I believe we exist in this vibrational universe as vibrational beings, in which we are all connected. We are all interlinked with our earth in a physical, spiritual and energetic relationship whether we choose to believe this or not. This goes for all the living forms of life on our planet and in our universe. Everything plays a role in the evolution and growth of existence.

Once you reach this state of alignment, where you are able to feel your own physical connection to the energy of our universe, you will be able to utilise your vibrational guidance regularly.

A significant benefit for you as a connected being is that you now have your very own support team. You have accessed your very own divine guidance crew, aligning you with your highest self as well as re-establishing your direct connection with our Creator, reconnecting yourself with our Highest Entity. Your celestial support team has nothing but love for you and always has your best interests at heart. It is a divine force that you can always count on whenever you need.

This force is something that has always been a part of you but exists at a much higher level outside the boundaries of the physical world in which we currently reside. It is a realm where existence is maintained through a state of pure love. As physical beings, we normally connect with this part of existence through our subconscious dreams, mediation or during our creative and inspirational moments in life. Conversely, once you reach true alignment, you now have re-established your consciousnesses awareness of the existence of this spiritual realm. You now have a direct line of communication, with vibration being the tool for communicating. This is the purest state of existence.

Your support team of connectedness has always been there for you but often, this is something that we must rediscover along our way. Connecting or reconnecting with your team ignites a transformational response. Newborn babies know of this connection since they are naturally connected as they enter the physical world.

Yet it seems that as we develop, grow and mature during our lives, our learnt and developed behaviours and beliefs, passed down to us via generational and social influences, seem to drown out our spiritual support team. There is an extensive group of energetic beings gathered in your team, waiting for you to rediscover your connection with the vibrational universe, existing in the realm where our Creator resides, ready to transform your physical life experience. All we need to do is allow ourselves the opportunity to reconnect with them, not fear them. If we re-establish this individual connection on a vibrational level, we can gain the maximum benefit of their powers during our physical earth life.

As a connected vibrational being, you'll be able to use your connection as:

- a guide to positive intentions and outcomes
- a confirmation of powerful conversations and special connections with other living beings
- a guide through the maze of life when you need some help and direction
- a universal healer for your body, with the ability to remove your pain and anguish
- a divine energy boost, able to fill your body with a pleasurable euphoric sensation whenever you desire without a cost, without consequence, with no hangover or comedown.

From the writing of my documented journey, you will be able to understand the steps through which this evolution takes place, including the letting go that frees us of our past.

I will share with you the tools I discovered, so you too can use these to achieve this level of connection for yourself.

This connection is as much a physical connection as it is a spiritual one, reaffirmed with the energetic vibrations that become visible for all to see. Our body is like one of those big giant transmission towers and when we are tuned in, connected and receiving our signals, our entire body vibrates. These vibrations are felt all over the body, down the arms and legs, up your neck, as your skin becomes alive.

When the energetic signal is received, the physical effects are represented by what you may describe as goosebumps, but this is much more than a shiver. What I learnt as part of my experience was that the physical change to my skin was one part; the second part is the internal clarity and conscious awareness that is uncovered while the euphoric energy is pulsating throughout my body, and into my brain.

This feeling will elevate you, lifting your consciousness to such a high level of connection, one that you most likely have never experienced or felt before or even knew existed. A place where physical pain is no longer felt. Where the mind fills with complete clarity and knowing, yet seemingly remains so quiet and peaceful at the same time, a sensation of pure warmth and bliss – this experience is something to behold. It is pure positive energy transmitting through your body.

You can pull this energy down onto you like your own protective armour. This is your protector, your spirit guide and your connection to the divine.

I consider this feeling of vibration as something that we can all achieve. I know that this spiritual relationship is something that no artificial substance can match. You don't need to pop a pill, drink alcohol, snort or jab a vein to experience this.

Setting the scene

One of the first pieces of divine wisdom I received on this path was that we are a spirit in a body, not a body with a spirit. Our spirit lands in our foetus on the day we are conceived. Such an amazing life-creating moment, where divine energy, including our unique soul, enters what will become our new body (shell).

I believe that the embryo is born with a clean slate since the lessons of the past life have already been set out to overcome. For example, if you have failed in the last life, and it has been decided that you are to return as something new to relearn lessons, you are given every chance to succeed in your new form. I feel that there is no preconceived idea of pain, no existing memory of trauma or hurt. Plus, I think the unborn foetus is pure of heart. I have come to an understanding that along with the physical connection to both parents through the intertwining of their atoms, enzymes and molecules as part of the creation of life, there is an additional connection.

A divine linkage constructed by the forever-flowing stream of celestial energy between spirit and Source. The eternal relationship between the foetus's spirit and the Highest Power, the Creator of All, the Holy One. Because the spirit in this instance has only recently transcended from the realm in which all of creation resides, the celestial connection is still so pure in love and power, just completely raw energy.

The matter's structure is the purest form available, an ultrafast-flowing lightning bolt that is very much alive and coupled with the source of all creation. This intertwined connection with the Highest Power ensures the baby receives all the divine love and positive energy that's required whilst in the womb before the unborn baby arrives in this physical world.

When the baby is born, like most newborns on this earth, they are born into their family. We hope that all newborn babies are born into an environment with loving family members who will nurture and guide their newborn through the journey of childhood, protecting their child from any negative outside influences that could harm or stifle the child's development and growth. As well as protecting the child from circumstances that could traumatise the young child's heart and soul. We hope that they will, in fact, encourage their child's development and most importantly love their child unconditionally.

Unfortunately, humanity has come to know that this is not always the case. We know that for a significant number of children around our world, either from the time they are born or during their developmental years, there are some individuals who, for their own reasons, choose to damage either their own children or someone else's.

Discovering the Cycle of Repetition

Sometimes this inflected damage is unintentional but unfortunately, it would seem for others this damage is deliberate. Something that I began to question was no matter how unintentional or intentional these actions were, could it be possible that these were just the result of repeated behaviours? Is it possible that the offending person themselves are just damaged broken souls?

Was there also a real possibility that many of these embedded patterns of behaviours had been passed down generationally, almost as a rite of passage or to set the expectation that life had to be hard which created the formation of a cycle?

I gave this cycle a name: the Cycle of Repetition. This title would include the cycle of repeated mistakes, repeated abuse, repeated damage, negative beliefs and repeated bad traits.

As I began to explore this possibility, I uncovered what I believed to be one of the fundamental challenges that's been set out for us as part of our journey. That is to break this Cycle of Repetition.

If we all began to focus on identifying and breaking the Cycle of Repetition, we could potentially give the next generation the freedom and the ability to develop without the negative behaviours and debilitating trauma that the generations before had to endure.

We need to expand our awareness so that we can identify and stop passing down these cycles of repeated behaviours, nullifying these inherited mistakes, abuse, negative beliefs and behaviours so we can gift the next generation the best chance to develop as spiritually and emotionally connected beings. Giving them the chance to create their own beliefs, make their own mistakes and not have to overcome the repeated ones from generations before.

As part of my journey to uncover this Cycle of Repetition, during the previous years of my life, I had started to compile a list of dot points. These dot points consisted of all the individual 'Moments in Time' and significant life events from as far back as I could remember, right back to the beginning of my life. My list included all the memories that I was able to recall, both positive and negative.

Unintentionally, this list was simply going to be used to write a story. Unbeknown to me, the list that I had compiled would later become the foundation for my awakening journey, playing a significant role in my pathway to alignment. This list offered me the ability to peel back the historical layers, untangling the experiences of the past so that my soul could be set free. This untangling would reignite the dormant divine connection that had been nullified by the distractions of life, allowing the powerful connection to return to its original form, just as it was when I was the unborn baby.

Freeing my soul – looking from the outside in

As confusion, fear and panic were raining down on the globe during the coronavirus pandemic of 2020, the state of Victoria in Australia faced two extensive lockdowns, the first in early March. I, like many other Australians, considered myself very fortunate to be living in a country as special as Australia, while this pandemonium was taking place.

Just like many others around me, I had never experienced such a situation before. The whole concept of being locked up in our individual homes was something new. Like many others during the first lockdown, I know I ate too much, drank too much and watched too much subscription TV, just trying to ride out the wave.

With the end of the first lockdown in June, a feeling of normality was back in the air. However, this return to normal life would be short-lived. After just a few weeks of reopening, we were told that the virus had escaped the controlled areas and was running rampant in the community once again. So as a state, we were plunged back into lockdown 2.0. However, this time around, I was presented with an opportunity; I could repeat the same choices I'd made during the first lockdown, or I could do things a little differently.

I chose the latter. The main change that I put in place was a decision to use this time inside to focus on myself. I decided I would use this lockdown period as a time to reflect, slowing down from the day-to-day rush of normal life, while understanding that I was fortunate enough to be able to do this. One of the projects that I had been preparing for was the writing of my life story.

Step one – dot pointing my memories

To me, my life had experienced some significant moments and, as therapeutic as this process would be for myself, my original intention was to share my story. Yet I did not know what I was about to uncover by undertaking this exercise.

While I was reviewing my list of events, more and more memories from earlier years came forward out of my long-term memory bank. The dot points were in their rawest form, just single words or small sentences from lived experiences. The plan was then to use them individually as the foundation to expand on, in detail, each specific experience, influencer or role player in my life.

The dot point format gave me the time to process each significant event individually, since I was working through some considerably traumatic events. All the memories were listed in chronological order. This was particularly helpful in managing the flow of my story while I was writing. As many memories from my early years were extremely painful, being able to write about a specific event and then put the pen down as I processed the feelings without losing track was extremely beneficial.

The first and most important factor of this writing, as I mentioned before, was to include all the memories and events, including the ones that I did not want to remember, the ones that I had tried to block out throughout the years of my life. These were the memories that had acted like chains around my soul, inhibiting my connection and my spiritual freedom. No matter how painful or challenging it might have been for me to recall them, they were a very important inclusion.

Step two – writing and releasing

The next important step that I discovered during my writing was that my journey needed to be written in the third person. Plus, I did not need to use any names; I could just use labels. As an example of what I mean, I was either the baby, the boy, the child or the teenager. My parents were titled 'the mother' and 'the father'. Everyone else was labelled with their role – the brother, the brothers, the uncle, the aunty, the cousin, the best friend, the friend and so on. Individuals' names were only used once as I felt that these two real-life angels required such recognition.

These two adults were external adults outside of my extended family, who I felt safe and comfortable with. They didn't use me for any self-gratification, nor did they have any ulterior motive by paying me special attention. These two adults had not taken any legal commitment to care for me or care for my wellbeing, plus there was no family or bloodline connection; however, they cared for me like a son and treated me extremely well.

Why in the third person?

I discovered that writing that piece in the third person was an extremely important tool for uncovering my unique *epiphany* moments. This enabled me to be able to look at my life vicariously from an outsider's perspective, *from the outside looking in*. Reliving my life not as me but as an external third person, I was able to process my individual life events, the unique Moments in Time both good and bad, from a new perspective with greater clarity and a sense of observational understanding.

There could be nothing left on the table as part of this process. The third person concept was especially helpful as I wrote about my childhood years, including my first painful memory held deep within me about a significantly violent experience from my childhood that I needed to release. This event that I was writing about was an incident that had occurred at around the age five when my family had travelled to Melbourne Airport to see off some relatives as they left for an overseas trip. This was going to be the first of many painful memories associated with my father. Nowadays we would classify this as child abuse on a small child five years of age. Plus, along with the physical assault was repeated aggressive verbal threats that if I would not stop crying, the hits would continue. A physical, mental and an emotional assault.

This was definitely a no-win situation for me as a child. How could I stop crying if I was being violently assaulted? Surely an adult would know this. The traumatic damage that was inflicted on this young life by a person who was supposed to be a loving protector was devastating. In the aftermath of this event, the violence continued throughout the years that followed.

Having my epiphany moment

It was hard for me to write about this memory, even from the third person perspective, trying to not relive the embedded historic feelings of violence and palpable fear. With tears flowing down my face and my emotions overcoming me, suddenly, out of nowhere, came a voice so loud, it was as if there was another person in my lounge room.

"What happened to the father when he was a child, and was he just repeating the same mistakes?"

Then there was a pause. As if time stood still for a moment. Gifting me the opportunity to consider the questions that I had just been asked. For I had never considered this perspective before.

Then just as a new sense of understanding was entering me, the voice said to me, 'And what happened to the father's father, and the father before him?'

'How far back does this go?'

Immediately I stopped crying as I begun processing the questions that were presented. *As I sat back into my seat, I asked myself, where did that voice come from? What are these questions and what is this perspective?* Since it was just me alone with my pen in the house.

This was my epiphany moment. A momentous occasion.

These questions would form the basis of my Cycle of Repetition principle.

I considered, what happened to my father during his developmental years?

Had he been treated the same way?

Was he just repeating the same mistakes that he had done to him, and did his father also just repeat the same mistakes? How far back did this cycle go? Was this behaviour something that had just been accepted and passed down generationally as the way fathers were meant to be? Was my father just a damaged soul, unable to break the cycle?

Armed with these monumental questions, a new realisation and sense of understanding quickly entered me. I realised that the answers I was feeling may very well be correct. With the picture quickly becoming clearer, I was able to package all of my father's indiscretions, all the violence and negative behaviours into a box and at last close that chapter forever. Accepting that he knew no better, I completely forgave him for all of his actions, and in turn freed myself from all the associated historical trauma. This was an enormous moment!

Immediately, I began to apply my newfound perspective to other historically significant events that had unfolded during my life by asking the same questions about those individuals. Were they also just damaged souls, unable to break their own Cycle of Repetitions? Had they been victims of abuse or terrible events during their earlier life? Was the only pathway forward they could find one that included continuing the rampage of destruction to make themselves feel better or comfortable within themselves?

What was it that they experienced in their life that led them to believe their actions were acceptable? What caused them to become so broken? Could they not find a way to stop their cycle? Did they even know there was a cycle?

As it turned out, I believe I discovered, in a state of higher consciousness, that they too were indeed damaged souls with their own emotional baggage that had been carried through life. The individuals had just repeated the same soul-crushing actions that had been enacted onto them, as children and as teens. Forging them down a dark pathway unable to see the light beyond their experience. With this understanding I forgave them, I completely forgave them, not for what they did but because they didn't know any better.

Reaching my epiphany moment and receiving these revelations led me to uncover one of the most important challenges we have in our lives: as a society, we should all strive to break the Cycle of Repetitions attached to negative beliefs and behaviours.

If we can challenge ourselves to break our Cycles, our emotional evolution will continue to evolve.

By accepting this challenge and working towards a positive outcome, imagine what the next generation could accomplish when not faced with the same adversity.

After the intense emotional experience from writing about those memories, I felt that I needed to take a break from writing to regroup my thoughts. What I was about to discover, though, was that embarking on this emotional journey had been SO WORTH IT!

I discovered the natural evolution of what happens next once someone frees their spirit and unchains their soul. The life-changing transformation caused by releasing the buried pain, trauma, grief and hurt completely outweighed any emotionally hard work I'd invested to uncover those painful memories.

Unknowingly, I had opened the door to the next level of my life experience. By walking through this door, I had been transported to a completely new world. A new world where I could recharge, reconnect and align vibrationally with all that is – this being the real world. A direct connection to the one that we call God, the Creator, Source and the Almighty. The name we assign to this deity is inconsequential, but the feeling is unmistakable. Little did I know at this stage of my journey, what beauty was about to come and be revealed!

My spirit unchained

As Victoria's lockdown continued, I eventually picked up my pen and continued writing more of my life story. At the time, I was thinking nothing further about what I had already discovered, yet I was feeling a complete sense of peace and emotional freedom.

While writing about more of my life experiences, this time focusing on the commotion of my teenage years, I suddenly realised that I didn't need to write anymore. No matter how wild, out of control and intense those years had been and, at times, the subsequent years in my twenties and thirties, a new level of self-awareness had become known to me. For the first time, I recognised and accepted that all of my life choices after my childhood trauma had been influenced by the emotional baggage that I'd been carrying. And since I was now unplugged from those learnt behaviours, developed conditions and ingrained traumatic experiences, I could finally forgive myself and let go. With my spirit free, I had nothing left to mask or hide from. I could finally live from this day forward connected as the new me.

On the outside, it was business as usual but unbeknown to me, new life experiences were about to be revealed. Experiences that I had never even dreamt of before, let alone known, were possible. At first, I'd only describe these moments as magical, almost unbelievable, even crazy talk; however, they were real, absolutely real. I was living them and experiencing them firsthand.

Land for sale – my first connection

My first such experience, *Moment in Time*, was during a phone call with my mother. We'd been working together as a team for many years and together we'd completed a number of projects. Throughout 2020, we'd been searching for some land with development potential down at the beach with the intention of building something special for all the family to enjoy.

During the first week of October, one such block caught our attention online. We both liked the look of the land, which led to further conversations about the possibilities as well as what our next move would be to secure it.

It was during this phone call that I had my first physical divine experience. Our conversation started just as they always did, with warmth and care before we started speaking about the land in detail. I was looking at the images on my phone screen when I suddenly felt my entire body become amplified. It was as if every skin cell and atom in my body awoke itself, beaming with light and love. This was a feeling that I had never felt before.

As my arms lifted while I was filled with this external energy, I exclaimed, 'Mum, I don't know what is going on right now, but it really feels like we need to buy this property.'

Mum intriguingly replied, 'What is it?'

To which I responded, 'Wow, I don't know what is happening to me right now, but my body has come alive. And it really feels like we should buy this place.'

Mum reiterated, 'Okay, Mike, I agree. I trust you!'

I was totally overcome with some sort of external energy, from outside of this world. A truly amazing experience. The complete sensation was overwhelming as the power took over my body, filling me with a euphoric warm glow that ignited all my body's sensory receptors.

This moment was my first ever *vibrational connection*.

Seemingly from out of the blue, something else was reaching into me. Astounding me more was the fact that I was not doing anything to influence or make it happen. Wherever this energy was from, it was a totally natural feeling, since it was just me, standing outside on my front doorstep, talking on my phone and breathing fresh air.

The feeling of this amazing energy and power was something almost indescribable, completely overwhelming at first, plus I didn't know what any of it meant. Then just as quickly as the energetic connection arrived, it vanished. Just like that, it was gone! I was left standing there bewildered, wondering what had just happened.

For those of you wondering, we were talked out of the land purchase by our adviser. They were concerned that it would be too difficult to achieve what we wanted due to the caveats on the property title. We accepted that feedback at the time because we trusted them but also because I didn't even know what it was that had touched me let alone if it was some sort of existential guide or not.

Then during the final days of late October – my *second amazing connection* occurred. To give you some context, I had an affiliation with a racehorse called Steel Prince. Steel was going to be running in the Geelong Cup. This majestic horse had to win this race in order to secure a spot in the biggest race in Australia, the race that stops the nation, the Melbourne Cup!

My experience, though, is not based on this horse winning the race but on an amazing connection that occurred during this event with this special animal.

Race day had arrived. Still being in lockdown I was at home, ready to watch the live telecast. The horses were being paraded around the mounting yard in preparation before they were to be loaded into the starting gate for the race. I was standing up watching the screen as this impressive horse was bought into the grassed area. Then as the horse looked forward, I felt an immediate connection with the animal. My entire body was suddenly filled with that same powerful energy that I had received weeks before with my land experience.

Oh geez, I thought, *this is happening again!* My whole body had once again been overpowered by an external energy completely out of my control. Such a huge sense of euphoria was now pumping into me from somewhere else; my body's sensors were once again electrified!

I questioned, what was connecting to me? What was happening to me?

What happened next, I cannot fully explain how or why. But as the horse nodded his head, a message was delivered to me, as if it was his way of saying, 'I've got this. I am going to win this race.'

To feel so connected with this beautiful animal and to receive such an acknowledgement while in such a state of Vibrational Alignment is an experience to behold. I felt such pure clarity and connection. My whole body was electric and amplified. In fact, by now my body was pulsating with energy. As the horse ran, I remained in this amplified state for the entire race.

This experience was something else, so out of this world, and was making me think that there was something special going on here. With that acknowledgment came an overwhelming sense that animals and humans are connected as one. I felt that the life-enabling spirit that was within the horse was the same life-enabling spirit that was within me. With this, I felt total bliss. This was a very special experience and yes, for those of you wondering, this special horse did win his race.

Then, just as had happened with my first connection, the energy disappeared once again. The moment was over. Leaving me in total peace. After such an elevated experience, I was quickly accepting that something amazing was being shared with me and that my entire life experience was beginning once again.

Now this was the second time I'd felt that euphoric connection and this time around, I could see the signs a little clearer. I felt that based on what had just occurred, this was a sign to show me that when I experience the vibrational connection, there are positive outcomes.

I was being shown that I could trust whatever it was that was unfolding since it was going to be a positive experience. As I inquisitively questioned what this connection was, I felt it was leading me towards great outcomes. I was sure that this was also a sign for me to be comfortable with my vibrational connection as it was nothing to fear.

I didn't know it yet, but I now had an open connection with Source that would guide and support me for the rest of my days.

My eyes were now starting to truly open, and I was beginning to see things with a new level of awareness. Within my moments of pure connectivity, there seemed to be an abundance of signs and messages coming in loud and clear.

Once again, after this experience, life for me returned to normal. The good news now was that our 'Lockdown 2.0' was over, we were finally being released from our homes and the restrictive conditions that we had all been living under.

Looking through a different lens

The following week, I arranged to meet up with my youngest brother. He had been working through his own challenging journey, with its own ups and downs. On the day of our catch-up, which was a Friday, he didn't show up. I was upset and frustrated, but internally I couldn't help feeling a sense of guilt to some degree. Some of his engrained learnt behaviours had been heavily influenced by him observing me in my younger years and how I had previously dealt with my own pain from our childhood especially during my teenage years.

Nevertheless, I decided to let go of how frustrated I felt about his actions and accept that his choices were something that I could not control. I had to focus my attention on the only thing that I could control, and that was how I felt. With this in mind, I opted instead to visit the cemetery so I could attend the grave site of my grandparents.

Pre-covid I would regularly attend their grave at least a couple of times a year, sometimes even more. Unfortunately, in the year 2020, no one in the state had been legally allowed to attend any cemeteries due to the COVID lockdowns.

I purchased some flowers and made my way over to the cemetery, eventually arriving at their plot. Here I spent some time with them, saying hello, freshening up their flowers, cleaning the marble and wishing them both well, thinking nothing further of my gesture. I considered the rest of my weekend to be normal with nothing out of the ordinary. On Sunday, after I finished dinner and watched some TV, I made my way to bed, quickly drifting off to sleep.

It was during my sleep that night, however, that I received an undeniable message:

'Start looking at life through a different lens – things are more than what they seem.'

My dream was one, many would describe as lucid. I remember there was nothing and then, suddenly, there I was sitting in the back of a black van with my two brothers. We were seated in the back on black leather seats, with someone else unknown driving. The three of us were laughing, joking and mucking around, all extremely peaceful, having a great time together. We were as we are now, our current ages. We weren't represented as children from our past or anything like that, the Moment in Time was now.

Instantly, I noticed that both of my brothers were so happy and comfortable together. The two of them looked so vibrant and healthy, plus we were all behaving like we didn't have a care in the world.

They were both sitting on one side of the van, smiling, laughing and making joyful hand signals and peace signs, while I was seated on the opposite side, using my phone to take happy snaps of the two of them. It was pure joy.

While we joked and clowned around in the back of the van, out of nowhere a bird flew in through the side window, landing on one of the headrests attached to a rear seat. It remained comfortably perched right next to one of my brothers, calmly bobbing its head backwards and forwards. We all looked at each other laughing and questioned, 'What is this bird doing?' It seemed so comfortable in our presence and clearly just wanted to sit with us.

As I leaned back in my seat to capture another happy snap of my brothers on my phone, the bird came into view of my camera lens, instantly shapeshifting into my Nonna (grandmother) who I had visited on the Friday before. Her head was slightly turned to the left side, she had a huge smile on her face and both her hands were raised with her thumbs up as if to say, 'HEYYYYYYYYY, I'm here!'

I immediately pulled my phone down in shock and exclaimed, 'WHOAAAA, what was that?' Then looking with my normal eyes, I once again could only see the bird sitting on the top of the seat, bobbing its head backwards and forwards. Captivated but confused, I cautiously raised my phone again. BAM! It was Nonna once again, her head turned to the side just as before, a huge smile on her face and her thumbs up. 'HEYYYYYY!' I felt that this was a special message from beyond, a thank you for coming to visit her.

My interpretation of the subconscious message from my lucid dream was a significant moment for me at the start of this my amazing journey. The seed was now planted in my mind, to start looking at our physical world through a different lens. Everything is not as it seems.

Could there be a real tangible connection between our physical world as we know it, the afterlife, and our subconscious dream world?

Chapter 3

A NEW BEGINNING

Day 1 – Energy overload

Day one was a Monday morning in the last week of November. I'd woken up at my regular time, around 7:30 am, ready to begin my week. There was nothing that seemed out of the ordinary, nor can I recall anything notably different about the morning.

I rose out of bed, with my body feeling the same as it always did. I quickly shifted my attention to completing all my regular morning tasks before I clocked on for the day. At around 10 am, Mum arrived at my place, as she did most weekdays. Her role within my company had shifted, which meant she could operate from the office at my place.

By late morning though, I started to feel different, then out of nowhere it was as if I was having an influx of external energy. My head felt like it was spinning around in a washing machine, and I was now struggling to focus. It was as if my mind was moving too fast, not allowing me to concentrate on any subjects for very long. This was not normal for me, as I recognised nothing was being achieved.

Feeling a little confused about what was happening by 12:30 pm, I said to mum, I do not know what is going on today, but I feel like I have far too much energy flowing through me I just can't focus; it feels like I'm going around in circles, I think I need to go to the gym and burn through some of this!'

Mum smiled at me and simply responded, 'Okay, no worries, see you later on.'

While driving to the gym, I started to notice that the lights around me were all very illuminated. It was as if I was somehow sensing the energy radiating from each light that I passed. My eyes had never felt this sort of sensitivity before, almost like my vision had been turned up internally to maximum clarity. Plus, if it was possible, I felt like I was absorbing that energy.

Like a large battery, plugged into a recharger, I now had an abundance of external energy flowing into me, overloading my internal levels. This was a sensation I had never felt before.

It wasn't long before I arrived at the gym and made my way inside. Walking up the stairs, I was instantly drawn to the treadmill. Something was telling me to run. It's important to note that before this day, I hadn't used running as part of my regular exercise for over fifteen years. Yet as I stood on the treadmill, I remembered back to my early twenties when I had run a 2.4-kilometre time trial in eight minutes fourteen seconds; achieving something near this was going to be my eventual goal – this would not be today, but I would work towards this over time. With the expectation set and seed planted, all I had to do now was start running! One thing that I didn't consider, though, was, that I had achieved that time eighteen years ago!

After completing my run, in fifteen minutes, I still felt so energised and pumped. There was no way I was just going to stop after that; I had an abundance of energy to burn through. I ended up staying at the gym for the next three hours. Then by the time I returned home, my mind had calmed, and I was finally able to relax.

Day 2 – An energy overload again

Day two started with a lot more clarity when compared to the day before. Even though I was unsure as to what this energy was or why it was happening to me, I was accepting of this transformation.

I prepared my to-do list for the day. This list needed to be comprised of all the outstanding tasks from the day before, along with all the new items that had come in overnight. There were at least fifteen tasks that I needed to complete – new sales contracts to be raised, accounts to be updated and several other items that needed to be finalised.

As I began working through the list, I could sense that I was really in the zone. Powering through each item one by one, once completed, tick, completed, tick, it was effortless. I remember thinking if the circumstances were different, this list could have taken a week to complete. Satisfied with the situation, I effortlessly flowed through the morning period.

Then just after lunch, I felt a shift. I'd reached the maximum energy level again; now I was overloaded. With my body giving me a sign that enough had been achieved. I turned to Mum and said, 'I'm not sure what's happening once again, but think I need to go back to the gym.' And with that said, I left the house.

This time on my drive to the gym, I noticed that once again something was happening to my vision. Not only did I feel like I could see everything clearly, with absolute clarity. If 20/20 vision is regarded as being perfect, I felt like mine was 40/40. The visual reality of what I was witnessing had never been clearer, the colours, the lights and the shapes of the world around me. I was thinking, *Wow, how are these lights all so illuminated? What is happening?* I now felt an internal connection to an energy that I had never even dreamt of before.

It was as if the nonvisible energy of the universe was flowing into me, causing my body to absorb and soak it up like a sponge. This was an energy that I couldn't see, but for some reason now, I could feel. This phenomenon was something out of this world.

I stopped my car to bask in my state of pure connectedness, a whole-body transcendental experience that once again activated all of my body's sensory receptors. It was in this moment that as I waved my hand through the air in front of me, I witnessed the energetic trail follow behind my hand. Somehow, I knew what this was. It was as if the spirit of my hand was trailing behind my physical self. I sat in awe as it seemed that my spirit was both inside and outside my body. A truly supernatural rendezvous.

Even though I was feeling elated, I knew that I needed to regroup and pull myself together. Finally, I quietly made my way inside, while still trying to process and maintain a sense of normality about the extraordinary experience that I had just been a part of.

Inside the gym, I repeated my running challenge that I'd started the day before, improving my overall time from the previous day and continued with other exercises. Once again, staying for over three hours, just to burn through the abundance of energy I had.

Day 3 – Seriously tested

Are you ready for what is coming, or will you go back to your old ways?

Wednesday morning at around 5 am while sleeping, I suddenly became overtly aware of my subconscious dream state (often referred to as a *lucid dream*). While fast asleep, I felt as if I was wide awake, inside a completely white arena, observing my body. I could see my arms and legs; I could feel my skin and I could feel every touch on my body. I felt very conscious, in my subconscious state.

The final test before the Big Reveal

Then I saw a needle appear. I watched as this needle pierced my skin, as my blood was extracted and then mixed with the chemicals inside the syringe. I witnessed as the drug entered my bloodstream, immediately feeling the effects of this. I felt an insane rush of euphoria overcoming my body, as my heartbeat increased from the instant oversupply of endorphins that were released into my brain, exploding my mind.

I quickly woke up, startled, and somehow still feeling the drug effects in my body, I exclaimed, 'What the F**K was that? What just happened?' It was such a surreal experience. As my reality became clearer, I immediately reminded myself, 'No way, that did not just happen. I'm in my room, I'm fine.' I repeated to myself that I hadn't ingested anything and the only thing that had occurred was that I had experienced an extremely vivid dream. I focused on controlling my breathing, on slowing my heartbeat down and on relaxing, eventually managing to get myself back to sleep.

Subtly, I called this dream the final test before the Big Reveal because of the impact this journey has had on my entire life experience. My entire belief structure has been uprooted and rewritten. My perception of life as I knew it and as I know it has been reconfigured, it is as if I have been reborn.

I knew that this was a subconscious test gifted to me with the intention to see if I would go back to my old ways or if I was ready for what was about to come!

Day 4 – Brunch with an angel

A day of new beginnings

On Thursday morning, I'd planned to have brunch with a special friend of mine called Tara. Still captivated by the dream I'd experienced the night before, I started the day with my usual routine. My body was feeling mostly normal, apart from the fact that I still felt the energy all around me. And the lights, the lights still seemed so much brighter. I was beginning to accept the fact that my mind and vision had been opened and that I was now experiencing the physical world with significantly greater clarity and knowledge, both mentally and physically.

I arrived at the café early; this way I could greet Tara when she arrived. Once we started talking, I shared with her the journey that I had undertaken during the months of lockdown, including the writing of my earlier book. I then started to share about the physical events that had been occurring to me over the previous months, including my experience with the land purchase and my connection with the racehorse.

As we sat there conversing, I could feel the energy level inside me begin to rise. The vibrational connection that I'd experienced with those two earlier events had once again returned, yet this time with extreme strength and an all-encompassing euphoria. What was special about this time though, was that Tara was witnessing this with her own eyes. I knew then that my connection was something that could be seen by others as well. As I shared my lucid dream experiences and how I had been feeling during the week, I continuously felt the powerful sensation of euphoric existential energy bursts as they continued to shoot down my arms and legs. *Zap, zap, zap* – I was repeatedly hit by the divine lightning bolt.

While overwhelmed by these sensory sensations, Tara continued to ask, 'How do you feel?'

'Elated and elevated,' were my repeated responses. Vibrationally, I knew now that this connection was for all to see, visible from the changing skin on my body that coincided with the bursts of energy pulsating through me internally. Most of the euphoric bursts would last for about five seconds, but there were some that lasted for what seemed like thirty seconds to a minute. The energy level within the café was rising now too. We were reaching the maximum level.

Understandably, Tara was a little concerned and freaked out by what she was witnessing at first. This was something that she had never heard of or seen before. But when Tara could see that I was fine, she relaxed and jokingly suggested that she would start calling me Electro-man! We both laughed at her new nickname for me.

As we sat there and conversed about life and family, I could feel that my vibration level had risen to such a high frequency that I could see what I can only describe as a white aura surrounding Tara. She was glowing, angelic and radiating. This feeling was pure euphoria. To experience someone sitting in front of me with no visual surroundings, radiating with whiteness wrapped around them is something to behold – a physical experience interacting with a real-world angel.

At my most heightened level, there were moments where I felt I was both in and outside of my body. My heart was beating so fast as I witnessed Tara glowing. The euphoric feelings were so beautiful. For the first time, I had discovered that I could connect with whatever this energy was by sharing true conversations, with meaningful words, by telling this story. The energy bursts were so powerful and often that when it was time to leave, I struggled to walk.

I sensed that this was a magical day, a day that would become part of my new beginning by introducing me to the new world and a new way of life as a connected being.

Even with all my questions about the origin of the unknown energy that was flowing freely within me, I was not scared. For some reason, I felt so protected and safe. I knew that whatever door I had opened by freeing my spirit and unchaining my soul something magnificent and truly unique was being shared with me that deserved to be cherished.

This was my new way. I was ecstatic to be able to share such a powerful experience with someone who was so special to me, in such a magical way. I was pretty certain that I was now truly at peace. Feeling this way, I couldn't help but to be humbled and thankful that the Highest Power had seen fit, to allow me to experience such a divine moment.

At the time my burning question was, how long would this last?

Day 5 – Living spirits – who comes back as who? – a connected world

I woke up the next day feeling extremely refreshed and peaceful. After the experience of the previous day, I could not even begin to imagine what magic was going to unfold for me on this day but what I did feel though was that no matter what was coming, I'd be open and ready to receive.

Casually, I progressed through my day just like I would have done on any other Friday. Then in the afternoon, I made my way to the gym again to continue with the daily run challenge that I'd set for myself. This time I set the timer on the treadmill to eleven minutes and completed my run. I had decided that every time I ran, I'd reduce the running time so I could keep reaching toward my goal.

After the run, I spoke with one of my nephews and shared with him the challenge that I'd set, along with my running efforts to date. I asked him, 'When do you think I could achieve my running goal of nine minutes?' He suggested, 'Maybe by the end of the year?'

To which I emphatically replied, 'End of the year? No way! I'm thinking I want to achieve this by the end of next week!'

What I did not realise now was that I had unknowingly set my intentions to reach my goal within the week, a challenge that was now well underway.

With my run done, I headed off home and prepared for the evening. I had arranged to meet up with a special friend of mine, Monique. I'd planned to pick her up and head over to the beach where we'd meet up with some other friends.

As we drove, I started to share with Mon about my week so far, along with all the other connected events from the months before. When suddenly, our conversation shifted gears into what I would now describe as a vibrational conversation. We started to talk about heavenly subject matters namely the connection between humans, spirits, animals and all things living on this earth. 'Do you believe we are all connected?' one of us asked. We delved into a high-level conversation about the connectedness of animals and humans, including spirits who have transitioned and the possibility of them returning in another shape or form. Each correct sentence was confirmed with an affirmation delivered by a vibrational burst of energy hitting my body like a euphoric spark of electricity. Bammm! Bammm! These were magical moments, and ones that I was so pleased to be sharing with Mon, especially after my day before with Tara. Another person witnessing my divine connection.

By the time we arrived at the beach, the atmosphere was electric, while the afternoon was fast becoming one of the most perfect evenings. We leisurely made our way down to the shoreline to join the other two sitting by the ocean. As we reached their spot on the sand, it was as if the sun appeared to be shining directly down on us. In that moment, it really felt like we were the centre of our universe.

Even still, just between the two of us, Mon and I had continued our own little side conversation, as we experimented and explored the vibrations that I was experiencing. Each vibrational burst was like a lightning bolt of pure love. What could we do with this? Would whatever this was playing with us respond if we asked it questions?

We decided we would try to pair animal and human spirits, asking, 'Who comes back as who?' Does a beach lover come back as a seagull? Does a surfer come back as a shark? These were some of the pairings that were suggested and vibrationally acknowledged. There were some pairings that we suggested that did not vibrate and there were others that vibrationally paired with ease. This was such a joyous, fun, connected evening and a unique way to spend our time together. By this stage of the evening, my vibration level was so elevated that there was nothing that had ever compared to this physical experience before.

Day 6 – An introduction to *ease*

Slow it down

After the magical evening of Friday night, I awoke Saturday morning feeling completely free. I could sense the 'chi' energy radiating from within my bedroom. My mind was so clear, while I knew that spiritually I was in such a beautiful place. I was continuously receiving an abundance of warm love from an existential connection that I'd never felt before. My body, mind and spirit were feeling a complete level of oneness with the entire earth.

The cells in my body were individually alive and vibrating, plus there was an all-encompassing knowing that a truly magical morning was about to unfold. As I finished my shower, I started to sing a song that I'd never heard before. In fact, this was a new song that no one had ever sung before.

Immediately, I thought, *Wow! This is a special song. I need to record this.* Then, as I reached for my phone, I had to try to rewind the song back to the start in my head. Successfully doing so, I pressed the record while allowing the song words to flow. Below is the complete song that came through me, from a very special place above (recorded 28/11/2020 4:04 mins):

Title: **SLOW IT DOWN**

Slow it down, slow it down
If I sing this song for you
Slow it down, slow it down
If I want it to be true

I sing this for the love
And I sing this for the life
I sing this for the world
To come together in night

Slow it down, slow it down
Won't you sing this song with me?

Slow it down, slow it down
This is where we gotta be

We can think about the future
Or we can spend our time in the past
We can focus on our memories
Or create ones new that last
We can control our thoughts
And what it is we become

Slow it down, slow it down
This is the holy one

So, I sing this for the moment
And I sing this for the trees
I sing this for the plants, the animals and sea
I sing this for the ocean
and I sing this for the sand
I sing this for the fish
And the waters of our land

Slow it down, slow it down
This is the holy one
Slow it down, slow it down
This is for everyone

If I could be the father
and you could be the son
If I could be the holy
The holiest one
Don't you ever question
Or judge another man

The powers up above
Have already got a plan

Slow it down, slow it down
This is the holy one
Slow it down, slow it down
This is for everyone

What I can do for you?
What I would like to be?
I'd like you to see the ocean
While floating above the trees
You might become a bird
Maybe a surfer in the shark
A beach lover in the seagull
It's all just my life

I think the greatest pleasure
Is coming back a bird
You can then travel
All across the earth
Fly into Antarctica
Then over to the sands
The sands of the desert
Of the Holy Land
North and South Pole
Alaska, USA
Over to Russia
And Europe far away
Come to see Australia
New Zealand, everyone
And all the other lovely places of Asia all as one

We got China, Fiji, Cambodia, Japan and Thailand too
India and Pakistan,
Sri Lanka's special too
We'd finish off in Africa
The starting place of Earth
I did this song for everyone
My gift to the world

Slow it down, slow it down
This is the Holy One
Slow it down, slow it down
This is for everyone

Maximum energy level

As one might imagine, channelling this song was a humbling experience, both emotionally and spiritually. Having not been a religious person or someone enamoured with God, something powerful was happening and I was completely submitting myself to the whole experience without expectation.

Feeling extremely overcome afterwards with the divine message of love that I'd just received, I had to give myself some time to sit in the enjoyment of what had just been shared with me, while absorbing all the euphoric energy that was streaming down unto me.

After such a vibrational start to my day, I was eagerly looking forward to what else might be shared with me along the way. I had plans to meet up with my good friend, Jimmy. I had not shared anything with Jimmy yet about my new connection, so I was eager to share my new experiences with him and gauge his reaction. I knew that Jimmy was a searcher already, who had been on his own personal journey of discovery over the years.

We'd made plans earlier in the week to meet up with another friend, Sabrina, at a local shopping centre for a catch-up. While Jimmy and I were in the car together, I started to share with him about my connection and the vibrations that I was receiving. I included the events of my morning with him, with the receiving of the words for *Slow It Down*. This topic of conversation naturally lifted the energy level in my car to a somewhat heightened level of connection.

It was during this elevated point of our ride that Jimmy decided to share with me a video clip from an international speaker, someone whom I'd never heard of before. I guess he wanted to share this with me as a test to see what might happen, interested to see how my body would react or maybe to see if this could provide any answers for him and for me.

As the words flowed through my car speakers, my connection was instantaneous. Whatever it was that was inside me resonated immediately with the topic and words that were being spoken. The international speaker was talking about connecting with Source and Vibrational Alignment subjects that I had no knowledge of, apart from what it was that I was personally experiencing. The timing of this introduction was magnificent. I was filled with powerful bursts of euphoric energy. This transmission raised my conscious level into a state that I'd never known existed.

Connected energy – we are all vibrational beings

Mesmerised and overcome by our incredibly special drive, we made our way inside the centre and met up with Sabrina. With the sensations still moving through my body and the freshness of our connected car ride still in the air, it was not long before I started to share the news of my journey.

Even with the real uncertainty and exemplified rawness I exerted while talking about what it was that was happening to me, I tried not to be nervous. Internally I questioned, what words could I use? What would people think? What if nothing happened? Would this connection just disappear?

Still finding my way, I felt it best to start by highlighting my newfound belief that we are all spiritual beings. That we are all a spirit in a body, not a body with a spirit. Immediately, the others could see my vibrations as the energy flowed through me. My interpretation of this meant that this was a meaningful conversation, and one that I was very pleased to share while it was around.

Change what you consume – Step 2 – from the ten steps

I cannot explain how or why, nonetheless, my decision was ratified by a vibrational acknowledgement that I was heading in the right direction.

It was on this day that I realised we should look to change and clean up what we have been consuming. This included moving to a more plant-based diet. This felt like a new way forward, the beginning of a new healthier diet for my body.

I was starting to more clearly understand the role that plants and trees played as part of the oneness. It was evident that we had been gifted a huge natural resource of fruits, vegetables and nuts to consume. Food that could provide many of the nutrients that we need to survive. Do not get me wrong, I think we can still eat meat, poultry and fish as we desire; just not in the quantities that we are consuming today. An example of this would be our depleted oceans caused by the excessive commercial fishing that goes on around the globe. Less is more sometimes.

We should all consider that spiritually, every one of us is connected to all the living animals and fish that we consume. Each living fish, animal and creature has the same life-creating spirit inside their shell that we do.

During the drive back to our area, our conversation continued elevating the energy level within my vehicle to such a heightened state that the physical reality became surreal. Special words were flowing, words such as Source Energy, the Universe, the Energy That Creates Worlds and A New Reality. The vibrations were now pulsating, and I was naturally convulsing from the abundance of Divine Energy that was flowing through me.

Together, we reached a critical mass moment where I felt that there was such a heightened level of energy that I had to pull over. I stopped in a large car park, then turned my head to the left and saw Jimmy with his hands on his knees in complete tranquillity. His palms were facing upwards as he sat in full receiving mode, soaking up the energy inside my vehicle. I had to get out of the car and just walk around. My body was feeling like a large energy beacon, radiating and vibrating.

Time was slowed down; in fact, the concept of time was non-existent. It was as if the movement of time had completely stopped. The surrounding sounds were clear, yet there was no white noise. My mind remained completely still, calm and overwhelmed with a feeling of oneness. What had begun as just a drive in the car to meet with some friends had turned into a remarkable spiritual experience, one of the highest orders.

Although I was still just trying to understand what was happening to me. What was this power, this special connection, this Vibrational Alignment?

Chapter 4

SHARING MY CONNECTION

Day 7 – Unlimited euphoria with no cost, comedown or hangover

Day seven was a Sunday that was well-positioned to be another memorable day along this amazing journey. I set my intentions in the morning, including sharing whatever this was, with my youngest brother Mathew. I knew all too well about the current path he was walking, which made me desperate to show him what I'd discovered. I was even hoping that whatever this was could be the catalyst to ignite his own flame. I wanted to show him that there was a different way.

I wanted him to see what is naturally achievable when we allow ourselves to be free of our pain and trauma. My only desire was for him to see that we don't need drugs, alcohol or anything artificial to make us feel good. Plus, I felt that if he achieved this level of spiritual freedom, he could re-establish his own free-flowing connection with the oneness of our universe, so that he may see and truly believe that our Creator really can provide us with access to as much healing as we require. I believed it was important for him to know that this divine stream could be accessed for unlimited guidance, healing, love and pleasure, as much as he desired.

Sharing my awakening with him was the main intention that I had set out for this day. I felt I knew what messages I wanted to pass onto him. Now, it would be a case of whether he was ready to hear these words or not.

Would he be in the receptive mode?

I remained steadfast and hopeful as I gathered my possessions and jumped into my car, making my way over to his place. The plan was

I'd pick him up and we would drive into the city together to meet up with our cousin Sandra. Mat knew nothing of my experiences so far, so I was excited to see his reaction. It was about midday as I turned into his street. I could see that he was waiting on the corner and as I parked, he quickly jumped into my car, eager to reconnect.

Straight away we headed off into the city. By the time we reached the freeway, I started to share some of my experiences. Then without any initiating or forcing, my powerful connection quickly joined in on our conversation. I could feel his genuine excitement combined with confusion as he witnessed my connection for the first time. I knew this was something that he had never seen before, as it wasn't that long ago that I'd never seen this before either.

He inquisitively asked, 'What are you feeling?'

I started to explain to him that the feeling was like nothing I'd ever experienced before. The feeling was an intense overwhelming whole-body experience, as if my spirit was being hit with a lightning bolt of warm, fuzzy-feeling energy. Intrigued, he watched on as I was continuously zapped by the divine power as our conversation flowed. I knew that what Mat was witnessing would be a lot to take in. We eventually arrived in the city at a local eatery where we had planned to meet Sandra. As we parked, we both spotted Sandra patiently waiting out the front, eager to greet the two of us before we made our way inside.

Seated at our table as we waited for our food, I continued with the conversation from the car drive so that this time I could also include Sandra as well. Internally, I was really excited because every time I was able to share my experiences with a new person, I was somehow able to relive the lived experiences once again. Then as an added bonus by speaking the words, the vibrations would start flowing like a confirmation that this story was an important one to be told.

Once lunch finished, we headed outside. I knew by the look on my brother's face that he'd been trying to process what he was witnessing for most of the lunch. I guess as part of his way of processing, he turned to me and said, 'Every time you get blasted, it looks like you're climaxing!'

Laughing, I thought, *I'm definitely not but maybe it does look like that. Yet this is only because the energy bursts are so strong.* We all just laughed. I shared, 'This feeling is like pure love pumping though my body.'

At this early stage of my journey, my connection was so strong that it was uncontrollable.

I was beginning to uncover that the universe can and is willing to work with you to help you feel good. I was finding out that you just needed to put yourself in the receptive mode. Sandra jokingly referred to me and my energetic connection as 'MEGATRON', something from another world.

Maybe this was exactly that?

With our lunch finished, my brother asked if we could go visit our uncle and aunty who lived nearby. I felt that since our afternoon was going so well, I was more than happy to oblige. As we made our way over to their place, I imagined that this was just going to be a quick visit to see them. So quick in fact that I had no intention of sharing anything with them on this day as I was still unsure as to when and where my connection would reveal itself. Even though I'd been talking and sharing with different people each day, I was still so unsure as to whether there would come a time when my connection would just disappear.

We parked out the front of their shop and made our way inside. We both could see that our aunty was busy talking with some customers, so we quietly said a quick hello and then made our way out the back. We gently walked up the stairs so as to not make a noise so that maybe we could surprise our uncle if he was home. As we knocked on the front door, almost immediately we were greeted by him, with a big smile on his face. I could instantly feel that he was very happy just to see the two of us together.

Then without a delay and without warning, my body started to vibrationally connect, responding to the genuine love and energy in the room. Suddenly, he looked at me with a confused face and asked, 'What's happening? Are you okay? Have you had drugs?'

I quickly replied, 'No way, absolutely not. Something amazing has happened to me. I believe I have freed my spirit. I feel like I am connected now to something much greater than I've ever known!' I shared with him that this sensation was not something that I could control by turning it on and off and that this connection was an energy force from somewhere else that had been revealed to me. And with that reveal, my entire life experience had begun transforming.

Intrigued, we all spoke for a little while, then said our goodbyes and headed back home. As I dropped Mat off at his place, I was hopeful that what I'd shared with him would trigger some sort of inquisitive response in his mind by stimulating a desire within him to want to discover this new way.

I wanted him to know that there was nothing to fear except fear itself and that he would not be judged by undertaking such a journey himself. Plus, if he discovered the desire to want to walk such a path, this would be something I would share with him without hesitation. I hoped that he would be open to the possibility to uncover that he too is worthy and able to feel this divine love and guidance.

We can change our future – with our forward-facing time machine

Early Monday morning while asleep, I experienced yet another important message via a lucid dream. During this experience, the message that was highlighted to me was that we are all gifted with a forward-facing time machine, one that can change the projected path and outcome for our future.

The dream began with me sitting in the back seat of a small white car, with two ladies unbeknown to me seated in the front. One lady was driving; the other was her passenger. I didn't recognise who the two ladies were – I was purely there to observe the events of the drive as they unfolded in front of me. We were driving along a windy coastal road. The driver and passenger were deep in conversation plus the driver was playing with her phone, which was causing her to be very distracted.

We experienced several near misses as we travelled along the winding road, right up until the point where we entered a sharp right-hand bend. I could see that the driver was totally unfocused as she misjudged the bend. The passenger-side wheels slid out onto the gravelled curb and with that instant feeling of losing traction, the driver panicked and clipped the side of an oncoming rock with her car. That loud impact caused her to overcorrect, sending us into a 360° spin, then once the car had finally stopped, we were left facing towards the cliff's edge. Under the stress of the moment, the driver panicked and floored the accelerator instead of the brake, causing us to drive headfirst over the cliff's edge.

As we drove over the cliff's edge time slowed right down. Realising that we were going to land roof-first onto the rocks below somehow, I was able to pause the unfolding end-of-life event just before impact as if I was watching a car crash scene out of a Hollywood movie. Then once time was paused, I was able to rewind the crash sequence of events, halting our guaranteed impending death.

Visually, I could see the car travelling backwards up the cliff face, reversing the flipping motion from the cliff's edge, landing back onto the four wheels on the road, then rewinding back through the 360° spins, back before the clipping of the rock, back to the start where both the driver and the passenger were talking, distracted and not focusing on the road.

As if this was a pre-recorded scene, the sequence of events were once again allowed to be played out in real time. Visually, nothing had changed but this time, I already knew the outcome. I was still just the observer in the back seat and in the beginning of the replay it was as if I could only watch without being able to warn them. Once again, I witnessed them passionately talking. I watched on as the driver played with her phone. I could once again see that the driver was very distracted, then as we entered the right-hand bend, I felt the back wheel leave the road onto the gravel, then the side of the car clip the rock, causing the driver to overcorrect, sending her car into 360° spins and then finally stop directly towards the edge of the cliff.

This time, however, I could react. Immediately, I launched myself forward between the two front seats and pushed the automatic gear stick into reverse, knowing that the driver was going to panic and hit the accelerator. I yelled out, 'FLOOR IT!'

The driver pushed the peddle to the floor as she had done before except this time, the car reversed backwards along the road, away from the cliff's edge, totally avoiding our impending death.

This changed the known, projected or anticipated outcome of an inevitable disaster.

I believe this example can also be true in life. If we have been down a particular road before, figuratively speaking, one where we have repeated the same actions in response to specific events or behaviours and expected different outcomes, we can stop, recognise the similar situation, play back the steps we had previously taken and look for a different play if we know that that path leads us to a certain outcome.

- Life often presents us with pivotal moments that challenge us.
- At times, we find ourselves heading toward the edge of a cliff – facing a critical decision or situation.
- It's important to recognise the road already travelled.
- If you feel as though you've already been over this edge before.
- Reflect on the choices you made in the past that brought you to the brink.
- Consider how those decisions shaped the outcomes you experienced previously.
- This time, instead of repeating the same actions and expecting a different result, let's try a new approach.
- Try to visualise your desired outcome using your different response.
- By taking a fresh course of action, you have the power to reshape your future

We have all been gifted with a forward-facing time machine. Our projected future does not have to be our future path. Use your time machine!

Day 8 – Spirit connections for the first time – a memorable day

As I woke on Monday morning, I already knew that today would be another day to remember, especially after my forward-facing time machine dream. My plan for this day was that I would share my magical journey to date and connection with some people who I hold most dear in my life, namely my mother and my special friend Wa. Wa was someone that I'd shared a significant amount of my life with.

My day began with my normal routine. I felt a real sense of excitement, which I believed was natural considering what was about to unfold. I was about to share my existential connection with the person who played a major role in my creation: my mum. As I completed my morning routine, Mum arrived at my place. I knew that once she had parked her car, she would make her way inside.

After we greeted each other, I started to talk about what had been happening to me over the weekend. Then as the words naturally flowed, I continued to share with her all the other special moments and events that had been occurring since I discovered the pathway to freeing my spirit and unchaining my soul. I included everything that had happened so far such as the land and racehorse experience, the divine tests, brunch with an angel and the pairing of spirits.

During this conversation, Mum witnessed my body's sensors become alive. This was a physical transition that she had never seen nor heard of before with anyone. Open-eyed, she gazed on in amazement and curiosity as the vibrations spread all over my body. She was completely mesmerised as my inner being, presented itself in its purest form.

Pure alignment – a vibrational spirit connection

In this moment of divine connection as Mum was witnessing something that she had never seen before, she asked, 'What is happening? What is this?'

I gently replied, 'I believe I have unlocked my spirit and freed my soul!' I reassured her that this was nothing to be afraid of and in fact, this was a beautiful thing.

Calmingly I explained to her that the powerful vibration she was witnessing was exactly what I'd experienced while I was on the phone with her discussing the land purchase and this was the same sensation I'd experienced while watching the horse race. I also shared with her that I believed that after some final tests at the beginning of the previous week to see if I was ready, this beautiful connection revealed itself to me in all its glory. The heavenly doorway had now opened for me to a whole new life experience.

I explained to her what I had discovered so far was:

- My special connection comes out when I have true meaningful conversations with others.
- When I ask for a guide to correct decisions about important questions.
- My connection comes out when I can feel true appreciation, love and feelings.
- A guide to positive intentions and outcomes.

I continued to explain that I believed my connection was something much more than just a connection for me; this was for everybody. My eyes had been opened and my mind had been awakened to knowledge, beliefs and ideas that I had never imagined or considered before.

I spoke about my newfound belief that since we are a spirit in a body, not a body with a spirit, then this makes our spirit our original life form. I asked does this then mean that on the day that our human body expires, do we simply just return to our original spirit form? And if so then what are the other possibilities with this? Could those of us still alive here on earth in our physical bodies then vibrationally connect with spirits who have already passed? If all the past living beings have simply returned to their original spirit form, do they then still exist all around us just living in a dimension where the concept of distance and time does not exist?

As we continued along this topic of conversation, we started to talk about Mum's parents. With their presence now being discussed, our conversation lifted to an existential level of absolute love. Mum spoke directly to her parents with pure love and admiration. As she spoke her words directed at me, I began to rise and feel the connection between her and her family. Elevating me off the ground surface, raising my heels so that I was perched on the tips of my toes. Divinity forces elevating the physical self in this absolute moment of connectedness.

I do not recall what words were said as those words spoken by Mum were not for me, but I felt that my physical body passed on to

Mum all the sense of emotions that her parents felt to her. This was an emotional, beautiful and truly special occasion for both of us.

This experience caused Mum to radiate with such genuine love and joy. I could tell that the experience was significant by the complete change in mannerisms of just actually 'being in the moment, experiencing the now' without fear or worry about what needed to be done. A truly profound experience.

After this event, Mum would go on to spend every day of this week at my home, leaving each day in the afternoon, then returning the following morning. Both of us, so eager to continue our true conversations, with meaningful words, this shared experience was opening both our eyes more and more each day. I knew that our normal day-to-day tasks had started to become so insignificant.

Later in the afternoon, once Mum had left, as part of my daily routine, I continued my running challenge. By this stage of the day, the energy was radiating from everywhere I looked. Something I'd never felt or been aware of before was unfolding right in front of me. Now I could feel the energy all around me.

> *'My eyes had been truly opened. I was now completely connected.'*

After my run, I met with Jimmy at the gym, where we talked for a while. This conversation could only be described as electric, vibrationally electric. I found, such was Jimmy's knowledge from his own personal quest of discovery, that he had been submerged in the world of new concepts and ideas. Because of this, it seemed on occasions he would share a new idea or topic he'd discovered.

I believe for him, the idea of being able to raise something with me and then to see if there was a vibrational connection, a resonation as such, was something he used as his own personal reassurance that there was something more out there for everyone to discover. For myself, I felt that if the topic he mentioned resonated with me, then I would explore the contents a little further by digging deeper down that rabbit hole.

Once our time together finished, I made my way back home where I had the idea to call my father. This call was going to be special. My intention with this call was to share with him that after everything, after all the events of my life, I believed I had uncovered why things had occurred the way that they had. I wanted him to understand that with this awakening, I had discovered my path to absolute spiritual freedom.

I was now completely at peace with him and my past.

By setting my spirit free, I could see him for what he was: someone who did the best they could with the information that they had. I believed that I had discovered that even though he was my father, he was also a damaged soul himself and that throughout his life journey, he had just been unable to break the Cycle of Repetition. I said to him, 'Dad, I think I understand. I think I know what happened.' Just using the word 'Dad' was an extremely powerful moment, as I had not called him 'Dad' since I was a young teen.

My body became amplified as we talked on the phone. I knew that this was my spiritual sign that I was speaking true, meaningful, powerful words to him. After I spoke about feeling like I knew why he did what he did years ago and that I understood now, I believed that he could feel the genuineness in my words and that I was at peace with him.

With that in mind, I wanted to extend an olive branch out to him by inviting him and his partner to my upcoming party that was being held with my family and friends. This event was scheduled to happen on the coming Friday evening. I knew that it was short notice, but I also knew that he hadn't been to a birthday of mine for more than twenty-two years.

While talking, I didn't actually explain to him what had been happening vibrationally with me. However, I was thinking that I might share this with him and my other guests at the party. What I did mention to him was, 'I think something pretty special has happened to me and maybe you would like to come along to be a part of it?' I continued by saying, 'It will potentially be a momentous evening and you played a significant role in my life so it would be great to have you there.'

His partner was talking in the background and wanted to know what was going on, but I believe that maybe my father knew or felt something had shifted as he simply said, 'Maybe the universe has aligned?' For my father to make such a statement, without me mentioning the words 'universe', 'alignment' or anything of the sort was perfect timing.

Once I'd hung up the call, I went back inside, feeling even more at peace with myself and the entire world around me. Once again, I felt a sense of complete oneness. Just that event alone, that specific phone call was a significant 'Moment in Time' along the journey of my life.

It was at this point that I thought about my ex-partner Wa, someone who will always be part of my family and my life, for as long as she would like to be. I called her mobile with the intention of meeting up. I wanted to share what I had discovered with her since she had been such an important part of my life for a significant amount of time.

When Wa arrived, she made her way inside and we started to talk. I shared with her the build-up to the revelations, including all the earlier special moments that had occurred with me. From the land-for-sale phone call, the racehorse moment, to the experiences that had transpired over the previous days. I felt that these experiences were truly special to share. After we talked for a little while, I wanted to bring her along on this journey too.

I knew how strong Wa's feelings were for her grandma who had passed, so after my elevated daytime experience with Mum talking about her mother and father, I wanted to also share this experience with Wa by using me to elevate to a special place to say 'hi'. A special place where she could speak and share her thoughts with someone who was so special to her.

Consolingly, I knew we could connect with her grandma by sending 'pure love'. I didn't know what was going to happen, but I knew I wanted to try. The moment that unfolded next was something to behold as the power of spirit entered the room. Being able to share this with her was a humbling experience.

As part of our evening together, I also disclosed the details of a powerful night that had occurred months earlier with me. This was the event that I'd refer to as A Heavenly Defibrillator, the lifesaving angelic experience that occurred in the early hours one morning in March 2020.

Sharing these words with Wa was something very special and I was grateful to her for allowing me the opportunity. As our night progressed, we shared some more conversations and a drink together. Eventually, Wa would head off home and I'd make my way to bed after such a powerfully connected day full of reality-changing events.

Laying in my bed, I thought about all the conversations I had earlier in the day with Mum, including her talking to me about my decision to still drink alcohol even with such an active spiritual connection. During one of our earlier conversations, Mum had questioned, 'Should you still be drinking with this connection?'

I had replied, 'It's fine, I'm allowed to drink. I'm exercising every day, I'm running, I can have a drink.'

Boy, would this belief soon change. I guess since my evolution was always unfolding, everything could not be revealed all at once.

Day 9 – A day to remember – no more blockers

I woke Tuesday morning to begin the day in my new way. This was now the new normal for me as I prepared myself for the unfolding of my day, eagerly excited about what new reveals might present themselves. There were still the regular tasks that needed to be completed too. One of the more mundane tasks I believed was the putting away of the dishes from the night before. This morning would be different though.

As I walked into my kitchen, I knew that the first thing to do was to put the clean dishes away that had been washed and left to dry overnight. This gave me a clean kitchen to work with so that I could prepare my breakfast. I began clearing the dishes one by one, including the glass that I had used from the night before.

Picking up the glass with my right hand, I reached towards the cupboard to put it away, just like I'd done many times before, when all of a sudden, without warning, the glass I was holding exploded and popped in my hand. *Bang!* As glass shattered everywhere, a piece of the shattered glass bounced off my right cheek.

'WOAHHH, what was that?' I exclaimed. Shocked at what had just happened, I jumped back, startled. 'I take it, this means no more drinking?' Then, almost as immediately as my words were spoken,

I received a powerful acknowledgement that this was, in fact, the direct message that I was supposed to receive.

I stood completely still in pure amazement, astounded by what had just occurred. As I picked up another glass, I questioned, *did I smack my hand too hard against the cupboard?* This time, I repeatedly whacked my hand against the cupboard, trying to recreate what had just occurred but nothing happened. The message had already been sent and I had received it.

It would be from this day forward that I would no longer feel the need to consume alcohol.

By this stage of my journey, I had now:

- Freed my spirit and unlocked my soul
- Shifted to a more plant-based diet in tune with caring for my body
- Begun exercising daily
- Stopped consuming signal blockers, including no more drinking of alcohol
- Received the awareness that we are all connected on Earth as humans, plants and animals

My decision to stop drinking alcohol on this day would be an even more significant one considering that I was going to be celebrating my birthday on the approaching Friday night. I documented the glass-breaking experience in my notes, then gathered my possessions and left my house for a morning meeting that I had scheduled.

This meeting was going to be held in a major industrial suburb called Campbellfield, an area full of manufacturing, warehousing and logistics companies. The suburb itself is located within the northern region on the outskirts of metro Melbourne. After the meeting finished, I returned to my car and headed back in the direction of my office. I had set the intention earlier in the day that I would share my newly discovered connection with my other brother Seamus. He can be very black-and-white at times and straight down the line. 'If you can see it, it's real. If you can't see it, then it's not real.' I was wondering, how I would be able to share this divine connection with him?

What would he think? He would see the vibrations, but would that be enough?

As I was driving along the road heading towards the freeway entry, I passed an old historic church, which for some reason, I immediately felt drawn to. I turned around and navigated through some back streets so that I could drive onto the church grounds.

Located at the front of this humble church was a small cemetery. It looked like there were maybe twenty to thirty people buried there based on the number of gravestones.

As I drove up the driveway, with the graveyard on my right-hand side, I felt the energy enter me from this powerful site. This was something I'd never experienced before. My body's cells were visibly alive from the energetic charge that my spiritual sensors were receiving from this unique setting. I was immediately filled with a divine presence just by being in this location. The vibrational connection was so strong that I had to stop and pause as the energy flowed through me. This would become the first of many trips to this special destination. Already on a call to Mum discussing the outcome of the meeting that had just finished, I revealed to her that I had been drawn into this church for some reason, maybe to help with my plan of sharing my connection with Seamus.

The fact that I was on the phone to Mum the whole time whilst in this historic site meant that I was able to share this beautiful connection with her as well. The feeling of euphoria was everywhere; it was like I was surrounded by a divine energetic presence that had entered me. Visually and emotionally, I could feel that my energy levels were through the roof.

After revelling in my connection by just being in the moment, I was ready to continue my little experiment, testing where and what natural environments turned on my sensory receptors. I continued driving forward in my car, making my way down the driveway that ran alongside one of the external walls of the church leading to the rear carpark. I wanted to know if I could also feel my vibrations from the energy connection within the church grounds, not just the cemetery.

This was all so new to me.

Then just like before, once I arrived at the rear carpark I could feel the energy level lift and the vibrational connection continue. 'Wow,' I said to Mum. 'Whatever this connection is for me, there is definitely a connection between myself, my spirit and this church.'

Now that I had experienced this event, with my connection, I suggested to Mum, 'Okay, I think I have a plan! I will ask Seamus to join me for a drive, where we can both go together to the local cemetery in his area, as there is a big chance that I will have the same connection there also.' With this said, we both agreed that that could work and said our goodbyes.

With the afternoon approaching, I contacted my brother and organised to meet with him at his place. Seamus's house was the tallest on his part of the street and by the time I arrived, my clammy hands were sweaty with anticipation about what was going to unfold. I was even a little nervous at first, thinking about what his response would be. Would my connection come out in front of him, or would nothing happen? What would I do if nothing happened?

I parked in his driveway, and I could clearly see Seamus standing outside ready to make his way down his steps to greet me. As we approached each other, almost instantly I could feel my connection become alive, causing me to say, 'Wow, this is happening already!'

He looked at me confused and I said, 'I didn't think this was going to happen just yet. It's nothing bad, mate. In fact, it's beautiful; it's something very special.' I reassured him that it was all natural and that what I was about to share with him was something very empowering!

As we drove off together, I told him about my journey so far, including all the steps I'd taken to arrive at this very point. My greatest first step being the freeing of my soul, undoing the chains of my long-held trauma and pain. He knew all too well what we had experienced as children.

I said, 'I am not sure how to explain this, but I had a special reaction this morning at a cemetery so I'd like to take you up to your local cemetery so I can show you.'

As we arrived at the cemetery, I couldn't help noticing how perfect the moment was. The sun was shining bright, and we quickly discovered a quiet place amongst the gravestones, where we could talk together without interruption. What we spoke about that day was between the two of us but what I will share with you is that we shared a message of love for family past. It was here that I also learned that messages of love need to be direct with volume and purpose. Clear and concise words open the spiritual connection.

Afterwards, we hugged and continued talking together. As we drove back to his family home, we talked some more about my journey and I explained how I had been discovering that my new connection was there for me in many positive ways, including as a guide for direction, as an affirmation of positive intentions and as a confirmation towards great outcomes. I believed that he too could reach this level of connection if he so desired and establish true inner peace.

I shared my recent awareness of the importance of a more plant-based diet. I was aware that this was something he had already been doing for quite a while now. We spoke about the events that had recently been unfolding, including the exploding glass incident and the message that came with that. Eventually, we finished our time together and as he exited my car, we said our goodbyes. Driving back home, I couldn't help wonder about how he was feeling. What was he thinking about the afternoon that we had just experienced together?

As the evening progressed, a friend of mine, Adam, reached out to see if we could catch up at his place. Funnily enough, the house he was living at was at the end of the street just off my brother's road where I had been earlier on that day. His house was just at the top of the hill with a view out towards the impressive green mountains of the Dandenong Ranges. I suggested that it would be fine to catch up and started making my way over. Eventually, I arrived at around 9 pm. He was outside already in the driveway, so we were able to greet each other immediately.

We had only just started talking when out of nowhere and to my surprise, he said, 'Wow, Mike, your vibe is glowing. You are radiating, brother.' Adam continued, 'The mood here was so negative before, but you have just shifted all that energy around!'

I was taken aback by his words as I had not shared any details with him to date about any of my journey. However, I knew that his words were genuine. I stayed for a little so we could continue our conversation together and then eventually it was time for me to head off home.

This would be my final experience for the day. My day had been full of so many connected moments; from the glass exploding with the confirmation that it meant no more alcohol. My physical reaction and the energy felt from both inside the cemetery and church. The sharing of my connection with my brother Seamus, to my connection with spirits past and present. As well as the special words spoken by Adam.

Day 10 – An affirmation that we are together forever

Wednesday was a gentle day spent at home taking care of business. This, however, did not stop some memorable conversations from being shared with Mum throughout the day. One of our main topics of discussion was a fear that I was starting to develop. In fact, this was now my only real fear. I was starting to question and worry about if my divine connection was going to leave me. Was I going to lose this magical experience? As unexpectedly as this out-of-this-world connection arrived, would it up and leave me just as quickly? Would I wake up one day to discover that my beautiful connection, my new way of existing was no more?

As we discussed my fear, I realised I needed to ask the question out loud, 'Am I going to lose my connection?' I felt no response. Immediately, I asked, 'Is my connection here to stay?' Almost as instantly as the words came out of my mouth, I received my vibrational confirmation.

We are together now, forever.

If you hold anger and judgement, you will be tested

The afternoon was unfolding beautifully, right up until the moment I was delivered some disappointing news via a phone call. You see, I'd just managed to secure the attendance of one of my two brothers and his family to come to my party that Friday by personally visiting him to explain the importance of his family's presence on the night. He was questioning whether he would attend the event due to his personal feelings towards our youngest brother, who, on his own roller coaster of negative choices, had emotionally scarred his family.

I had to remind him that I had friends flying in from interstate and yet one of my brothers who lived locally wasn't going to attend. Plus, I reiterated that I was bringing our whole family together after the year that was. Having him and his family join everyone else on this evening was extremely important to me.

That afternoon, I received a phone call informing me that my youngest brother had fallen off the rails again. Allowing my frustration to take over me, I called him full of anger and in an aggressive way, I told him that his choices were going to cost him dearly, including his relationship with his family, his sanity and if he wasn't careful, his life.

I also advised him that based on his actions and choices, he wasn't invited to the party anymore since I had previously explained to him how conflicted the family was now with him. I had already stressed to him that after all his destructive behaviour, I had to personally convince people to come to my own birthday, which was not an easy task nor an enjoyable one. So, if he was to take a step backwards, there would be consequences like not being part of the evening. This wasn't about me being the judge, jury and executioner, it was more about protecting the feelings of the entire family as a collective.

For me personally in that moment, there was a real mixture of sadness, frustration and anger. The event scheduled for Friday night was a joint birthday party for my cousin and me, bringing together our extended families and some close friends after the year of lockdowns. Plus, on top of this, remember I'd also invited my father to this celebration, which in itself was a momentous feat, as he had not been to a birthday or family event of mine for more than twenty years. So, to have my two brothers, mother, father and other family and friends together was always going to be an important evening.

Also, I knew what was on the line: the relationships that were hanging by a thread. I was well aware of how some of the others within the family unit had already been pushed to the end of their tether and how the dynamics of these long-standing relationships had now changed. There are no winners in this kind of situation; everyone involved just gets hurt because deep down, no one wants to exclude anyone from the family. But significant damage had been done.

After my heated phone call, I headed to the gym. I needed to let off some steam and clear my mind. I completely avoided everyone, putting the frustration of the phone call behind me. I headed straight to the treadmill and started to think about my running goal. So far, I'd managed to get the time down to around eleven minutes for that distance, creeping closer each day to my final goal. The focusing on my target and running as fast as I could seemed to clear my mind of any external thought or confusion. I finished my run and then headed back home for an early night. I had noticed that my body clock had come back into alignment. As I laid my head down to sleep that night, what I didn't realise was that I would soon be tested once again.

While I slept, I received another lucid dream. During this dream, suddenly I could see my pale legs. I looked up to observe the room I was in when I noticed I was sitting in a space that was completely white in colour. As I looked down to my left, I saw my naked arm. Cold steel pressed against my skin as the needle pierced my vein. Instantly, I could feel the rush of the drugs as they entered my bloodstream. With that instant sensation, like an explosion in my subconscious mind, I immediately woke up, thinking, *Woooo, no way. Holy shit, what was that? That's not real. That's not me. That did not just happen.*

I knew right away that I had been tested once again. Even as my eyes were open in the darkness of the night, I could still feel the taste in the back of my throat. My heart pounded in my chest as if I'd actually just been injected with an artificial stimulant. I understood the message loud and clear – *You know how hard this is for your youngest brother. You have overcome this yourself. If you come from a place of judgement and anger when dealing with him, you will be tested to see if you are going to break! Will you fold? What will you do?*

With my new perspective and appreciation for the struggle he was enduring, I quickly formulated a new plan for the coming party. I calmed my mind and returned to sleep. The lesson had been learnt for that evening. I would try to make this the last time that I came from anger and frustration when dealing with him.

Day 11 – Reaching a compromise, but you won't do it alone

Thursday morning, I woke and started my day with a powerful affirmation that had been shared with me. I found that speaking these words aloud helped my body, mind and spirit align vibrationally.

- Feels like ease
- Feels like compassion
- Feels like connection
- Feels like knowing
- Feels like whole
- Feels like completeness
- Feels like love

Once I finished my morning routine, I headed off to an appointment with my Chinese doctor. I found a balance between both Western and Eastern medicine worked for me. I'd planned to share with him what had been occurring and the path I'd walked so far to get to this point. This would be the first time I'd shared my connection with a health professional.

I didn't know what was going to happen or what to expect! What would he think? What if my vibrations don't show and nothing occurs? There were many questions in my mind as I speculated what his potential answers might be. While parking my car outside his practice, I began imagining how I would start this conversation with him. I considered that maybe the best way might be just to start talking and trust that the correct words would come as they were needed.

Just as I anticipated, as we began talking, the words started flowing and my connection became alive, joining us in our conversation. This was a significant moment and would be the first of many discussions we would share together talking about my holy divinity.

My worries and concerns about how I would be received were quickly alleviated with his resounding acceptance of what I had uncovered, divine peace and oneness with the wholeness of who we are. Once we finished my consultation, I thanked him for the opportunity to allow me to share my gift with him and then headed off to the gym to repeat my daily run challenge.

Today I was planning to crack the ten-minute mark. I'd prepared myself mentally for a fast run and in doing so, I was completely absorbing the surrounding energy. Beginning my run, I was very focused. I had set the target in my mind and on the machine, so now all I had to do was run. Keeping up a fast pace throughout the entire run, I smashed through the ten-minute barrier by reaching my final goal, of running the 2.2-kilometre distance in the time of nine minutes!

Having not run for many years and setting my target, I had achieved my goal. Feeling pleased with myself, I felt it was now time to set some new targets. As I packed up my bag, ready to leave the gym, I began thinking about what these new goals might be. While I was thinking, I crossed paths with a friend of mine, Simon. We started talking about what was new in his life, plus I shared some of what was happening in mine.

I'd not shared with him the details of my personal journey yet, but I could feel the vibrations attached to the genuineness of the words of our conversation. We decided to go grab some lunch together, when out of the blue Simon suggested to me that it felt like I was really electric and alive! In my mind, I thought these were interesting words for him to use since these words were some of the exact same descriptive words that I'd been journaling to describe how I was feeling since my journey began:

- Feeling extremely alive
- Feeling extremely connected

- Feeling like everything is electric
- Feeling like the energy is illuminated
- Feeling the energy

After our lunch finished, I headed back to my car to make my way home. I had an idea about how I was going to deal with a certain situation from the day before. As soon as I arrived home, I called my youngest brother. I wanted to continue our conversation from the day before, but this time with my new perspectives that I'd learnt from the dream message during the night.

Since the phone call from the day before, I had put some thought into what had occurred and what could possibly be a workable solution. Of course, in the end, I wanted both my brothers with me on this special evening.

Reaching a compromise – but you won't do it alone

As he answered my call, we said a quick hello and then we moved straight to the point.

I stated, 'I've had a think about what was said yesterday, and I realise I was wrong to come from a place of anger and frustration. I still want you to come on Friday night. However, I will need you to do something for me. I don't want you to drink any alcohol on the evening. I want you there level-headed. What's happened this week has happened. I can look past that; however, on Friday night I want you there with as clear a mind as possible. I'm asking you to agree not to drink on the night as part of this compromise. However, you will not do this alone; I will do this with you.'

I reaffirmed to him that, 'It does not matter to me that the evening is a celebration of my birthday. I won't drink any alcohol with you as I would not ask you to do anything that I would not do myself.'

Instantly, I could hear that he was surprised in his voice and taken back by my offer. I sensed he was shocked, but he quickly responded in agreement with, 'Yes, okay, I can do that! Thank you.'

I also put forward that in the few days remaining before the night, he would stay on track, to which he agreed, then we said our goodbyes, ending our call.

Reassuringly I knew that mum had overheard our conversation and I could immediately tell that she was both relieved and pleased with this new proposal I had put forward. I shared with her in detail afterwards how I had reached this compromise, including the test I'd received during the night before. We both expressed our feelings about how we hoped he would stay true to his word.

With my head cleared and my plan in place, I comfortably headed off to have some dinner with my friend Jimmy. Tonight, we'd agreed that we'd explore more of my special connection. I knew that since Jimmy was on his own journey of discovery, he had explored many different concepts and practices.

One of the practices he'd previously experienced was Quantum Healing Hypnosis. He had explored this for his own reasons; however, the concept of this practice is to embark on a spiritual journey by connecting with your highest self, exploring the sub-conscious realms focusing on the healing of your spirit. This practice uses past life regressions as the means to overcome and heal. Since I knew that my spirit was already freed and that I was vibrationally connected in my conscious state, I was very eager to see what I might uncover during a sub-conscious hypnosis experience.

Day 12 – My signal is now open and receiving

Today was a very important day on my journey. I wanted to start by reflecting on my connection, exploring all the special parts, and testing the words, thoughts and moments that really allowed me to feel my alignment with my highest self. Since the fear of me losing my connection had been alleviated, I was now ready to keep exploring the possibilities.

I started by writing down all the moments that I'd experienced in the previous days, along with the earlier energetic experiences that had occurred. Documenting who I had shared this with and what had occurred on these days was an excellent idea because I knew that my connection was special. Plus, I felt this was an important story and one that needed to be told.

Sitting down in my space at home, with a still mind, I began to allow the thoughts enter my consciousness, including what subjects triggered a vibration. 'Things that trigger my vibrational response' was the title I used above the content I was recording. It was as if I was documenting my experiences like a test subject:

What was triggering my vibrational response:

- My connection to the truth, with words and conversations about meaningful subjects
- Knowing that I was connected to an energy that I could feel but I could not see
- My connection with spirit
- The affirmation of being in receiving mode
- The illumination of the lights – absorbing all the energy into me

Now I was truly evolving, beginning to appreciate that this was my new way!

I was genuinely excited for the journey ahead. I was picturing one where I could share my discovered connection and the message of divine love and internal peace. With the natural pleasure of the euphoric energy flowing, the freedom of knowing and the power of my connection my future was shining.

As the day progressed, I started to prepare for the evening. My party was coming up, bringing together my extended family and friends after our strange year. How special this would be!

Arriving at the venue, at around mid-afternoon, I wanted to make sure everything was prepared for the evening ahead. I'd hired out a unique establishment in the city that offered a mixture of all the comforts associated with a seasoned venue along with a sub-tropical forest feel, from the scenic plants and trees spread around the courtyard area. Everything was set for the night ahead.

It wasn't long before my guests had started to arrive and mingle. After about an hour had passed, I received a call from my youngest brother. He had arrived with his partner and was out the front. I quickly made my way outside to greet the two of them. After we said our hellos, Mat and I reaffirmed our commitment to each other to remain sober for the evening, to which we both agreed, then we ventured inside. What I enjoyed most about our agreement that night was that knowingly or unknowingly other immediate family members showed their support by joining Mat and me in our commitment to each other during the night.

Using our forward-facing time machine – we can change our future

Throughout the evening, I shared a story with some of my guests about a special lady I had met. She was a young mum with two little girls of her own. She'd come from a long line of generationally unemployed individuals and had been unemployed herself for quite a few years; however, she had experienced her very own beautiful awakening moment.

During her moment of inspiration, she'd made a personal commitment to herself to change the trajectory of her future path. She wanted a different future for herself and her girls, something other than what had been unfolding in front of her eyes.

With her intention set, she made her plan. Using the initial effort she had invested, along with some additional help and guidance that was provided, she managed to successfully open her very own business. This was a momentous achievement for herself; not only had she broken the generational cycle of unemployment but she was now also self-employed. She was her own boss. She had broken the cycle of repeated behaviours and negative beliefs, unwilling to conform to the engrained mentality that she would always be in a struggling family. This achievement in itself was a fantastic story.

However, the part of this story that I loved the most was how her positive choices and behaviours, the ones that had motivated her to create a different story for herself and a new future, had influenced two other little creative beings.

For the first few weeks after opening her own business, her daughters would ask her every day, 'Who's your boss, Mummy? Who do you work for?' And she would cheerfully reply, 'I am my boss.' The girls would then reply, 'Yeah okay, but then who do you work for?' They couldn't seem to get their head around the concept that mummy could be her own boss. They both struggled to understand that this was even possible. However, after a few more days of repeatedly asking the same questions, something finally clicked in the little girls. Now their perception of reality, what they could achieve and what was possible for them in their future had been reimagined and altered moving forward.

This was a beautiful thing.

I really love this story because it shows how our attitude and choices can easily influence those closest to us in a positive awakening moment. It does not always have to be negative behaviours or attitudes that are repeated or passed on to the next generation. We can have many positive influences.

I believe that at our core; we are all creative beings. We came to this earth to enjoy the experience of everything that is on offer. We came to create. Whether we create a life for ourselves, or we create a family, create opportunities, create meals, create friendships, create artistically or create love.

We have all come to create our own story.

Chapter 5

FEELS LIKE EASE

Day 13 – Finally a peaceful birthday with my soul freed

I woke on this day engulfed with an overwhelming sense of peacefulness. Today was my actual birthday and for the first time in my adult life, I was at total peace with myself and who I was. This would be the first birthday I would celebrate without searching for an artificial high. With this sense of understanding, I was relishing in my newly discovered serenity.

In addition to this internal peace, I also had my connection to something greater than I'd ever known. A connection that I've since come to believe was there all along just hidden under all the emotional baggage, behaviours and beliefs that I'd developed and inherited over my life's journey. As I laid in my bed at peace, I reaffirmed my intentions for the day.

By this stage, I was so responsive to my vibrations. There were many things that I was still unsure of, including questions about what it was that was actually connecting with me and how I completely connected with them. I was searching for new ways to connect instead of using the keywords and statements that I'd uncovered that seemed to activate my connection.

Looking through the journaling of all my vibrational moments, I could see that many of these elevated moments were occurring during actual conversations and interactions with different people. Basically, anyone that I was interacting with on a connected level. I was comfortable with this; in fact, I believed that this was perfect as this level of comfort allowed me to share my experience with more and more people.

With my true self now unleashed, I was looking for more of these naturally connected moments, without the internal blockers that fed any negative self-beliefs and feelings. I had nothing left to forget, no regrets and no pain from anything that had occurred in my past. I was finally free.

> *'Your spirit is the divine life force inside you,
> your soul is the essence of you – it's what makes you, YOU.'*
> **– M. Smith**

I was sure that because I had allowed myself to find that internal peace, the reward of calmness had allowed me to reach an elevated level of spiritual freedom. I was discovering that by reaching this point, the natural progression was allowing me to connect with and receive from all things around me.

During the day, I received some calls from close friends that were out of the state. One call was from my close friend Darren, who had arrived in the country from Europe but was still going through the quarantine process. A strange scenario that had now become the new normal for travellers. During our call, I gently shared some of the journey so far; however, I was careful not to talk too much with him over the phone since I'd planned to speak with him face to face once we were together. We were already organised to reconnect the following week up at the Gold Coast in Queensland. As our conversation flowed, I could feel the vibrations come out. With the genuineness of our dialogue and the purity of the words spoken, the positive energy streamed.

By now, my day was already unfolding beautifully, plus I knew that soon the evening would be upon me and that at night, I would reconnect with Wa, just as we had planned earlier in the week. We shared a lovely effortless evening together, just the two of us enjoying each other's company. After our meal, I suggested to her that maybe I could bring her to a special place that I'd discovered. This was the old church and cemetery that I'd previously written about.

It was during my first visit to this site that I discovered just how truly spiritual and vibrationally connected this location was. I was eager to find out what might occur the second time around. Would the experience of vibrational connectivity be repeated, or would there be nothing? I wasn't sure, but I was certainly excited to find out!

Quietly confident that I would be able to relive this special experience with her once again, on our drive there, I spoke about my first experience at this historic site including the powerful energetic field associated with the address. While we talked, I became aware of my mind as it elevated to a level of complete clarity and awareness; this experience was tied to the increased energy associated with my physical connection, vibrationally.

The feeling of one's mind being completely open and in the receiving mode is such a beautiful state of existence. Being present in the 'now', existing only in the moment, without obstructions. Basking in the complete sense of oneness and appreciation, while relishing in the vibrational sensations from the internally flowing, euphoric energy.

Once we arrived, I turned off the main road into the driveway of the historic site. The driveway was just a thin gravelled road lined with small trees on the left-hand side and an old, dilapidated fence for the cemetery on the right. The cemetery seemed more like a private burial site than anything commercial. It's a petite site where a chosen few have been buried over the last 200 years; about twenty-five gravestones exist, each one seemingly belonging to a significant person or family associated with the church. For me, it didn't matter who was buried there as it was the overall level of energy associated with the site that had drawn me in, with its energy of such great magnitude.

Ahead was the old church building, built from solid rock stone and originally constructed during the 1800s. The church itself was rich with its own powerful energy. The energetic power flowing at this place of worship is something in itself to be cherished and basked in.

As we reached the first stop along the gravelled drive, we were roughly at the halfway point of the cemetery, I parked my car for just a few minutes. I had parked in this exact same location on my first visit, when I discovered this powerful site. I wanted to repeat the same actions step by step in my attempt to recreate the same outcome.

I wanted Wa to see with her own eyes, the revelation and physical reaction that is very real. I wanted to share with her the evidence that there was something much greater at play here, along with reaffirming that we are all connected and that part of what I am feeling is a true connection to spirit.

> *'I felt as if I had discovered a confirmation that death was not the end, and that death really was just the beginning of our next journey.'*
> **– M. Smith**

With the energy level rising and my vibrational connection clearly visible, I noticed that Wa turned her head away. I was aware that this would have been a lot for anyone to comprehend. After what seemed like a couple of minutes, I started my car again and instantly my vibrations reduced. As we headed along the bumpy drive towards the rear of the church, out of curiosity I asked her, 'How come you turned away?' To which she replied, 'I didn't want to see you get taken away!' I gently laughed and quickly reminded her that I was not going anywhere. I reminded her that this beautiful connection was something to be revelled in and enjoyed not feared or hidden from.

As we entered the rear of the church, the energy began to rise again. This time, I noticed it was not at the same intensity as when we were parked in front of the cemetery. However, the rear of this church ground was still a high-frequency space. I was extremely pleased to have been able to share this connection with Wa and that my second visit to this site was just as connected as my first. I began to understand that for me this site was significantly relevant along my divine journey.

I turned the car around so we could head back towards the main road, and once again we passed the cemetery. Suddenly without any initiating, my connection with the energy of this environment ignited my vibrations, connecting with the celestial spirit.

On our drive home, I thanked Wa for letting me share this exceptional experience with her. I knew that an experience like this was something to be seen to be believed. Witnessing an open connection with Source, with spirit and with the Creator of our existence. It was not long before we arrived at her place where once again, I thanked her for the evening and for allowing me to share some very special moments with her.

I waited as she exited my car and made her way inside, that way I knew she was home safe. Now I had the opportunity to sit and enjoy the experience that just was and all the events of the evening. I could feel that I was once again becoming elevated. The feeling of total calmness, peacefulness and being at one with everything consumed my body. This was such a beautiful day!

Day 14 – Slow it down

An extraordinary Sunday morning was planned for this day. Since recording the lyrics to my song *Slow It Down* at home the previous week, I was heading into the music studio today to lay the vocals on the music track that had been created by my music man, the Doctor. Since I hadn't heard the music yet that he'd created for my lyrics, I was excited to soon hear what sounds he had put together based on the words. This was co-creating at its best!

With my lyrics in hand, I made my way inside his studio. We talked for a little while and then the Doctor shared with me what he'd come up with. As soon as I heard the sounds, without hesitation, we jumped straight in and started to put the song together. After laying down my vocals, we both listened to the new track. This was a highly vibrational moment. We had turned a thought into words and now into a song. I believe that receiving the vibration was an acknowledgement from Source that they too were pleased as well.

Sitting in the moment, I felt the euphoria disperse throughout my entire body. Every day was a new connected adventure now. I eventually left the studio and headed home, as I needed to pack, prepare and tie off any loose ends that required actioning before I was to disappear for the week. I was heading off Monday morning for a holiday. I'd already organised a beautiful trip up north to the Gold Coast, in sunny Queensland to recharge and reconnect with the sand, ocean and earth as well as with some special family members and friends.

Asking the question: Can we use only our minds to connect and feel the energy of the universe?

As I packed for my trip, I stopped to take some time to reflect on the previous day's experiences, reaffirming my newfound connection with the Almighty. Even though all of this was still so new for me, I wanted to see if I could trigger my connection using just my mind, without spoken words, conversations or specific environments.

I sat down and attempted to quiet my mind. Ensuring my immediate environment was totally still, I used a focus breathing technique to clear my mind of any thought. This ensured that my mind was now a blank canvas. I envisaged the following worded thought inside my mind: *I want to feel my connection with Source, I want to feel my connection with the Universe.* Almost instantaneously, I could feel my cells become alive and I could feel my connection through vibration.

By now I was quickly becoming convinced that my physical vibrations were the acknowledgement of my divine connection between my physical body and my highest self. Once again, the bursts of euphoric energy pumped around the inside of my body. I was in love with my connection, and I loved my new way. There was no looking back now!

My life experience had been reset with my new beginning and as my evening progressed, I continually reached out for my divine connection. I repeatedly focused on using my thoughts while quieting my mind, having now discovered another way for me to establish my connection, to feel touched, to feel blessed, to feel the heavenly love.

Day 15 – Leaving to reconnect with the ocean and the sand

I awoke this morning full of life and joy. I was ready for my reconnection holiday. I'd already set my intentions to reconnect with the ocean and sand and in my mind, I was already there.

In the days before, Mum had asked if she could drive me to the airport, to which I willingly accepted. Once she'd arrived to my place, I loaded my luggage into her car then we headed off to the airport together. As we drove towards the city, I wanted to share with her the speaker that I'd recently discovered. Since the words from the speaker seemed to connect with me on a vibrational level, I wanted to share this experience with her while we were travelling together.

Experiencing a vibrational reaction to spoken words from someone speaking on a pre-recorded clip was certainly something that I'd never quite experienced before. I thought that sharing another connected moment with Mum would be another powerful event. I asked her to play a specific clip that was online. Then, almost instantaneously as the speaker started talking, my cells became alive. Vibrating and connecting with the spoken words. The celestial energy filled my body, like an open tap gushing with an abundance of euphoric energy flowing through me from above.

My relationship with these words can only be described as a celestial match. With every sentence that was spoken, it was as if I was receiving some sort of confirmation that these words were important. I was sure that this message was full of valuable information that I needed to give my attention to and begin to understand. Would I be spreading a message soon too?

I believe: 'We can have more, experience more and feel more connected than we have ever known.'

With my eyes wide open now to a new life experience and with my vision so illuminated, one of the questions in my mind was, 'Are those in society who are referred to as the "Illuminati" just seeing the lights brighter, seeing the universe for what it really is? Are they all connected beings as well? Is their spiritual eye wide open? Do they know the truth behind our existence, that we can have anything, do anything or be anything that we desire?' On a few different levels, this would seem to make sense.

Inside Mum's car, the energy level was electric. We were experiencing an amplified drive together, sharing the experience and my connection. Even though I was the one who was receiving the physical vibrations at that very moment, I was happy to be able to share this experience with Mum once again as she witnessed this unfold. I began to wonder if she was starting to want to feel this connection too. Could Mum connect like this? What would she have to do?

Would it be possible?

I thought, of course, this would be possible! This is for everyone!

We eventually arrived at the airport, where we said our goodbyes and I headed into the terminal to catch my flight. Feeling so connected from the car drive-in and the experience that just was, I could sense that this was going to be a powerful trip already.

Once landed in Queensland, I collected my baggage, grabbed my hire car and headed over to the hotel where I was staying. The plan was that I'd be spending a couple of nights at the same hotel as Darren, then I'd leave there and spend the remaining days/nights at the second residence.

The second address on my holiday was much closer to the water; in fact, the doors opened onto the sand. I had chosen this location specifically for my re-connection with the beach and the ocean. After I checked into my room, I began feeling excited about the evening ahead. Tonight, I was going to be able to share my newfound connection with another special soul in my life.

I set up my room, then quickly headed down to the gym for my daily run. Since I'd achieved my goal of the two-kilometre time, I wanted to set a new target. This time I wanted to try to run for longer distances now; I wanted to improve my body's natural endurance. This time round, I set up the treadmill for twenty-five minutes at a solid running pace. This length of time might not seem like much to you, but for someone who had just started running again, this time was going to be the longest duration I'd run non-stop for over eighteen years.

Feeling fresh, tied in with a proud sense of accomplishment, I decided that I'd continue this new challenge each day over the next few days. However, each time I'd continue to increase the length of time I was running for, along with the speed at which I was running.

Having finished my run, I freshened up in my room and then arranged to meet up with Darren for the evening. He'd already completed the quarantine period in the weeks before and was now free to partake in normal life, re-joining the rest of the community. We organised to meet up in the hotel lobby and from there we'd walk over to the casino with an assortment of restaurants and bars to choose from.

After greeting each other in the lobby, talking about life and catching up on all the latest news, we made our way across the street into the casino, then up to the restaurant area. Darren had already reserved a table for us at one of the very popular establishments. Upon our arrival, we were greeted by one of the friendly wait staff and escorted to our table.

It was during our dinner that I'd planned to share my journey so far with him. Once we had ordered, I began by sharing the news of my connection, discussing the divine power and the guidance that came with my connection to Source. I spoke about my journey so far, including the steps to date that I had unknowingly walked:

1. The freeing of my spirit – establishing my connection with my highest self.
2. The learning and understanding of generational behaviours and cycles.
3. My awareness that helping others is one the most important things that we can do in life.
4. My awakening to the reality that we are all connected – my land and Steel Prince experience.
5. My newly started exercise running regime.
6. The changing of my diet.
7. No more blockers.
8. My newfound sense of guidance.
9. My newfound trust in the universe.
10. My personal discovery that there is more to our existence than what we can see.

Connecting with him in this manner was something truly special and I could feel from my vibrational response that the words were not lost on him. This was something powerful!

Day 16 – Connecting with words

The previous evening, I'd planned to spend this day just relaxing, recharging and entertaining myself. I wanted to continue exploring the connection with my highest self by listening, hearing and feeling for the words of relevance. One of the ways I was going to achieve this was by listening to the speaker that I'd found. She was someone who seemed to be talking about subjects that I'd already uncovered myself, so for this reason I felt extremely connected with her.

She was unknowingly helping me along my journey towards understanding and accepting what it was that I was experiencing. I felt a real sense of connection to her spoken words and many of the messages that she was delivering. I was still trying to get my head around some of her topics though, as I felt some of the messages were too self-focused. Although, I was beginning to understand that maybe the reason these messages were being delivered in such a way was so that people could potentially understand that wanting to feel good is perfectly fine. Feeling good, feeling love is what life is all about.

I considered that maybe the message I needed to hear was that it is not selfish to want to feel good. You are allowed to feel good; you can want to feel good. If others choose to accuse you of being selfish because you want to feel good, then that's on them, you can leave that with them and that's okay. Hopefully one day they will realise that they too are allowed to feel good.

Realising that you don't have to live your entire life existence in a state of sadness or anger just because others are. You could wish better for them, but you could also try to understand that they are making their own life choices. However, I also believe that doing whatever you want to feel good should not be done to the detriment of others. We should not need to bring others down, just so we can feel good.

What I started to wish for was for people to discover for themselves that once you free your spirit and align with the Highest Power, you can reconnect with your inner being and discover who you truly are. I knew that from this vantage point, anything was possible – you could even establish your own unique vibrational connection between your body, mind and spirit.

I thought about how I'd like everyone to be able to feel the divine touch of the universe, as often as they desire. Since I knew that the connection we have with Source is unlimited, I was sure that there was no way we could ever run out of the most euphoric feeling you could ever imagine, the purest positive energy imaginable. This was why I created the Wounded Butterflies – Overcoming Adversity program, as a guided pathway to freeing your spirit and unchaining your soul.

Why wouldn't someone want to naturally experience the sensation like you're floating on cloud nine? Where your mind shifts into a space of pure clarity, where the answers to questions are known and given to you in a stream of abundance for you to receive. When the divine touch acts as a confirmation of positive intentions or outcomes. It's absolutely beautiful.

Knowing that once you'd re-established your divine connection, vibrationally, you would not want to ever let it go. It's all you ever truly need to feel good. I knew that once you've connected, you could discover what words worked for you; however, I was aware of the powerful effects of speaking the sentence, '*Universe, heal me please.*' I was certain that these words when spoken from a place of connection, activated the divine healing energy.

Beginning my day on the Gold Coast
Heading out of my hotel that morning, I decided that I would make my way by foot into the local café area nestled in between the city buildings. I wanted to really immerse myself in the moment as I explored the city while absorbing the feeling of being so vibrationally connected. Listening to the sounds and words that naturally heightened my senses.

I wanted to be consumed by the energy, relishing in the power as I attracted the radiating energy that was being expelled from the surrounding lights and infrastructure, seeing them all shine so bright with so much life.

Eventually, I arrived at a café aptly named the No Name Café, I was immediately drawn to this location and for a good reason too! The positive energy flowing around inside this café was immense, so much so that I could instantly feel my connection. Looking back through my notes from this day, I noticed that I'd referred to this café as my 'ENERGY CAFÉ' underlined and in capitals which was my attempt to highlight just how vibrationally important the experience was for me, with minimal words.

This was one of those moments where, even though there were not many words said inside, there was no need for words; we were connecting on a higher frequency. In fact, I had made a special connection with one of the staff on duty. Our connection was established with such ease. This was a profound experience that we explored together.

Day 17 – Non-vibrational beings

I awoke the next day feeling immediately connected. Once again, this morning the lights visually felt so illuminated. My eyes were like sponges just absorbing the radiating energy. As my body consumed this sensation, my vibrational sensors immediately became alive and activated. I comfortably got myself ready and made my way to breakfast at my new Energy Café.

My walk there was spent relishing in the feeling of being inside my zone. I was soaking up my energetic connection focusing on purely being in the 'now'. This was such an elevated experience now that my connection had become so powerful. The atmosphere inside the Energy Café that day was electric! After my connection from the previous day with the staff member, I knew that this morning would be just as exciting. It's quite hard to completely explain the feeling of being vibrationally connected and plugged into all that is, while just sitting at a table eating one's breakfast.

I felt as though today was going to be one of the most significant days on my holiday. Even though I was living connected moments each day, there were some days, where specific events were at such a heightened level, that my vibrational connection could not be ignored. These days stood out as game changers. It felt like today would be one of those days, since I was going to share my connection with my cousin Lisa.

We'd planned to meet at the art studio she managed around lunchtime. Lisa knew that this would be her quiet period, so we could catch up then. The studio was strategically located on the corner of a bustling city street, with a constantly changing window designed to grab your attention. I arrived around midday and after our catch-up on life, including how she was going and what had been happening since we last spoke, a couple of her clients walked in to see her quickly.

Seizing this opportunity, I browsed around the gallery to check out what was new. There were several artists in her studio that I liked, so I wanted to see if they had released any new work. Once her clients had left the studio, we resumed our conversation only this time, I began sharing with Lisa about my journey so far and all the different events that had unfolded. Before this, Lisa had only been told about what I'd been experiencing from some of our other family members but now, it was time for me to share this with her firsthand.

A vibrational conversation

I started by sharing a statement that had become so familiar with me, that we're all a spirit in a body, not a body with a spirit and as I have previously written about, explaining to her that I believed this meant our spirit is our controlling force, our spirit life force is infinite. Our body, as special as it is, is just our shell. These words had become the words I used to introduce the conversation of what it was that I was about to share. I had used them on many occasions by now, as they seemed to flow at the beginning of each conversation with a variety of different people. Where these words and wisdom had originated from was something divine in nature.

As I spoke these words, they instantly helped me to vibrationally align and connect. Plus, I knew that once connected, my conversation would flow freely. I knew that my vibrations would be alive and that these moments were extremely special, with the topics shared extremely real. I spoke about the euphoric energy, along with my vibrational connection that just seemed to come alive after the spiritual path I'd discovered inside my home, after freeing my internal spirit and unchaining my soul. I shared with her my connection to the universe and with all that is.

Curiously, Lisa asked me, 'What does the feeling feel like?' as she could see the physical change.

I did my best to explain that it felt like nothing that I'd ever felt before, a feeling that I believe did not originate from this physical world. The sensation was like a lightning bolt of pure energy hitting my body and blasting through me. The feeling offered me complete clarity in my mind. I exclaimed that it was something much greater than I'd ever known!

We discussed the similarities between this natural sensation and the artificially delivered sensation supplied from manufactured drugs, such as narcotics. It's almost as if they have been pharmaceutically designed to mimic this natural sensation to trap people so that they are forever chasing the artificial feeling. Locking people into years of addictions, even lifelong addictions in their search to feel good when this sensation is already naturally there and available now for anyone to access without a cost or consequence.

This would help explain why they are all so addictive. If naturally, we all feel this connection as a newborn baby, then the memory of this divine sensation is implanted deep in each of our minds. So, when a drug user opens that door for the first time, they are potentially not aware of what historic memory they are about the reactivate. I continued by saying, 'Think of what could change if we could all discover that we don't need to consume, snort, inject or smoke any chemical in order to feel this feeling and that all we needed to do was just free ourselves internally. If people only knew that they could connect with this energy naturally, could this make a huge change in human behaviours? If everyone could become a true believer, think of the possibilities. Imagine having an open tap to Source. A stream that can fill you with the energy from the universe so that you can experience the divine touch as often as you desire throughout your day without the fear or consequences that come from drug addiction!'

Continuously I spoke about the fact that I had already begun to believe that drugs and alcohol were just signal blockers, designed to jam your frequency and muffle your divine connection, highlighting that these would play no further role in my life.

Together, I shared my newfound discoveries, how I emphatically believed that we are all connected as humans, plants and animals to Mother Earth. The complete end-to-end biodiversity ecosystem. I felt that no matter who or what we are, we all exist with our own internal life-giving spirit. I suggested that although we may communicate in different ways, we are actually all connected, as we contribute and play our role here on earth.

We are all interconnected spirit beings.

I mentioned to Lisa that now I felt that my spiritual awareness was so alive and open now, that I couldn't even bring myself to kill a spider. I shared with her that now I have an agreement with them, if they stay outside, I'll stay inside, then we have a deal. No one's getting squashed!

Lisa laughed and agreed that she, too, was already feeling the same way!

Continuing our conversation, I shared with Lisa about my vibrational connection to our *divine* Creator, along with my belief that there is already a grand plan in place. I believe that as individuals if we can find true Vibrational Alignment, this will transition the earth into a significantly higher level of consciousness and awareness.

This brings each of us individually into our own receptive mode, while universally connecting all of existence unleashing unlimited potential. I believe it is from this point that we can start to live out our true existence. It is from this connected state of being, that we can begin to feel the complete universal guidance that is available to us.

It is from within this level of consciousness, that one can truly experience the divine messages as they are being shared with them. Knowing that we are universally supported, in achieving what it is that we desire to achieve. From our non-physical to physical perspective. Whatever the original intentions were that we had set out for ourselves to achieve before we descended to this earth, I know that we all have the divine assistance from above available to us to achieve these outcomes.

We conversed about my belief that if we are spirits in a body, not a body with a spirit, then, could it be possible at a spiritually high level, one in which we cannot see but one in which we can feel? Could our spirit connect with other spirits both past and present? Even as I write these words now, I'm reminded by my connection to the divine, that this is the way, feeling guided by my vibrational connection.

It was during this point of our conversation that we spoke about if this is the case, then once someone is in the receptive mode and connected, can they then be used by non-receptive people to connect with transitioned spirits? Even if this is just for the purpose of a non-receptive person having the ability to visually see the vibrational acknowledgement of a current spirit's existence. A vibrational acknowledgement that their verbal message has been received from the spirit world!

Once we'd spoken about this possibility together, we sent our own connected message through the universe to some spirits that had already transitioned past family connections using this divine connection. This was a truly special conversation. This experience was something to remember. After such an elevated event, we organised to meet up again later in the evening and with that, I headed off for the rest of my afternoon adventures.

For me, I had found our conversation, experiences and the time spent together to be extremely enjoyable. A truly connected occasion. The thought of continuing this vibrational experience in a few hours' time was something that I was eagerly awaiting.

As the day progressed, I spent my time exploring, connecting and getting back in touch with the earth. Then before I knew it, the evening had arrived, so I made my way over to their home. It would be at dinner this night that I would have the signal blocker understanding reaffirmed for me.

Entering their home, the vibe was great, warm, welcoming and friendly. It was only once the conversation started with others inside that I realised:

Some will be ready – some will not

Since my connection was still so new for me and something unheard of, I understood that this might be a lot for some people to process and take in immediately. This was fine; I knew that there would be some people who would need time to process. Some people would be open to understanding, some people would feel some sort of connection and some people may already be connected or have experienced a similar connection. However, I was also aware that there would be some people who would not be ready. These people would still hold their doubts even if they witnessed my connection with their own eyes, they would struggle to accept. Then finally, there would be those who may never be ready, to believe, listen or understand.

- Some people are connected.
- Some people believe and want to explore the possibilities more.
- Some people are on the cusp of their own awakening.
- Some people are not yet ready.
- Some people may never be ready in this life.

I knew that Lisa was open and receptive to my awakening; however, there were others who were not and once I felt the direction of the conversation going down a specific path, I pulled back, reset my mind and allowed myself to just enjoy the evening at the level that it was to be at. This change was okay too. This was fine, this had to be fine, as this too, would be part of my journey, experiencing moments like these! I had to accept that the words and the messages that I was delivering would not always be accepted by those around me.

Chapter 6

CONNECTED SOULS

Day 18 – Children are so connected

As the sun rose, I rose, opening my eyes to the glistening morning rays that had penetrated through the huge glass windows directly into my room and across my face. After the night's sleep, I was feeling completely refreshed, considering the mixed bag of emotions that I'd experienced from the day before. Two extremely different interactions when comparing the elevated conversation that was shared with Lisa during the day to the complete opposite with her partner in the evening, a conversation that was almost a mockery of what was unfolding.

However, I reaffirmed to myself, that this was okay – in fact, this was fine. I needed to experience these moments along my journey to see if I would alter or change my course of direction. However, I knew that they would just reinforce my belief that I was on the right path. By now I knew too much already, too many things had been revealed to turn back now.

I was aware though that not everyone would be ready, willing or able to accept this new version of my reality, a reality where we all exist vibrationally connected to the one Creator. An existence where pain, trauma and old-school behaviours and beliefs are replaced with divine love, guidance and wisdom, an everlasting stream of celestial energy for us all to tap into and constantly receive.

Today was planned to be another momentous day! I was going to meet with one of my closest friends Shane, his partner, Hannah, and their young boy, Steele. Shane is like a brother to me; in fact, I am very close with his whole family and with this in mind, I was extremely excited to see where our afternoon would take us once we reconnected. Although before beginning the journey to their place, I'd decided that I would spend the morning getting reacquainted with the energy of the ocean once again by walking down to the sea.

As soon as I reached the sand, I kicked off my shoes to allow my bare feet to reconnect with the warm golden particles that covered the shoreline. I have always felt an affiliation with the ocean. I find that my entire relationship with the water is based on an internal grounding process, one that always allows me to forget about the external noise and just be in the moment.

I found myself standing with my feet at the water's edge, watching the ocean as the waves rolled in. As each wave broke, the cold water rushed over my feet while I stood there listening to the trance-like sounds of the sea. Hearing the waves crash one after the other is such a magnificently peaceful experience. As each wave breaks it is the coming together of the ocean's might and power combined with the ocean's tranquilness. A sound, movement and moment provided to us by our earth, for free, for all of us to enjoy.

After my time on the sand, I made my way back to the apartment so I could collect my vehicle and begin the drive down to Shane's place. Shane and his family were living in a beautiful part of the world where the ocean meets the trees, mixing the beach experience with a forestry nature-filled lifestyle.

During my drive, I continued to tune myself into my receptive mode. I wanted to be in the highest state of consciousness for my arrival since I was planning on potentially sharing my journey with them all for the first time. That was if now was the right time. I knew that I would feel the signs. I made my way down to their place via the coastal roads. By taking this path, I could visually stay connected with the ocean for the entire drive.

Along the way, I encountered a number of unmarked locations with spectacular panoramic views that I could enjoy. Unique spots where the ocean met the land, as well as some strategically placed lookout points to stop and appreciate the natural scenery. Absorbing nature's natural artwork like an interactive 4D masterpiece. I arrived in town early before anyone would be home and quickly decided to check out the immediate neighbourhood as I wandered around the local shops and down to the beach area, just taking it all in.

I came across a petite retail store; it was a health food shop selling fresh organic produce in the form of food dishes and fresh smoothie drinks. In addition to food and drinks on sale, there was a large number of photographic artworks mounted on the walls and on display throughout the store. As I began to browse through the images that were on display, I instantly received a vibrational signal that there might be a special hidden gem inside this place.

Apparently, the owner of the store who just happened to be working behind the counter on this day was also a very skilled photographer. As we started to talk about some of the images that had caught my eye, he began to share the background story behind each of the shots. Things like where he was when he took the photo, the weather conditions on the day and the time he spent just waiting for the ideal moment.

While we were conversing, I could feel that I was vibrationally connecting with the words he was speaking. I could feel his genuine love and passion for his work. He recalled the specifics of each shot in great detail, like the morning he patiently waited for hours floating in the ocean just for the perfect moment. It was as if it was only yesterday that he taken each photograph.

As I continued to explore more of the images, I could feel some of the photos start to vibrationally resonate with me. Some of the photographs were so powerful, it was as if they were radiating their own energy from Source. Then I came across one particular image that was pulsating with so much energy hidden inside. As I locked on to this photograph, I stood in appreciation of what it was that I was experiencing. This was something that I'd never experienced before, a vibrational connection radiating so strongly from just a photograph. The image itself connected with me straight away, a combination of the earth's natural beauty, the powerful ocean and the peaceful sky.

The image consisted of the sun's radiating energy spreading pink and purple waves of colours across the morning sky right down to the horizon so that the waves of the sky could connect with waves of the ocean. The image made it seem as if on the horizon the set of skyline waves and the ocean's own waves had melded together joining as one, creating this powerfully energetic connection.

An amalgamation of universal energy coming together as one.

The vibration I felt with this piece was so strong, that after I revelled in the energetic connection for a few minutes, I said to the artist, 'I'll purchase this one, this is a powerful shot! This image is way too strong for me to leave here and not bring home with me today!' I could sense that he was pleased to hear these words and happy that I'd connected with some of his work. I thanked him for sharing his experiences with me and headed off.

I walked down to the beach and out onto the warm glistening sand, soaking up the tranquillity of the entire area. I was filled with gratitude for the special day that had been so far. After a short while, Shane arrived home, so I made my way up to their place. Because of COVID and the lockdowns, it had been way too long since I'd last seen him in person.

As soon as we started speaking, young baby Steele walked over to say hi. Steele was still so young and a little shy, but this didn't stop him. He is such a special child, one whose natural ambiance seems extremely connected to all that is. As he looked at me, wondering, *Who is this person?* I noticed that there was a kangaroo cartoon playing on the TV in the room. I quickly decided I'd break the ice by transforming myself into a kangaroo and bounce around the room with him. As I bounced around, he started to smile and then immediately ran over to me to dish out an almighty big hug.

What happened next was a connected moment like no other, another new vibrational experience along my journey. As I bent down to pick him up with my left arm and raise him up for a hug, I felt the divine euphoric energy pump down my entire left arm. The sensory receptors in my arm were amplified. I could feel the divine connection flow down my arm that was holding him. What a magnificent moment. This was such an unexpected heavenly experience, an event that I was not anticipating. This was a divine energy transfer from being to being.

Since I hadn't even spoken to Shane yet about my recent discovery or any of the events that had unfolded, I felt that this time wasn't the right time to share my connection with him. I knew that the right time would come but that wasn't right now.

I cherished that special moment with baby Steele, just like I'd cherished all the special moments that had been shared with me for the first time, as part of my new beginning.

- The first time I had been vibrationally connected with all that is
- The first time I felt my vibrational connection with positive intentions
- The first time I had vibrationally connected with the energy of the universe
- The first time I had been guided by vibration
- The first time I had vibrationally connected with spirit
- The first time I had vibrationally connected with a cemetery
- The first time I had vibrationally connected with a church
- The first time I had connected with another being vibrationally
- The first time I had been vibrationally healed

These were all special moments for me and I was living a brand-new life experience.

Everything was new now; it was as if I'd been reborn.

Because I was experiencing so many new moments and special connections for the first time, I continued to record as many of them as I could, either as they appeared or just after each experience. It felt like I was now experiencing the real world, in its truest form, oneness in the most naturally euphoric divine state.

Day 19 – Inside a church – a house of God

After experiencing such a magical day the day before, I was looking forward to what this day might bring. How could I not be? Today was the final day of my holiday; however, I was not upset by this since my time away reconnecting had been so memorable.

I was content knowing that the days spent away had been special but there was still one more thing left for me to do before I was to depart. Due to the COVID lockdowns, all places of worship were closed for in-person attendance, which meant I'd only been able to experience my connection with a church from the outside. My grand plan for today, however, was to test how my connection would react inside an open church. Since I'd previously experienced such a divine connection in the carpark of the historic church I discovered, I now wanted to see what sort of experience would unfold once inside.

Aware that a church was a holy place, where individuals acknowledge sacrifice and forgiveness while finding comfort and security. I thought that since I was aligned with my highest self and as connected as I was, what would I feel inside a church, such a religious sacred place? Would I receive a divine acknowledgement or message that I was on the right path?

I checked out of my room and left my accommodation for the last time. Then once I'd loaded my belongings into the hire car, I was ready for my final day. I was planning on heading back down to Shane's place for the day after making a special pitstop along the way. I had searched online for an open church, one that I could stop at on my drive, if only just to walk inside. I thought if I could quietly enter the building, without any expectations, I'd walk around to see if I could feel any connection to any specific areas inside.

A little while into my drive, the rain started to pour down hard. This was unlike all the previous days of my stay since every other day I'd been blessed with the most perfect weather. Today was going to be extremely wet. Unperturbed by this, I stayed committed to my plan. *What's a little water?* I thought. It wasn't long before I located the church and made my way inside.

Unsure of what to expect or if anything was going to unfold, I walked in, searching for any areas that resonated with me, vibrationally. I wasn't going to force anything with spoken word; I was just going to allow my connection to unfold, in its own way. I quietly made my way over to several pictures that were mounted on one of the walls.

As soon as I approached the image of Saint Mary MacKillop, euphoria started passing through my body. I could feel my connection. *Wow,* I thought, *this is really something else.* This was exactly what I was looking for. Even now as I write about this moment, euphoria spreads through me.

This was exciting; something special was happening inside this church. I reviled in my connection with the image of Saint Mary for a short time and then moved onto the next picture hanging on the wall. Humbled by what I was experiencing, I wanted to continue this little adventure.

The next image that I moved to didn't provide a resonated response at all. Surprised by this, I gave the image some more time to engage. After a short while, I moved back to the first picture of Saint Mary. Once again, my body connected vibrationally with her image. This powerful affirmation reaffirmed my belief that Saint Mary was a special lady. I walked around inside the church, not speaking a word, just observing while revelling in my connection with the divine energy that existed inside the holy house.

Even though the church was empty, it was at this point that I realised the morning service must have just finished before I arrived. By now there was just the pastor, an older lady and myself inside. Once I saw the lady leave, I made my way towards the exit doors. The pastor was at the door, thanking everyone for their attendance. I greeted him with a gentle hello. After we shared some words together, he handed me a small gift. I decided that I would keep his gift as a special memento of my first time inside a church experiencing my vibrational connection.

I was humbled and pleased that this experience had occurred. Just to have had any sort of physical connection inside this establishment was something to behold! I scribbled down some notes in my journal of what I had just experienced, then continued with my day, spending the remainder of time with Shane and baby Steele until it was time to return home to Melbourne.

My time away had achieved everything I could have asked for and more. I felt that I'd come to know more about what my special connection was and I was beginning to understand how I could be guided by this existential power.

Day 20 – A connected evening – believers and non-believers

Upon my return to Melbourne, I knew that I was tuned in and more connected than ever. The Saturday morning started with my routine, engaging my connection with the Highest Power. I tuned in my alignment, feeling my physical connection with Source before embarking on the day's tasks.

This daily routine that I was committed to was still evolving for me. However, at this stage, I'd combined some spoken words into a morning affirmation that I found could connect me within seconds. 'Feels like love, feels like warm, feels like connection, feels like ease.' Even if my connection was just for a moment, this was enough to satisfy my desire. That short burst of euphoria would let me know that my divine connection was still with me and that my journey was continuing to unfold.

Although I'd been vibrationally reassured that my connection was here to stay, I couldn't help being a little fearful in these early days that one day, my celestial bond might just up and vanish. I didn't want to lose what I'd discovered. This was simply an internal fear that I would need to overcome. I knew I'd just need a little more time.

As the day progressed into the afternoon, I ventured over to Mum's partner Jose's house. We were all gathering there for his birthday. Members from both sides of the family were coming together to celebrate his day. In the back of my mind, I was eagerly awaiting to see when my vibration might reveal itself during the evening.

I was increasingly becoming more comfortable with the sharing of my story, yet I couldn't help to consider, *what would people think?* Even so, I shared snippets of my journey with some of the people in his home. I noted these conversations in my mind as 'vibrational moments'. Before I knew it, the afternoon had become the night and many of his guests had said their goodbyes, leaving a small group of us inside. The conversations were still flowing along, as well as the drinks and as the night progressed, one of the discussions turned to the subject of religion.

Religion is clearly a topic that many people hold close to their hearts. Many have their own opinions regarding their beliefs about where we are from, about God, what they believe is the path to God, Jesus Christ and other religious matters, including the other religious deities. Depending on the situation, many people seem to express their opinions about these topics with strong conviction, even aggression at some times. Which is interesting, as I believe that once you truly discover God, you will know that God is love and God's only desire is for you to know that you are loved. With pure love, there is no anger or aggression. With God being an all-loving divine entity, I believe that God does not want you to fight your fellow human in his name. God would just prefer for you to spread his message of divine love and acceptance for all.

Most of the conversation was being had in front of me, not with me, as we all sat around the dining table. Since I was just observing, I sat and watched as the discussion became more and more boisterous. This heightened level of passion was understandable, knowing how people hold onto their learnt beliefs, convinced that their way is the right way.

Out of nowhere, the conversation shifted to words that were directed towards me, about my experiences so far. Words that indicated that I was playing with things that I should not, suggesting that I was playing with fire and the dead. I had not even spoken a word yet, since I'd just been observing the conversation and watching as the volume increased and the words intensified. With the conversation now directed towards me, I decided to stand up and speak to everyone who was seated around the table.

'I am not playing with things I shouldn't be. I'm not tempting fate or playing with the dead. This isn't something to be afraid of. In fact, quite the opposite.' I gently raised both my hands up to my sides, smiling. 'My connection is with pure positive energy. What I've uncovered is a gift in response to the work I've done to free my spirit and unchain my soul.'

Mum looked up at me with her warm brown eyes. The others at the table were watching me intently as I continued.

'This gift is not just for me but is, in fact, for anyone and everyone. I've just been given the opportunity to speak about it and share it with whoever wants to listen.

I spoke about the fact that this awakening had opened my eyes and my mind to an entirely new world. I was now seeing things clearly for the first time, feeling more connected with the earth than I ever had. I also now understood that money, although important, was not everything. This constant effort to acquire more wealth was not the be-all and end-all. I now felt that discovering our divine connection was a much more satisfying and important life goal plus, I now believed that one of the most important things for us to do in our life was to help other people.

To clarify what I had meant, I explained, 'You help your family and you help your friends, but if you help a stranger, that's a very powerful gesture. Whether that is by lending an ear, giving up some of your time, giving some money, food, shelter or just by acknowledging them and saying, "Sorry I can't help you right now", that support or acknowledgment is food for their soul and in turn, benefits your soul also.' This great act reminds the person that you are helping that they are worthy too, they are equal just like you and that there is hope for them.

As I spoke these words, I heard José say, 'That's beautiful.'

I stopped and asked, 'Sorry, what do you mean?' to which he replied, 'It's beautiful to hear you say that money is not everything. That's beautiful, man.' As he spoke those words to me, it was then in this very moment that my vibrationally aligned self came out and joined the party.

I replied by saying, 'I can really feel that you genuinely mean that statement.' At that point, my vibrations flowed and it was as if the concept of time had stopped and all things stood still. I was standing in front of five people who were sitting down in front of me, just gazing at me taking in the moment.

As I panned my eyes across the room, I could see a single tear fall from my mother's eye. I watched as the tear gently rolled down her cheek, as she softly spoke the words, 'Wow, look. It takes over all his body. It's all over his face too!' I knew this was something special they had all just witnessed. A vibrational moment with the Highest Power, a physical connection with our Divine Creator.

This moment was also very memorable for me, to be given the opportunity to share this with them all. Sharing a moment of pure vibrational connection with our Creator was a heavenly but humbling experience. Such was the power of this moment, that once the experience had finished and I'd stopped speaking, I sat back down, where I could immediately observe how the conversation had completely shifted. The energy level in the room was full of love, calmness, warmth and peace.

In my notes for the day, I scribbled the following dot points about the shared experience that had unfolded from the events from the evening. I recorded them simply as:

- WITNESSING THE ENERGY
- WITNESSING MY CONNECTION
- WITNESSING TRUE CONVERSATION
- WITNESSING MY SKIN

At the time, this was how I was recording my vibrational moments. I didn't know what else to write. I felt that I at least needed to write down something, even if these weren't the right words. Eventually, I arrived back home, still feeling extremely connected; in fact, my body's sensors were still so alive after what had been such a special evening. I focused on calming my thoughts, using some focused breathing techniques to help quiet my mind. This was a task that, by now, I could achieve quite quickly. Once I felt as one, I laid down and rested for the evening.

Day 21 – What's your superpower?

As soon as the sun was up, I was up. After having experienced such a momentous evening the night before, I was once again ready for whatever new moments would be presented to me that day. *What an exciting way to approach each day,* I thought.

Unplugged from the physical world, plugged into the feeling world

Believing that the foundation of life was built upon experiencing different Moments in Time, I now held a firm understanding that as we live out our life journey, we experience a myriad of different Moments in Time a mixture of negative, positive, happy, sad, angry and peaceful moments. But it is how we process these moments that mould us into the person that we become. Especially those moments that force us to truly face ourselves and respond accordingly; these are the important ones to note.

Each moment we experience either consciously or subconsciously, with awareness, connects us to the different facets of our mind, body and spirit. Then as a cumulative effect once we have freed our spirit and unlocked our inner power this then allows ourselves to shift paradigms, moving from the physical world into the feeling world. If we allow this transition to unfold and don't stifle the shift, we then become truly connected beings. As part of this gift, we are then able to re-establish our connection with the source of all creation, the one many call God. I believe reigniting this link is one of the key purposes of the meaning of life.

It is from here that we are now communicating directly with Source via our own unique divine connection or what I have come to acknowledge as 'Vibrational Alignment'.

Exploring choices

A very insightful person once said:

> *'When something happens to you, you have three choices. You can either let it define, destroy or strengthen you. The <u>choice</u> is yours.'*
> **– Dr Seuss**

Since hearing these words many years ago, they have remained with me and now as I venture through my journey of enlightenment, I have found special purpose to these words. They are a reminder that we almost always have a choice and with that choice, we have options even in our darkest or most troubling times. It is these moments that can either define you as a person and your life's purpose, destroy you as a person and your life or strengthen you, strengthen your character, your resolve and your life.

Thinking more laterally, as I continue my journey, I am beginning to consider a more generalised concept that includes all moments:

> *'Life's moments can either define, destroy or strengthen you.'*

Good or bad, positive or negative, joyful or sad, devastated or invigorated; the list of our emotional interactions with our world is endless and with each moment we can choose how to use that experience in our lives. Take, for example, my newly found sense of purpose and divine connection. My everyday life experience had been completely reimagined and was now unfolding like an adventure novel. With new surprises revealing themselves along the way, who might I connect with on a vibrational level next? What signs might appear throughout my day and at night while I sleep? I had opened the door and was now truly living my purpose.

After completing my morning routine, I headed over to the gym for my daily run. Now I was running at least four to five kilometres each day since the chore of running had transitioned into becoming fun. With my daily run complete, I headed home to get myself ready for the afternoon's gathering.

I'd made the decision that I would gift the vibrational photo, which I acquired while away in Queensland, to my cousin Sandra. I decided that I'd share this powerful image with her to pass on the pure positive energy that radiated from inside. Maybe she would experience this as well.

Picking out my best outfit for her event, I made sure I had everything I needed before grabbing the photo and heading out the door. On the drive over, I contemplated what her reaction might be to the image I was going to gift her. Would she feel the same connection with the energy of the image as I did? By the time I arrived, their house was full, and her event was in full swing. The music was flowing as I walked inside, so I carefully navigated my way through the crowd to Sandy. After warmly greeting each other, I passed her my gift and quietly shared the back story of the image.

It wasn't until later that afternoon that I was caught off guard. While having a conversation with one of her guests I was asked, 'So, what is your superpower?'

Wow, I thought, *that is a fascinating question!* Would they really want the answer to this question? Could my discovery that unlocked my higher self be my superpower? Taken back by the connotation, I subtly flipped it over to him, asking what his superpower was. All the while, I was still pondering his question and the fact that it had really resonated with me. Limiting myself by thinking with the ego, I thought, *how can I answer his question without sounding crazy?*

What would he think? How would I start to explain my story to this stranger?

What would he say if I told him I had freed my spirit and unchained my soul?

What sort of response would I receive if I shared with him full detail that I can now feel the divine energy flowing to me and through me since I'd stumbled across the pathway to something called Vibrational Alignment? What would he think if I shared with him that I now feel so connected to the entire universe and I'd discovered the key to unlocking our real-life purpose and experience? How would he react to the news that now, through the sacred sense of vibration, I could feel true conversations and connect directly with our Divine Creator? Could I share with him that I have discovered a vibrational guide that navigates me down the pathway of positive intentions, choices and outcomes?

What would anyone think if I were to say that I felt like I was unplugged from all my childhood trauma, all the engrained childhood beliefs that were instilled in me, all my inherited negative patterns of behaviours that were instilled both generationally and socially within me? Would a relative stranger accept my belief that I was now plugged into the feeling world, connected to the divine energy of our universe, something so much more powerful and special than I could ever imagine?

How would I put all these words into my conversation? I felt that the right words would come soon enough and when they did, I would be ready. I just had to take my time and let my evolution continue. I finished the conversation with my 'superpower' friend by lightly sharing some of my connected journey so far; in return, he shared with me his superpower. This was the power of becoming 'Artistically Creative', such a beautiful power to have indeed.

Day 22 – A new way

Monday started with the completion of my morning routine, speaking my words, experiencing my connection then knowing I was on point. Feeling the divine touch opened me into a receiving mode, ready to be blessed. Once my morning tasks were completed, I left my office ready to begin my day of discovery and adventure.

Today I'd organised to connect with James. We'd been tossing around some ideas about how to spread the word, sharing my experience and the steps that I'd undertaken to achieve my connection. My intention was to develop a format that included the steps that worked for me in a program that anyone else could follow and use as a guide to help set their own spirit free. I knew my life-changing connection was a beautiful, all-natural, powerful force that was readily available to anyone who wanted to walk the same path.

Plus, my mind was the clearest that it had ever been and along with that clarity came the opening of my mind's eye to a reality that was much more than I had ever imagined. In many aspects during my moments of pure connection, it was as if I was witnessing the world through the eyes of Source for the first time.

Once I finished at the gym, knocking over my run challenge, I headed to the local café. This is where I'd meet James today. We discussed some of the ideas that we'd both been thinking about. At this stage, everything was just a concept. I felt excited at the possibility of doing something together; however, I knew that things still needed to be further explored and allowed to evolve.

We started by writing down our individual ideas on our notepads. This part of the creative process is always fun when two people bring innovative ideas about what something could grow into. These ideas can form the foundation of something powerful if everyone is on the same page. No matter what was to happen, I felt that the idea of creating something from my personal journey was the right thing for me to do and just bouncing ideas off each other was a good place to start.

This was the beginning of my new way to helping people.

Day 23 – Witnessing the energy

My day started with the excitement and anticipation of not knowing what new experiences would soon be in front of me. Even with this unawareness, I was ready to be in the moments as they appeared. I had now become accustomed to beginning every day with gratitude and connection. Feeling the power of divine love was the perfect start to the day.

The underlying fear that I had held about losing my connection was now close to disappearing. By now I knew how to connect anytime I wanted to, plus I'd received the vibrational confirmation that my divine connection was here to stay. There was NO GOING BACK from here!

While completing my connection, before starting the day, I decided to relive some of the powerful conversations I'd already been a part of earlier in the previous week. These conversations had been vibrational when the original words had been spoken, so to relive and enjoy the euphoric energy that had been generated was a beautiful way to reconfirm the true power of the words that had been spoken.

I had discussed the idea of doing something very special for a close friend's children at Christmas time. Vibrationally, I had felt their appreciation in the words as they accepted my offer. Making positive memories for children at Christmas was what that day was all about. With the vibrational confirmation, I knew that my positive intentions had been well received.

After that experience, I felt a real desire to share my connection with someone who was extremely close to me. This person had experienced significant loss and did not have the opportunity to say anything to the loved one they'd lost. I spent some time in my morning starting to mould the idea from my original desire to share this with them.

I contemplated sharing with them what I believed I had discovered on my journey so far. That death was not the end; spiritually, we will all continue after our physical experience expires as we transition into the next phase of our existence. I was also open to the possibility of playing a part with them, in sharing a vibrationally connected moment, if they desired, I would be happy to oblige. If I could, I would be happy to be the conduit between the two of them.

Originally, this entire concept seemed so surreal but now as I elaborate in this book, much time has passed so I am very comfortable. I now know the door that I've unlocked, plus I am aware of the connection that I have.

I can also say that I would not change anything from my past, as everything has led me here. All moments, events and outcomes, all the ups and downs, all the highs and lows, all the pain and sorrow, everything that I had experienced has led me to this very point in time right now. This magical moment, where I can vibrationally connect with the energy that creates all. An angelic space where I can see my world clearly through the eyes of Source. A reality where I can speak the words, 'UNIVERSE, HEAL ME PLEASE,' and within seconds, my body connects, my vibration levels increase and all throughout my body, the euphoria circulates my internal network.

How could I change anything from my past? I couldn't and I wouldn't!

After such an exceptionally connected morning, I had some operational tasks to complete. However, at this stage of my journey, I was starting to question if my day-to-day tasks were really important at all. In the full scheme of things, they seemed so insignificant, in my new BIG PICTURE. Was I doing what I needed to be doing? Or was I going off track and wasting time with these day-to-day tasks that I'd given myself to complete?

Within seconds of asking my questions, I was vibrationally guided with the response that I should just enjoy the feeling of getting ready for the next adventure and understanding that everything in my life experience was unfolding just as it needed to be. I needed to remember that there was nothing that I would be asked to do that I was not ready for. Everything that I was now experiencing was all part of my original intentions that I had set out to achieve, long before I'd ever arrived into this world in my physical form.

These confirmations and reassurances were important for me; they were something that I took comfort in. I also knew that my day-to-day tasks provided me with the means and opportunity to achieve what it was that I wanted to achieve. Giving me the freedom to explore my life in its current format as each day was unfolding. These were important facts that I needed to remember.

Right now, nothing is meaningless, everything is right on track.

As the evening neared, I found myself outside at the same time as my neighbours, two lovely sisters from South America, genuinely good people with beautiful energy. We started to talk about what they had been up to and how their week had been. Somewhere during our conversation, I decided that I would take a leap of faith and share my journey with them. I wanted to share with them what it was that I had uncovered and what it was that I was experiencing.

Unbeknown to me, the two sisters were open-minded and they themselves had an interest in energy. As I spoke about the story of my year so far, it did not take long for my vibrational connection to join us and for the energy to start flowing for all to see.

Just as I started many of these conversations, I began by sharing my belief that we are a spirit in a body, not a body with a spirit. I continued by explaining what I meant by this. I continued with my journey so far, the freeing of my spirit and the unchaining of my soul, sharing with them some of the process that I had discovered along the way. I explained how I'd reignited the connection with my highest self and how I'd opened a door to an incredibly special connection, a vibrational connection between my physical form, my spirit form and all that is.

I shared several of the events so far including, looking through a different lens – all is not what it seems – along with the details of the evening I had recently experienced when we were pairing the spirits of humans and animals. I spoke about how now with my newfound awareness, I believed there was a much deeper connection available for all of us.

The sisters then shared with me some of their experiences with energy, mostly around using the healing powers of energy. Healing with energy was a totally new concept to me. This was something that I had never thought of before or considered. However, now this notion seemed so logical and immediately gathered my interest.

Could I use this energy for physical healing purposes as well? What was achievable? Is this even possible?

They shared that they had, in fact, experienced an energy healing session in the past and that the process had healed physical pain that was being held within the body for quite some time. I decided that this was definitely something worth exploring.

Chapter 7

QUIETING THE MIND – DISCOVERING MEDITATION

Day 24 – Preparing for the next phase, a meditated state of mind – eyes open

Wednesday began with me achieving my energetic connection before the influences of the outside world had an opportunity to entwine with my physical avatar. I knew that an effective way for me to do this was by speaking the powerful words I'd uncovered, as they seemed to instantly connect me vibrationally with our Divine Creator. This alignment would then allow me to move through the many challenges of each day with clarity and focus. Once my morning routine was complete, I was ready for my day to unfold.

I organised to meet up with Jimmy. He was someone close to me, who knew the before and after me. He was one of the people who had witnessed the transformation firsthand. Some of these connected events had been so energetically charged that even non-believers who were witnessing were forced to ask questions such as, 'What's happening here? What is this that I'm seeing?'

We sat down at our local meeting place: a quiet little café tucked away inside a bustling busy centre. Comfortable with our setting, Jimmy threw out the suggestion that maybe I'd be interested in trying a meditation. By now, he knew that somehow, I'd personally been able to achieve a remarkably heightened sense of connection and peace from within both the conscious and the subconscious realms while seemingly just going about my daily life. He thought that maybe now was the right time to explore a deeper meditated state of mind, one with my eyes wide open.

I had never meditated in the years before; in fact, for all my life, I believed that I couldn't reach the level of stillness required to truly calm the mind. I had convinced myself that my mind always needed to stay busy, subliminally fearful that stopping or slowing down would force the dreaded quiet time upon me. The still moments where, whether willingly or unwillingly, you're forced to face yourself and be comfortable in your own skin and personal space, a conscious arena that gives an opportunity for the pain of the past to rise to the surface, often leading to negative choices and behaviours.

Although, since this journey had begun, I had, for the first time, been able to clear my mind and be comfortable with the stillness while removing the distraction of thought. The freeing of my spirit had allowed me to be completely comfortable with a quiet mind and actually enjoy the absolute clarity.

These elevated moments broke down the concept of time as I knew it. Time seemed to stand utterly still during these experiences, offering complete conceptual peace. With this in mind, I considered that maybe now was the right time to experiment with reaching a highly energetic meditated state, one with my eyes wide open, in an activity-filled environment.

In fact, I believed this would be fun.

As we sat in our chairs, we began by focusing on breathing the energy. This mediation process is about replenishing the energy levels within your own body. Your focus is on breathing new energy in, and then releasing the spent energy. Returning that depleted air back into the universe to be recycled and converted once again into fresh energy, ready for consumption. This is an internal recharge for your entire insides.

This process requires a quiet mind that can focus wholly on the moment. Without distraction, you can be anywhere: in a café, on public transport, in the office, watching TV or in the park.

Steps to the 'Refill Your Internal Energy Level' meditation:

Step 1 – Clear your mind of external thought

You can do this by using the power of breath. However, there is a trick: we need to breathe the way that our body was originally designed to, using the full capacity of our lungs. As you inhale, ensure that your stomach expands. Your chest area should remain completely still; this will ensure that you use your lungs' full capacity.

- Breathe in, push your stomach out and expand.
- Hold the breath in your lungs for five seconds.
- As you breathe out, your stomach should naturally deflate.
- Repeat this five times.

Step 2 – Think only about inhaling pure energy into your body

Now as you breathe normally, you are no longer just breathing air. Using your mind's eye, visualise the air you are breathing as pure positive energy and give this energy a colour. Golden yellow and white are pure energy colours.

Step 3 – Focus on seeing the energy enter your body

As you breathe, use the power of thought to visualise the pure energy entering your body through your mouth and nose.

Step 4 – Focus on seeing the pure energy travel to your lungs

Using the power of your mind, visualise the radiant energy travelling down your throat and into your airways like a bright light. Visualise the moment the bright light reaches your lungs.

Step 5 – Fill your lungs

Feel your lungs as they fill with the bright energetic light, transforming them into a glowing beacon. Your lungs are now filled with pure positive energy. Picture them as they glow from the light.

Step 6 – Visualise the energy entering your bloodstream

Now feel as the energy enters your bloodstream and circulates throughout your body. Your internal bloodstream is glowing with pure positive energy.

Step 7 – Recognise now as your entire body fills with this pure positive energy

Understand that now the energy has expanded throughout your abdomen, radiating this pure light. Picture the energy travelling down your legs, into your feet and then down to your toes. Bask in the warmth as the energy travels into your arms through to your hands and into your fingertips. Allow the euphoric energy to travel up your neck, into your skull, flowing into your brain.

Step 8 – Releasing your expired energy

As you breathe out, visualise your expired energy exiting your mouth. Give this depleted energy a colour if you will. Black is the colour I chose. Let go of your depleted energy as it leaves your body and returns to the universe so that it may be reworked into fresh, new energy ready for consumption once again.

Breathe in the pure positive energy – breathe out your expired energy. Repeat this process.

Be in the moment, focus just on you, your breath and the sensations that you feel happening inside your body. Continue this mediation, until you feel that you have recharged your internal energy levels. Remember the healing power of our universe is unlimited. You can recharge as often as you wish without a cost. The ability to feel good is something that our universe provides to us for free.

***

After our catch-up at the café finished, Jimmy and I said our goodbyes and headed off on our separate ways. Internally, I was feeling light, bright and energised from my introduction to this new meditation – with eyes wide open!

Meeting people who want to believe

As the day matured, I needed to prepare for the evening ahead. Tonight would be a catch-up with friends from all over the country, many for the first time since pre-COVID and the ensuing lockdowns. The plan was that we would all meet at a city pub for pre-drinks and then venture across town to a renowned Indian restaurant.

Arriving just before 6 pm, I quickly identified where everyone was. Friends had come together to celebrate being free and living life normally once again. Different conversations were taking place across our group as everyone eagerly shared all the latest news and gossip that had passed over the previous year. There was a new face too, one guy I'd not met before; however, it wasn't long before we made a connection.

Talking about the year that was, we quickly found some common ground, discussing how the strange year had affected us individually. While conversing, I thought, I'm going to share my journey and what I've uncovered. I wanted to see what another stranger would think!

I explained that I knew how hard the year had been for many people and I felt for them. But personally, I believed that the earth had been given a chance to breathe. This was evident around the globe with the pollution clearing as factories shut down, none more so than in India where a small town rediscovered their picturesque view of the Himalayan mountains. A view that no town folk had seen for over thirty years due to the smog and pollution that had built up in the air.

I explained that I had been given the opportunity to use my time in lockdown to focus on myself. To discover an amazing process, which unknowingly, freed my spirit and unchained my soul, introducing me to an entirely new life experience. A new world, one with a direct connection to Source. I'd been given the opportunity to uncover something extremely real and very relevant!

A new way of existing. A divine connection.

I gently spoke about the pathway that I had walked. The steps that I'd discovered one by one, and what these steps had unlocked: my connection, the energy, my awakening. We spoke about the universal law of attraction, about how when you apply effort, the universe gives you more and more of what you are consciously or subconsciously seeking.

In human terms, we would categorise this as good and bad.

We discussed the point that if you are constantly emitting negative energy, negative intentions, guilt or sadness, the universe just sees that for what it is. This is what you are choosing to surround yourself with so you must want more of the same, so here, have more. Remember the saying, 'When it rains, it pours'. Although by the same token, this universal law of attraction also works with positive intentions, positive beliefs and behaviours such as happiness and wellbeing. If you are consistently emitting positive energy, acting with positive intentions, love and happiness, then the universe will reward you with more and more of this.

You will be rewarded with whatever it is you are seeking.

An important note to remember is that you cannot bluff the universe. You cannot pretend that things are a certain way if they are truly not. The universe can see right through you. These divine powers cannot be fooled by mere mortals. You must be completely real and true to yourself.

I could feel that the words and topics we were discussing resonated with him. There was an immediate connection that we'd established, plus we were both in agreeance. I felt that potentially this could be the beginning of another valuable connection on my pathway forward.

Day 25 – Searching for more

The morning began with me receiving brief moments of connection and vibrations. However, on an energetic scale, these were low-level bursts compared to what I was used to. I knew that I'd learnt ways to induce vibrations, but the ones that I really enjoyed were the vibrational confirmations that came directly from Source in moments of pure alignment. These were moments where midway through an action or conversation, whether as a guide to positive intentions or beneficial outcomes, I would receive a vibrational acknowledgment. I believed this to be a divine sign from Source showing that whatever was happening within that moment was truly meaningful, or that the outcome would be positive. I understood that to live this way was an extremely special experience, to be in constant communication with our Creator.

These are moments when the vibration acts as an existential confirmation that the forces greater than what we can see are in agreeance with the topic or words being discussed, or when the vibration appears upon entering a specific site or location. Memorable moments that I have experienced at some highly energetic addresses include the church, cemetery, museum and other historical locations – places on our earth where history, memories and spirits are held.

I found myself searching, like a game of discovery looking for my next interaction. I was eagerly waiting with excited anticipation as to where and when the next connection would reveal itself. Today though, I was craving for more than just the small energetic bursts on offer. Compared to the power that I'd been used to, these were not enough to satisfy my desire. I wanted to feel the full force of the divine and since the afternoon was fast approaching, I decided I'd continue my search for more revelations by heading out to the historic church that I knew.

By now, the importance of my connection had overtaken most things in my world. This had become my sole focus; I knew that if I could maintain my vibration, abundance would flow, whatever that looked like.

I was quickly learning that this heavenly interaction could quite possibly be the key ingredient to discovering the next level of our existence. Discovering the magnificent power was a humbling experience as it provided me with an abundance of entirely new perspectives. With this power, I'd been gifted a completely new understanding of what my life experience was all about. To add to this, to feel the power of this divine touch without the consumption of anything artificial or any external influences was something surely to behold and be grateful for.

When we look at how humans conduct their daily lives, feeling good is what almost everyone on Earth is trying to achieve. For example:

- We make new friends and meet new people – love feels good.
- We create a family.

- We explore; we travel.
- We help others.
- We make positive choices.
- We make decisions about acquiring new material possessions, a new car, a new house, new clothing or a new toy.
- We pamper ourselves.
- We participate in physical activities or sports.
- Even any addict; for example, a drug addict, someone who is so desperate and in despair, uses drugs to make themselves feel good.*

*Many times, the addict will use a product or substances to assist in either distracting, forgetting or blocking out what it is that they do not want to remember. This, along with the artificial stimulation provided by the product or action, can come with a HUGE PRICE for the addict... This price can include their sanity, their health, their finances, their friends, their family and, in many cases, it can even cost them their lives!

So, hopefully, now we are in agreeance that as humans, we are all constantly searching for ways to feel good. Well, what is it that I've unlocked? What if I've found the key that has unlocked the universal secret to feeling good? What if I've discovered the universal stream of divine love, pure positive energy? A direct feed to our Creator?

How powerful could this be?

Would people want to experience this life-changing connection just like me?

Since there is no drug that you need to consume and there's no place that you need to travel to, nor is there any associated cost or fee, would others want to receive? Would they believe that it is all just within you, within each of us?

Uncover that special place inside yourself where you can reach a level of awareness and understanding for those who have influenced your life up until now. Bask in the feeling you achieve when you reach a level of forgiveness for the perpetrator by understanding that whoever it was that played a negative role or who had negative influences in your life was most likely just a damaged soul themselves. A broken soul who had not worked through their own emotional trauma.

It is important to remember that your pain and trauma is different to the next person, but it is all relevant. There is no comparison or grading of whose is more important or more severe. If it matters to you then it is important; everything is relevant to the specific individual.

Become aware that the person's actions actually reflected how they felt about themselves. It really was nothing personal towards you; they were already either broken, misguided or emotionally traumatised to know any better. They were just not strong enough to break their own Cycle of Repetition. One of their life lessons was to break their cycle; your lesson is to simply overcome what you have experienced and prosper!

Their lessons will keep repeating until they learn. You, however, as a connected being are already evolving above and beyond them, shifting into a whole new paradigm.

Believe that you are strong; you are not weak! You can be the stronger soul, the stronger spirit, the bigger person and BREAK the CYCLE OF REPETITION. By not repeating the same mistakes, by being the educator, the positive influence in the lives of the people around you, you can achieve this. Be open to the understanding that there is a plan in place already for us all. We all have been given a seat at the table; we just need to sit down and partake in the experience.

Imagine if we could all discover this divine energetic connection that is on offer to us unconditionally from Source. What if we could explore our heavenly connection as a guide when we need to be guided, heal us when we need to be healed and love us when we need to feel loved, using the euphoric energy of the universe whenever we desired?

How beautiful would this be?

Arriving at the church

I considered these thoughts as I made the drive towards the historic site. I turned into the gravelled road, driving slowly along the unmade surface, which was littered with small potholes, until I'd reached the cemetery. The left side of the driveway housed a procession of small trees marking the boundary, while on the right side, the boundary line was emphasised by the fence that belonged to the small, hallowed cemetery.

Once I reached the halfway point, the euphoria of this sacred location immediately entered my body, connecting me with what I had come to know as the spiritual energy of the divine. I was certain by now that this was an extremely holy location. The fact that I could feel the vibrational energy floating in the air, without the need for any words to be spoken, had to be something special.

With the whole concept still so amazing to me, accepting the fact that I was able to feel the energy vibrationally from such a blessed site was out of this world. Feeling abundantly content and extremely grateful, I continued driving my car towards the rear carpark where I sat for a moment to connect with the church. After basking in the church's energetic rays for a short while, I restarted my car and headed towards the exit. Knowing that I had such a majestical site freely available to me was indeed a heavenly feeling. This was an important day to experience. For this was a day where my connection had left me wanting more until the very end.

Day 26 – Connecting with Source

The morning started with alignment as my first order of business: Tuning in my physical body, conscious mind and spiritual self to the signals being transmitted by Source. Vibrationally connecting with all that is, was and will be. Feeling the euphoria provided to me unequivocally by our heavenly father. By now, the universe's energy was constantly flowing and like a radiating beacon of divine energy, I was regularly being told that I was glowing.

Understanding that I was discovering new things every day, with the gradual unfolding and learnings from new experiences, today I would attempt to play, connect and heal with the divine energy that surrounded me.

Playing with my energy vortex

I started this process by raising my vibration level to a position where I could feel the energy surrounding my body. In this heightened energetic state, I visually compressed the energy into a ball-like shape. With an open mind and an understanding that we are all pure energy, anyone can reach this state.

Our hands play a very important role in the processes of creation and healing, whether we are using the energy of Source or not. Our hands are our original God-given creative tools. We use our hands to create in a multitude of ways: to create meals, create art, create and play music; we write with them, we help with them, we build with them, we love with them, we touch and connect with the ones we love, we hug with them. So much is created with our hands.

So, with this in mind, I wanted to uncover if I could use my unique creative tools to harness the chi energy surrounding me, the energy of the universe that is part of our expanded wellbeing. I decided that I would test the hands' ability to heal.

Energy healing without touch – test subject: me

This would be a simple test, using my hands in a nonphysical contact process. To begin this process, I needed to locate an area on my body where I was experiencing some physical pain or a niggle. Once I located the area, using my hands, I hovered over this region, ensuring that there was no physical contact from my palm to my skin surface. I had to focus on using the divine energy to heal that specific body part.

With my clear and focused mind, I centred on my pain point, elevating my vibration level whilst maintaining my energetic connection above the surface.

Universe, heal me

Heal my body

Heal my mind

Heal my spirit

Universe, heal me, please

Through my newly discovered faith and connection to the energy of the universe, I could feel the divine power, as Source flowed through me. The powerful energy entered through my mind and then spread throughout my entire body.

This energy healed all aspects of pain in my body. Whether that be the healing of physical pain that I've felt, or removing any sensation of muscle tightness or soreness. I have felt the internal healing of the emotional pain and trauma inside my heart. I have been humbled more times than I can remember now as the divine power takes over, blissfully quietening my mind an existential experience while I transcend to a divine place of spiritual existence.

Could this be what life is all about?

Is the answer to the ageless question, 'What are we here for?' Simply about humanity, reconnecting with the divine consciousness? Removing the barriers of individualism so that we may all truly become part of the great oneness.

Is this earth our beautiful playground, one where our spiritual selves can enjoy all that comes with each physical life experience? A special home that we can regularly return to, so that we may experience different physical forms as we desire. Life as a human, an animal, a bird or a fish, maybe as a plant or a tree or whatever shape it is that we wish to experience.

I wonder as, human beings living on Mother Earth, as the pinnacle of creation, how many untapped and unknown resources are available to us? Resourceful powers that were once maybe known but have now long since been forgotten. Are the ancient abilities waiting to be rediscovered or learnt whilst we are here in our physical form? Could it be that all that is required for us to achieve this is for us to be vibrationally aligned so that we are open to receiving this new version of reality?

What if as we reach our individual awakenings, we could all become part of the togetherness within this connected version of reality linked with the divine power? Globally reaching a new level of divine consciousness as an entire race whilst still living out our physical lives. Not having to wait until we transition to experience the pleasures of heaven, divine love or the reconnection back with the universal oneness. What would our physical world look like then, if we all allowed ourselves to believe and connect to the one mind?

A global population connected to the one mind. Elevating the global consciousness to an entirely new stratosphere. Information, knowledge, love and wisdom would be shared instantaneously. Life as we know it would be rewritten. All beings able to receive the flow of universal energy and information streaming to us, allowing humanity to transition into an entirely new physical reality. All living beings working together as one with our earth and universe. The possibilities could be endless.

What a magical experience this would be.

Day 27 – A fresh start – pure positive energy

After yesterday's energetic events, including the moulding of energy like clay, the visualisation of the energy using my mind's eye and the absorption of energy enabling healing, I concluded that today would be a fresh start. I recognised that as soon as I opened my eyes, I was immediately swamped with an increase of my connection thanks to the events from the previous day, and yet the previous day had been an increase on the day before that.

By now, I was very aware that I was continuing to evolve, moving forward along my new path. Every day the universe was revealing completely new vibrational connections and moments. Each time allowing me to gather a new level of perspective and appreciation while the magnificence flowed through me. Being gifted with the divine touch and guidance by something much greater than I ever thought possible was extraordinary.

I knew that soon the day would come where I would be sharing my connection with people outside of my immediate environment. Sharing the special message I had been gifted, along with the steps I'd uncovered that had led to my connection with the vibrational world, sharing with anyone who would listen to my story. I was excited by the prospect and the possibilities of what was to come.

Even if now was not the time, soon it would be. For now, my only task was to prepare myself. Getting ready to be ready, I could have faith that everything was already being done. My task was to exist outside of the ego, to remain in every moment, enjoying the vibrational interactions as they unfold as well as the connected conversations as they occurred. I was relishing in this task and today would be no different.

Appreciate the day – by living in the moment
As the afternoon drew near, I reconnected with Jimmy, a modern-day seeker. Over the hours we spent together, I spoke about the importance of appreciation. With forgiveness came new perspectives of past experiences which then allowed us to transition into appreciation. From there, we naturally keep rising through to the levels of joy, then love, serenity and finally enlightenment. We discussed the importance of giving thanks for the moment, for the day, for yesterday and for tomorrow.

I shared with him some new words that I had begun to associate with appreciation.

Levels of Appreciation

Appreciate this day – I'm so grateful that today was my today

Appreciate that tomorrow will be tomorrow –
I'm so grateful that tomorrow will be my tomorrow

Appreciate all things that were yesterday –
I'm so grateful that yesterday was my yesterday

Appreciate all things that were your past –
I'm so grateful that my past was my past

Appreciate your parents – I'm so grateful that my
parents are my parents

Appreciate your friends – I'm so grateful that my friends
are my friends

Appreciate your earth – I'm so grateful that this
earth is my earth

I thank you for the gift that is my life

Day 30 – Tuesday 22/12/2020

Exploring quantum hypnosis

Tuesday morning came around before I knew it. I had an appointment scheduled for something very intriguing. It was a new experience for something that even as recently as a month before I had never heard of.

It had been suggested to me to participate in a quantum hypnosis session. These sessions were normally used as a healing tool, uncovering past life regressions and working through deep-seated trauma using hypnosis to connect with the individual's spiritual self in a subconscious state.

My case would be a little different though, since I'd already freed my spirit. This was creating a reality that meant I was spiritually connected in my conscious state. For this reasoning, I was eager to explore what might be uncovered in the sub-conscious realm!

I had prepared some questions too:

- What is this universal energy I am connecting with?
- Who or what is my connection with?
- What am I to do with my newfound connection?

I was eager to learn much more, however, I knew that I would in fact be grateful for any information I could uncover. Any new pieces of wisdom or understanding, I would appreciate. Like many other pieces to my puzzle, I was keen to see what this experience would reveal. I arrived at my appointment with an open mind and excited for what the day might bring. The practitioner was consulting from a room attached to her residential home. Questionable at first, however, I was not perturbed by this, as she had been highly recommended and was booked out for many weeks in advance.

Ringing the doorbell, I was greeted by the hypnotherapist, who introduced herself as Joanne or Jo, as she liked to be called. She was warm, welcoming and vibrant. Joanne appeared just how I'd imagined someone would who was working with the subconscious mind. Wearing a shiny vibrant top, she was radiating a natural positive energy.

Guided into her consultation room, I could immediately feel the positive energy flowing through the air. The room itself felt as if it was radiating its own warm glow plus the whole environment felt extremely comfortable. Against one of the walls was a small wooden table paired with a couple of chairs, then positioned almost directly opposite was a wooden bookcase full of literature about the universe, energy and other connected subject matter. Finally, positioned against the back wall was the patient's bed, stationed under a large, curtained window. I assumed that this bed would be for later in our session.

Jo suggested that I take a seat so we could discuss how the day would flow and what I was looking to achieve. Positioned in the centre of the table was a colourful fruit platter for both of us to enjoy as we conversed, since we would be spending the next four to five hours together. When we'd originally talked on the phone, I'd briefly explained my journey so far, just to give Jo a basic idea of what it was that I was experiencing; however, now I would share my entire journey to date with her.

I wanted to include all the different events so far, along with the original steps I had discovered that led to this Vibrational Alignment. I began by sharing the process I'd uncovered, which I believed was the catalyst to freeing my spirit. As the words flowed from my mouth, it was evident that vibrationally our conversation morphed into a connected experience for the two of us. I spoke about the unfolding of my divine connection along with the vibrational moments I had experienced including the land conversation, Steel Prince and then the unfolding of all the other events over the previous three weeks including the divine teachings that had been existentially shared with me.

While I shared my words with her, the vibration level increased as my inner being became alive for her to witness too. My higher being rose to the surface. I could sense the pure joy from her in response to me sharing my divine connection. Once I finished speaking, we were both ready to progress into the hypnosis section of the consultation.

During this part of our session, Joanne directed me to the bed in the room, so that I could lie down. The bed was positioned at the rear of the room underneath a small window that was curtained off from the outside world. Once I was comfortable, I was instructed that first I needed to clear my mind of thought. This was required in order to reach a subconscious state of hypnosis.

I achieved this by using a focused breathing technique known as 5/5/5. Breathe in for five seconds, hold that breath for five seconds and then exhale for five seconds. After five repetitions, the mind is clear. Now that I was resting in a relaxed susceptible state, we embarked on a spiritual journey. This consisted of extracting my internal spirit so it may travel externally from my physical self, using a guided word meditation. My spirit would be encouraged to fly along a multi-dimensional pathway whilst I remained in a deep hypnotic state until I felt the desire to stop and land in a specific space and time.

The intention of this exercise was to uncover a past life or past lives. However, the actual specifics would be revealed as the session progressed. The hypnotic experience was by far the most elevated part of our session together, a real multi-dimensional quantum subconscious journey.

The detailed contents of what we discovered as the result of my experience I will keep for another time. However, I will share with you that during this session, I was informed by an existential being:

'The possibilities are endless, as a connected vibrational being.'

Day 31 – Source is here to stay

Today was a milestone, for it had now been thirty-one days in a row of me living my new life experience connected to the divine energy. Thirty-one days in a row of experiencing something that I'd never known, dreamt of or even knew existed. I was now living my daily life experience directly connected to Source, living as a connected being, guided by the universal intelligence through my energetic connection.

By now I'd shared my discovered connection with many members of my family, close friends and even some strangers. I'd also spent my time developing my own daily practice, a morning routine to get connected. I explored the sensations as the feeling was received and then attempted to learn a deeper understanding of what this all was, what it was that was communicating to me through the power of vibration.

If you'd suggested to me a year ago that this is where I would have been today, I would've thought you were crazy, and I would not have known what it was that you were talking about. I now believe, though, that as these days pass and my connection evolves, I am becoming more aware of when a vibrationally connected moment is occurring or about to occur. I can ask the following questions and receive vibrational responses. Whatever this is, it's a powerful being not of this physical world:

- Is Source here to stay with me for now until the end? An overwhelming YES vibrationally.

- Is Source a guide for me to positive intentions and outcomes? An overwhelming YES vibrationally.

- Is Source sacred? An overwhelming YES vibrationally.

- Is this divine love that I am receiving? An overwhelming YES vibrationally.

This was my confirmation and guide to the truth!

I had many more questions in store for Source. What are your intentions with me now? What is next for me to achieve? Have I been gifted this experience to spread the word about your divine love? How may I be of service to you? Are there people out there interested in reaching this level of connection? Would others want to feel this divine love and live in this vibration reality next to Source? How do I best spread the word?

These were some of the questions in my mind and I knew in time the answers would come.

Nevertheless, since this was still so raw, I knew there was no playbook for me to follow or a guide for me to read. This was all just from my personal journey of discovery with the revealing of new elements and information every day. All I knew was that I had this feeling, this heavenly connection, which was so becoming, powerful and pure. Surely there would be others who would want to experience this too.

Even though this was now day thirty-one, I remained steadfast in my commitment to establish my link every morning before anything else had begun. I had convinced myself that if I could vibrationally connect in the morning, then I would not lose my connection during the night.

At this stage of my journey, I still craved this reassurance.

Days 32 to 35 – A time of celebration

The following four days coincided with an extremely joyful time of year, for it was Christmas. I'd be spending these days celebrating and reconnecting with family and close friends. Traditionally, our Christmas celebrations were spread over multiple days; this enabled everyone from different family groups to reconnect and spend quality time together without the rush of squeezing everyone into one day. These days included Christmas Eve's eve, Christmas Eve, Christmas Day and Boxing Day.

I noticed that during each different event, at some stage, either throughout the day or night, there was a conversation about my new discovery, as well as about the events that had unfolded for me. I was also realising that people had different opinions about what it was that I was experiencing, and I was beginning to accept that not all of the reactions were what you might call positive. Some were extremely excited and eager to discuss, some wanted to learn more, and then some did not want to talk about it at all. It was as if my experiences went against everything that they thought was real – maybe even the whole idea scared them, unsettling their own ingrained belief structure. The idea that there was something greater supporting us, that just wants us to know we are loved, was unsettling to their developed beliefs that life is meant to be a struggle or hard.

I considered without any judgement that these people were just locked in their ways, struggling with their own internal pain. I thought if only they would give themselves the opportunity to experience this too, what a difference this could make. I knew that since I'd discovered my pathway to peace, my own personal belief structure of what life was all about had completely changed. I was well aware of how powerful the shift was and how life-changing the divine connection was for me, opening my eyes to the real world, the feeling world, where we are all together as one.

Plus, there were some people who just could not understand. I knew that this subject matter, this new version of reality went against everything they thought they knew. The thought of how this could even be possible was something that they struggled to accept. 'How could this even happen to you?' was a question I sensed from some around. I understood this train of thought, as I too had asked this question to myself, but I wasn't deterred.

On my last day of Christmas for this festive season, I was celebrating with a group of friends so close that we consider ourselves family, Tara and Shane. This day's events were, by far, some of the most vibrational moments I had experienced across the four days. During our time together, we spoke about the journey so far, including the ten steps that I'd uncovered that I believed led me to *Vibrational Alignment* and the discovery of my divine connection. I could sense the different reactions from the people inside, as I witnessed their minds process the words that were being spoken.

Witnessing the vibrations

It was during this day that I had my first experience of seeing another connected being, even though it was only for a moment. While we were gathered at the family house, I ventured outside with Shane as I'd planned on sharing my new song with him as well as elaborating on my journey. This was a big deal for me as we had known each other for many years now, so to introduce him to my new version of reality was something that I hoped he would accept and allow just like I had.

We made our way out to the driveway where my car was parked so we could sit inside, listen to my new song and talk. As we sat down, we began talking about my entire experiences to date. I could feel the words connecting with him. I suggested we go for a quick drive so I could play him my new song *Slow It Down*. This was a special moment for me, sharing this connected experience with him, and after a short drive, we eventually arrived back at the house.

Parked in the driveway, we both stayed inside the car so we could continue talking. I could feel he was really connecting with the words that I was saying when suddenly, I could see his right arm and shoulder light up becoming vibrationally alive. I could see the same energy that was flowing through me pass through his body just for a moment, this was special. I knew he could feel this connection too.

'We are going to do something special together,' he said.

As he spoke these words, in my head, I was thinking, *wow, how did he know to say those specific words?*

Unbeknown to him, these were the exact words that another special friend had said to me during an earlier conversation in the weeks before about the future. However, I had not mentioned that earlier conversation to anyone. As we sat in the car together, vibrationally connected, I was in awe of the synergy that I'd just witnessed and of the fact that he had used the same words in such a connected moment. In my head, I contemplated, *this cannot just be a coincidence, can it?*

Day 36–37 – Discovering your energy field

During these days, I continued exploring the process of feeling my body's vibrational frequency. Focusing on tapping into my energetic field, as this enabled me to connect my physical body with my spiritual self vibrationally. My routine included not consuming the news of the world at the beginning of each day. Not feeding my mind with article after article of world events, mostly about fear, terror, war, death and destruction with a sprinkling of articles about celebrities, sports and real-estate properties that most only dream of. Ego-driven death and despair are mixed with subjects that are used to convince us of what it is that we need.

Focused on self-healing – feeling the body's external energy field vibrationally

I felt that if I could limit the consumption of this external noise first thing in the morning, then I could connect myself to the real world, the feeling world that includes:

- The physical self, including all the physical components we see around us.
- The vibrational self, connecting with the energetic frequencies radiating through you from the world around you.
- The spiritual self. This includes connecting with the spirit universe that surrounds you.

Since I'd discovered my energy field, I was now constantly practising raising my vibration to a whole new level. I was noticing that during these connected moments, my body was totally in tune, even pulsating with divine love. I knew that it was during these 'moments' that one could use the divine energy to focus on physical self-healing.

From this elevated place of consciousness, once all the body's sensory receptors become alive and energetically charged, every subatomic particle radiates with gratitude, love and acknowledgement. It is from this level that I believe we can completely heal our physical selves. I knew that I was still only in the very early days in relation to how far I could take this, but I was sure that I'd uncovered something extraordinary.

Day 38 – Feeling someone's energetic intention, vibrationally for the first time

During the previous day, I had met someone new, someone different while out in the local area. A young adult, who was definitely a connected being even if they didn't know it yet. We bonded with our eyes first and immediately I felt there was some sort of magnetic connection. Feeling the link but unsure as to what it was all about, we both continued on our merry way. About half an hour later, our paths crossed once again and this time the universe brought us closer together. We started talking, just a light friendly conversation at first, until this special person suggested that I ask them back to my place. Immediately I obliged, to which they accepted.

After throwing out such a forward request, they insisted that they did not know what had overcome them to act in such a manner, almost inviting themselves but they had just felt like it was the right thing to do.

Together we ventured back to my place, where we could continue to talk and get to know each other. It was during this conversation that for the first time, as we were seated fairly close to each other, I could feel this person's intention and vibration pass through me. Our physical energetic connection pulsated without any specific words spoken and with no contact or touch. The skin on my arms and legs became electrically energised and the amplified sensation that passed into me was a sense of elevated euphoria. This was another new overwhelming experience but not unbecoming.

In my mind, I was surprised but excited to have experienced this new sensation. To be able to feel someone's intentions vibrationally was something so unique and pure. After our evening ended, I pondered the thought that since we are all projecting our own unique energy field, surely it must then be possible to feel someone else's frequency and intentions through the power of vibration if their signal is strong enough. Especially if both parties are connected beings.

What a magical experience and an exciting way to bring in the New Year!

Chapter 8

RECOGNISING THE SIGNS

A piece of celestial wisdom that was shared with me early in my journey, which has now formed part of my belief, is that there is a plan in place for each of us.

Whether the plan includes the individual intentions that were originally set forth long before we arrived on this earth, or whether our life's plan is part of the great Creator's overall design construct for earth as a whole, there is a plan in play.

The freedom of choice

This grand plan comes with a catch: we always have the freedom of choice. As the great plan unfolds, we always have the choice as to whether we will participate or not, utilising the many signs that are shared along the way. These signs will flow in the form of divine guidance and existential assistance, but the question is whether we are ready and willing to receive, or will we stay within our existing comfort zones.

Even when we allow signs into our lives, we always retain the power of choice – the choice to accept and acknowledge the messages being presented to us at any given moment. When we encounter a fork in the road, we can decide whether to turn left or right, just as we choose whether to stay in or go out for the night.

Similarly, when it comes to our emotions, we have the ability to decide how we want to feel – to embrace happiness or remain in sadness. We also hold the choice to expand our minds and encourage personal growth, fostering evolution, or to stay in the familiar confines of our current reality.

Sometimes, that familiar reality may be filled with pain and sadness, yet we cling to it because we've convinced ourselves that this is simply how life is meant to be. But even in those moments, the choice is ours – to remain in that known comfort zone or to step into the unknown and discover something new.

To borrow a line from the film *The Matrix,* we all can choose to swallow either the red or the blue pill.

I believe this freedom of choice follows the foundation that is the construct for our entire universe otherwise known as Yin and Yang. Dark/light, life/death, happy/sad, good/bad, day/night, male/female, up/down, left/right – this list could go on for miles. Almost always we are free to choose. Then as sure as night follows day, the choices that we make have consequences and will determine the direction of the grand plan. Therefore, this divine plan is constantly unfolding, forever evolving.

I have come to believe that there will be many moments of guidance presented to us along the way, gifts to help us achieve what it was that we set out to achieve as part of our original intentions. The end result will just depend on if our eyes are truly opened and if we are ready to receive such support. Throughout my journey to alignment, once my spirit was freed, I allowed myself to transition into this special reality that I have aptly named the feeling world. A place of existence that amalgamates the physical world with the existential spirit world taking your life to the next level. We arrive at this place when we are truly free, ready to recognise the signs, guidance and special moments as they present themselves.

All I had to do was let go of the shackles of my past. The natural progression from this then shifted my mind into the receiving mode as I was now ready to connect. Fragments were then delivered to me maybe to see how I would respond. From there began a visual unfolding tied to the physical experience, seeing the signs as they appeared, both in my conscious and sub-conscious world (dream state). My antenna was finally tuned in. This led to the frequency of transmitting signals loud and clear, I suppose this was inevitable. However, nothing could have prepared me for the beauty that was about to present itself in the form of 333. This experience I will share with you later in this chapter.

I have discovered that these universal messages arrive in many different forms and for you, I have identified them as follows:

A. **Angel numbers** – Number sequences are commonly referred to as angel numbers. Divine messages are sent from above in the form of a sequential or common number pattern. An example of this is the number sequence triple two (222). This triple combination is commonly believed to be a sign from above that is reminding you that you are exactly where you need to be. It is heavenly reassurance reiterating that you are right where the universe wants you to be as part of the divine plan for your life's journey. A helpful reminder if you are feeling lost, distracted or having doubt.

B. **Affiliation numbers** – Affiliation or attachment numbers can be a single number or a sequence of numbers that you feel drawn to or an attachment with. For example, the number eighty-eight (88). Many people feel a strong connection to this pairing of numbers. In fact, many believe that they are a sign of great luck and good fortune. The birth number calculation can also help you create your own affiliation number, one that you may feel a connection with. Birth numbers are single digits ranging between 1 and 9. They are created be using your date of birth; for example, 01/01/1990 = 1 + 1 + 1 + 9 + 9 = 21 = 2 + 1 = 3 Birth Number 3.

C. **Dream messages** – These messages can be delivered either clearly and consciously or they can be delivered in the form of a cryptic clue scenario that requires deciphering. These messages can contain either positive or negative elements. If we are receiving divine guidance through a dream message, we may need to decipher the dream to discover the hidden message that is being shared with us.

Dream messages are a common way for us to receive subconscious guidance, support and information.

D. Conscious messages – These can be delivered with a physical world component of either vibration, a separate visual component and/or a sub-conscious element. These messages can include a combination of all the elements or even just a single component. Many believe that music and song lyrics, book content and inspirational ideas are received through the stream of conscious messages or downloads.

As an example of a conscious message, my real-world experience with the number sequence triple three (333) included physical world components with vibrational elements, visual numerical angel numbers and letters while awake within the conscious world, plus a sub-conscious dream message, with a physical world attachment as a point of reference. It is important to note that this triple three (333) experience was spread out over multiple weeks.

These messages can be linked to activating our recognition and acceptance of the more sacred instincts and human body responses – human functionality that has been supressed while we are consumed with the modern world of living.

Certainly, some of these signs are not new and have been explored in singularity or plurality by others. Yet the credibility that I attach to the actual realisation that in fact these are what I call 'real' is validated by the physical world experiences that I will share in this chapter.

I have discovered a way to feel, recognise and allow myself to receive this existential support and then utilise the guidance being offered as part of my entire life experience. This is a magical discovery.

On the following pages, I have written an introduction for you to the various signs.

A) Angel numbers – number sequences

Angel numbers can appear in many different ways, you could be glancing at a digital clock or timer and at the exact moment the numbers are paired or sequential such as 11:11, or maybe you are watching a sports game and during your conversation, you notice the time clock at exactly 4:44. They can appear while you are driving or travelling in some form of transportation, maybe at a specific moment you notice a passing registration such as ABC 222. The triple or quadruple number sequence or pairing of numbers such as 1212 or 1010 all have different meanings associated with them and represent their own unique divine message.

Becoming aware of these signs brings in a whole new element to your physical existence. Life becomes adventurous, like a game of discovery, as you tune yourself in. You don't even need to make any major changes – just be open to new ideas, reimagining what is possible and become aware of your surroundings. It is your choice whether you want to receive the message or not.

Some people have suggested that the power of angel numbers relates to the energy that revolves around the individual number beyond its numeric value. Personally, I know that once you make the shift, the numbers will begin to appear with relevance. The relevance is what the numbers represent versus the thought or action you are exhibiting. When the numbers form part of a message for you, there could be a combination of events that occur.

Firstly, you are aware enough to notice the numbers. Many numbers come and go throughout each day; these numbers don't just magically appear for you. However, at that specific moment, because you are aware and aligned, you recognise them. Your vibration is a match. Pay attention to the specific numbers, record them or remember what they were. When you have a moment, look them up and educate yourself on the unique meanings attached to each number sequence.

Capturing the numbers with your sense of sight is an immediate way for us all to receive a message of divine support. Try to remember what it was that you were thinking about or what your actions were at the very moment when synchronicity brought you together.

Can you identify any correlation between your thought and the sign?

Are there any other specific clues in your message? I will provide an example of this further along in my shared experience.

Secondly, at the time you're aligning with the numbers, if there is a message for you, you may feel a change inside your body. Pay attention to how your body feels. From my own personal experience when a direct message is received, the physical body feels a vibration flow through it as the physical shell connects with the whole of existence. During these moments, the physical experience combines with the divine numbers to carry a special message for you.

Angel numbers and their meanings:

111

The triple ones are a powerful sequence associated with manifestations – the triple one (111) or quadruple one (1111) are signs associated with new beginnings. You may have a new job opportunity on the horizon, a new relationship starting, or you may be beginning a whole new chapter in your life. This is your new beginning. Stay positive and true. Whatever your dreams are, they are currently manifesting into your reality for you.

222

The triple twos are a sign from your angels representing where you are at in your life, confirming that you are exactly where you need to be. This number sequence can appear when you are having a moment of doubt or dismay, pondering or concerned as you stress about where you are in relation to the overall pathway for your life experience.

Many people contemplate the question or ask the universe, 'Am I doing what I need to be doing? Am I where I need to be?' in search of purpose or divine guidance. When you ask this question look out for the triple two (222). This is a sign to reassure you not to panic; you are exactly where you need to be.

333

The triple threes are a direct message from your angels above. When you see 333, you can be rest assured that your angel guides are with you. Your current efforts, dreams and life path are being supported by your angel guides; your dreams and prayers have been heard and they are being answered for you. This doesn't mean you can relax or slack off. You still need to put in the effort. For your commitment a great reward is on the way for you, this will bring you much joy and fulfilment.

444

The triple fours are the divine support numbers and the message from your angels attached to these numbers is loud and clear: DON'T GIVE UP! Don't give up even if you feel like you are currently fighting a losing battle. Stay strong, stay true to yourself. You are not alone; your angels are with you. You're so close to achieving your dreams. 444 is the message that all of your hard work is about to pay off big time!

555

The triple fives are a sign from your angel guides to hold on to your horses and GET READY! Major changes and opportunities have entered or are about to enter your life. The triple fives are vibrational numbers that are all about you taking action, fulfilling your dreams and desires – a direct message from the angels to GO FOR IT. If the universe did not feel that you were ready for what was coming, you would not be seeing this sign. You will never be asked to do something you are not ready to do.

666

Triple six is not all doom and gloom. 666 has long been associated as the devil's number and a satanic sign. However, this is not the only association 666 represents. In fact, in the realm of angel numbers, 666 represents taking a break, taking stock and being aware of your thoughts and fears. Sometimes you can focus on negative components too much: your fears, your worry, the negative what-ifs.

As sure as you can manifest positive outcomes, experiences and circumstances in your life, you can also manifest the complete opposite, negative outcomes, experiences and circumstances in your life. Give yourself a break, slow it down and focus on the POSITIVE stuff in your life; this will ensure that you manifest positive outcomes in your life, not the negative ones.

777

Triple seven is a direct message from the angels bringing great news. The universe has seen all of your hard work, so you are to be rewarded. The angels are right there with you every step of the way and will continue to support you to ensure you stay on the right path. Seeing 777 is a sign you are in perfect alignment with the universe, and you can expect great rewards, good luck and plenty of wonderful opportunities and happiness.

888

Triple eight is the number of abundances, especially when it comes to your finances. The 888 represents winning in life; when this number shows up, you can get excited and expect great things to come for you. The number eight turned on its side is the symbol for infinity, which represents where our true source of health, happiness and wealth comes from. This coincides with the original source of infinite abundance that flows directly from our Creator, the Chief Conductor, GOD.

999

Triple nine is the angel number that represents the end. When you see 999, you can expect to close a chapter in your life. The sequence of nines is sign you can take comfort in; maybe you have been struggling in life trying to overcome a challenge, something hard and personal for you. When seeing triple nine, you can take comfort in knowing that whatever the challenge, event or situation is that you are currently experiencing may now be coming to an end for you.

Angel numbers – seeing the signs – 333

I will now share with you some extraordinary events that I've experienced with these heavenly signs.

This miraculous story was experienced over a number of weeks and includes angel numbers, vibrational messages delivered in a conscious state, as well as a subconscious dream message.

Writing about this experience for you is done so with only intention to help elevate the understanding that as we move along our life's journey, there is great support for each of us from outside the physical world. The same celestial entity that gifted us our spirit is also there to provide unlimited support and guidance as we progress along our unique trail, attempting to achieve our life's purpose.

This story actually started several years ago, back in the year 2015 when I had come into contact with a prospective client as part of my daily business. During my initial interaction with this prospect, I invested significant resources in negotiating a solution based on their business needs at the time.

During this time together, my investment included a number of site visits, attended by multiple staff members, as well as a number of administrative hours in preparing our offering for them. My company believed we had constructed a competitive solution for them and that we were in a prime position to secure their business. However, when it came to making a final decision, the prospective client decided to accept a competitor's offer.

This was fine. No hard feelings, as we all have a choice.

Business is business, disappointed as I was, we move on in search of the next opportunity. Fast forward to 2021.

Powered by my newly discovered connection, my mind was now open to all possibilities. Somehow, I was connecting with external forces that I was convinced had to be from a whole other realm. I already knew that special things were at play; however, I was about to discover that what was unfolding was so much more than I'd ever imagined.

The prospective client from my past had reached out to the universe and as fate would have it, was placed back into contact with my company. Since our previous interaction, the prospect had a number of negative experiences with my competition and was now wanting to revisit the opportunity with my business. Once again, we had been bought back together.

This time around though, after being burnt before, I'd decided that I would be approaching this opportunity very differently. Last time I had been very flexible in my approach to no avail. This time I would not invest too much time at all. I'd just package together our proposal, submit the details and that's it. If they agreed, they agreed and if not, so be it. I was not going to be overtly consumed by this specific opportunity.

So, after an initial phone call, I prepared our draft offering and submitted the details electronically. The offer was clear, listing the indicative costs, as well as including all the core items that they required. I knew that my proposal would ensure that we could service our new client with the highest level of customer care and support that they required.

After I'd emailed the quotation, a couple of weeks passed by before the client eventually reached out to me to organise a site meeting. By this stage they had reviewed the quotation, understanding the costs and inclusions, and now with this information known, they wanted to progress to the next stage. The manager requested that I attend their office, to which I agreed.

I arrived at their office the following day, internally still carrying my preconceived feelings about how I was messed around last time. Walking to their entrance, I reminded myself that I would not be played this time. As I stepped through the front door into their reception area, I was immediately hit with a divine lightning bolt. *Bang!* My entire body became alive with a divine message. Underneath my shirt, I became amplified. This caught me off guard as I knew this feeling meant something good was coming.

WOW, I thought, *what's this? This is going to be an interesting meeting!*

This was my first sign.

Immediately, I decided to leave all of my preconceived ideas and negative feelings about how I was going to handle this meeting at the front door as I made my way inside. My mind was now a clean slate. In fact, I was eagerly excited to experience whatever it was that was going to unfold and where this momentum was going to take me.

I was captivated by my special connection, whilst externally still ensuring that I was conducting the meeting professionally. As I spoke with the prospective client and their staff members, I continuously felt my divine guidance zap me with the divine love. Filling me with euphoric bursts underneath my work attire, letting me know this was the beginning of something special. I reaffirmed with the customer their immediate requirements to ensure that we were all on the same page. Then once we were all in agreeance, I left their office so that they could discuss the details between themselves. No deal had been officially agreed to yet; however, I knew exactly what they required so I could finalise our packaged solution.

Within the following week, I'd finished our letter of offer, covering off on all their needs and requirements. I submitted my final proposal electronically and continued on with my other activity.

Roughly a week after I had submitted my final offer to them, as I was driving my car along one of the major metropolitan highways, I received a call from this prospective client. As soon as I answered the call and our conversation began, I was hit by the divine lightning bolt. My body became amplified, filling with divine love. I wasn't sure what was happening, but I knew that this was something so magnificent.

I tried to remain composed while on the phone with the client and not get caught up in the power of the euphoric energy as it filled my body, attempting to maintain a normal toned conversation with them. In my mind, I was asking, *what is happening? What is this magnificence?*

The client said, 'Mike, we have decided to go ahead with your proposal.'

Then right at that exact moment, I received the message to turn my head. So, I did. I turned my head to the left and caught a glimpse of the number plate of the car passing me.

YSM 333

In that heavenly vibrational moment, the message immediately translated to me as… 'YES, MIKE SMITH 333!!' This was a definitive message, direct from above. My initials had been intwined in with the numbers. Such a magical moment, one that I had allowed myself to receive.

I was overwhelmed by this, but all the while managed to stay composed on the phone and simply said to the client, 'That's great news. I can really feel how eager you are to come onboard!'

Those letters and numbers were such a direct message that it was too hard for me to ignore. MS, my initials, and the angel numbers

333. Something godly had orchestrated this divine rendezvous. As I ended the call, I revelled in the euphoric feeling, simply amazed as to what had just occurred and with that, I continued on my way. This new deal was not complete yet. I knew that no sale was finalised until the paperwork was signed; however, a verbal acceptance meant we were well on the way.

After that memorable phone call, a week went by. This was normal in my line of business, and nothing seemed out of the ordinary. The next divine message I received relating to this entire experience was on the Monday evening of the following week.

That evening before bed I had been thinking about all the open sales opportunities along with all the different bills and expenses that needed to be paid. As I laid down, I was still thinking about my open opportunities and money. Eventually, I drifted off to sleep. It felt like I had been asleep for hours when during my subconscious dream state, I could feel I was transcending into another powerfully vivid lucid dream. There was nothing and then all of a sudden, there I was. I could see the client's business name appear right in front of me, I could see the client's logo, I could see the client's yard full of their trucks… I could see it all. It was so real; it was as if I was standing in the middle of their truck yard.

Suddenly, I had to wake up. 'Am I in their yard or am I still in my bed?' I asked.

Almost convinced that I was actually in the middle of their yard, I pulled myself back into my conscious state, into my physical reality and then immediately pressed the tablet next to my bed to check the time…

3:33 am

Not 3:32, not 3:34 – exactly 3:33 am. In my head, I thought, *WOOOOOOOO what are the chances of this? What is going on here?*

I was very surprised, wonderfully surprised, considering the number plate that I had seen in the previous week when speaking to the same client. Somehow, I managed to relax and drift away back to sleep for the rest of the night.

Later that same week, I spoke with the client, so we could schedule our next meeting. This would be at their office so we could sign all the relevant paperwork. Due to various details, the plan was to start with half of the proposed solution immediately and then the balance in six weeks' time. This was no problem; I could work with this.

The meeting was scheduled for 1 pm on the following Monday. I arrived at their office just before the start and navigated my way through their yard. Their yard was bustling with tip trucks constantly streaming in and out. Immediately as I stepped through their main entrance doors, the vibrations started, filling my body with bursts of euphoric energy. Underneath my work attire, I could feel the constant zaps as I tried to remain composed. Someone was having fun with this.

As our meeting progressed, the original plan of fifty per cent now and fifty per cent later was scrapped. The client had now decided that they would proceed with the full one hundred per cent now. The sale doubled in size.

Abundance was flowing! Once the signing of the new documents was completed, the client referred another new prospect to me… the abundance continued to flow. Everything was happening with such ease. When our meeting concluded, I headed out to my car, happy with what had just gone down. I sat in the driver's seat, turned on the ignition and looked at the time.

13:33

This time, the powerful lightning bolt hit me in a manner like I'd never felt before. *BOOM!* It filled me with a massive load of divine love. An existential power like no other. Now I was elevated, dynamically connected. Like a stream of heavenly energy flowing directly into me, filling every atom within my body with Source. This was a celestial message; I had allowed myself to feel and see the signs in both my physically conscious world as well as in my subconscious dream state. I knew this was something special. I knew what I'd experienced was big.

'Once the divine love is felt, that is all that is needed. When the vibration is received, the universe will set the wheels in motion to accomplish everything that is universally desired.'
– Source

B) Affiliation numbers

Another form of communication used by your celestial support team to transmit messages to you on a higher level is the use of relevant numbers. Affiliation or attachment numbers are digits that have a special meaning or connection to you or those who are close to you. These numbers might only be specific to you, like your birth number, or maybe you have a family member that has a specific number that you associate with them. I have a personal example with the affiliation numbers of eighty-eight.

Number eighty-eight is a significant number in itself; as I mentioned earlier, the number eight on its side is commonly known as the symbol for infinity. Infinite existence is never-ending just like our spiritual self. However, for me the number eighty-eight is stamped onto the gravestone of my mother's parents – my Italian grandparents, my Nonna and Nonno. Because of this, I associate this number sequence with them both, but significantly with my Nonna.

One evening during the summer of 2020, I was spending some time with Wa. I'd picked Wa up from her place and we were out driving together. While we drove around, talking, Wa asked a leading question. Only leading in the sense that she was really searching for the answer to her question for herself.

She asked me, 'Do you miss your grandma?'

Contemplating her question for a moment I then offered her my considered response. 'I don't really feel like she is gone. I feel that she is always around me, just not in the physical form that I knew her as. When I see the number eighty-eight, I know that this is her number and so I know that she is around.'

As we drove, I pointed out all the eighty-eights that were appearing in front of us. The number seemed to be on every second or third passing car, up until the moment that I decided to turn into a public carpark, where most of the cars in front of us had the number eighty-eight on their number plate.

I said, 'See? She is here, all around us. She is everywhere and she is sending a sign to both of us.'

We eventually left the carpark, and I continued to drive. I drove through a number of back streets and then as we turned onto the main road, we entered the right-hand turning lane. To the amazement of both of us, out of all the possible cars in the entire world that we could have pulled up behind, we were stationary behind a Caddy wagon that had a HUGE eighty-eight sticker on the back door, covering most of the rear door.

'WOW!' we both exclaimed.

Surrounding the huge number were four smaller eighty-eights in a diamond formation, at the top, bottom, and on the left- and right-hand side. This was a truly magical moment. Instantly, a vibrational acknowledgement was received as the message was sent and received. A connecting moment linking both the physical and spiritual world.

I was completely elevated by the heavenly connection I'd received but there was still more to come. As we passed next to the car, we could see that there were HUGE eighty-eight stickers mounted on the side doors and bonnet, with smaller eighty-eight stickers in diamond formations surrounding them. We both just laughed and smiled, recognising that this shared experience was something beautiful. This entire car was completely covered in the number eighty-eight.

'Once you are in a state of allowing, actively aware of the signs, your life experience becomes more like a fairy tale, one that is full of the possible, not the impossible, one that is not limited to the constraints of what you have been told to accept as part of your existence.'

– **M. Smith**

C) Dream messages – a sub-conscious state of mind

Dream messages are constantly transmitted when we close our eyes and sleep. Understanding, deciphering or remembering the content will come down to the individual receptive mode or lack of. An individual whose signal is blocked or jammed may struggle to decipher the message with any form of sense or clarity. One who is in a state of allowing will be best placed to receive and translate the information that is being shared.

Since my journey began, I have received many dream messages, transmitted to me from a place of higher consciousness, with many of the messages delivered to me in some form of cryptic puzzle – fun to solve, but not always clear at first. Messages that I needed to decipher. I have found that the dream messages usually contain a story, along with a choice, or a certain situation with a directive.

Most of the messages are delivered as a two-part puzzle or as a scenario with a choice with two potential outcomes.

Here are some actual examples:

1. Start looking at life through a different lens – 'all is not what it seems'

This was my dream where my brothers and I were happily traveling in a black van, laughing and enjoying each other's company. While taking pictures, a bird flew in through an open window and calmly perched on a seat. We were all curious about the bird's presence, but it seemed content. Yet when I raised my phone to take a photo, the bird suddenly transformed into our grandmother (Nonna), smiling and giving a double thumbs up. This transformation happened twice, and the message became clear: life should be viewed through a different perspective, as things are not always as they appear.

> *We need to start looking through a different lens –*
> *all is not what it seems.*

2. Change your projected future – 'We are all gifted a forward-facing time machine.'

I shared the details of this dream earlier; however, this dream is about the power of choice and the potential to alter the course of our future. The dream, in which I am a passive observer initially, offers an opportunity to intervene and change a tragic outcome through the ability to pause, rewind and then alter the sequence of events. Within this dream, I was shown how the awareness of a recurring pattern or outcome can empower us to make different choices.

The key message here is that our future is not set in stone. The metaphor of a 'forward-facing time machine' emphasises that we have the power to navigate through time, understanding the consequences of our actions and adjusting accordingly. By recognising patterns in our lives or situations, and consciously choosing a different path, we can change our projected future.

Einstein quoted his definition of insanity as, 'Repeating the same action and expecting a different outcome.' This highlights how, if we keep responding in the same way to the challenges or dilemmas we face, we should not expect different results. To break free from negative patterns or avoid destructive paths, we must change our actions – sometimes by taking an unexpected or different route.

In a broader sense, this dream invites reflection on how we approach challenges in life. By acknowledging that even when we feel trapped by recurring cycles or predictable outcomes, there is always room to change our direction – if only we are aware enough to make the right choice at the right moment.

This message was a reminder that no matter our projected path –

We can change our future.

3. Slipping down the rabbit hole – 'Trapped'

In this dream, I was not myself. Instead, I believe I was someone very close to me – someone I knew had been struggling with addiction. In the dream, they were walking casually across a grassy oval. The sun was shining, and everything seemed perfect. But as they took a step forward, their entire body suddenly fell into a circular hole. It wasn't a large hole, but it was big enough to swallow them whole.

As their body became consumed by the hole, they uncontrollably slid down into the tunnel, falling deep into the rabbit hole. The tunnel was narrow, and as they slid further, they could see the earth's dirt directly in front of them. They observed all the details of the dirt – worms, roots and other living organisms beneath the earth's surface. Desperately, they tried to stop or slow down, using their fingers and nails to grip the sides of the tunnel. But nothing worked; they couldn't catch hold of anything to stop their descent.

Eventually, the tunnel began to taper off, and they came to a stop. They were so deep below the surface that when they tilted their head back to look up, they could barely see the faint glow of daylight above. At this moment in the dream, I became them. Using all my strength, I pushed through the dirt and instantly returned to the surface.

The message was clear: The person I care about had fallen so deeply into the rabbit hole that they could barely see a way out. But I realised that if I accepted the challenge, I might be able to help guide them back to the light, back to the surface since they were trapped and couldn't get out on their own.

This was a difficult realisation because the person must be ready and willing to receive help. The support given must be in the form of healing, not enabling. If the helper becomes an enabler, it will only prolong the cycle and prevent true healing from taking place.

The message was –

they are trapped and cannot get out.

4. Parked but rolling backward – 'Losing Control'

Within this lucid dream, a specific family member was in the driver's seat of a passenger van that had pulled up into an empty carpark spot. Seated in the front passenger seat was the driver's mother. She was trying her best to be a positive influence and offer the driver beneficial advice; however, her words were not being received. In fact, she may as well have been talking to herself such was the driver's inability to interpret the information being offered.

The van had been filled with the driver's other family members; however, his father, his brother, his uncles and aunties, cousins had already exited the vehicle. Everyone had safely assumed that the van (driver's life) was at least stationary. Not moving forward but not moving backwards either. However, the car had actually started rolling backwards even with the driver still seated in the driving seat. The van was a representation of the driver's life.

I, myself, was still seated in the rear and could see that the van was now rolling backwards, plus I could see that all the family gathered around outside the vehicle were unaware that the van now rolling backwards. Hurriedly, I reached forward, aggressively yelling, 'Fucking stop!' whilst pulling the hand brake up at the same time in an attempt to stop the van (driver's life) from rolling uncontrollably backwards.

The message here was –

the individual has lost control.

5. Balloon balancing a controlled exit or bubble bursting – you choose

During this cryptic dream message, I was stuck between two large rubber balloons full of air. One was in front of me; one was pushed up behind me. I was squashed in the middle. The rubber balloon in front of me was shaped more like a rectangle than a circle.

Since I was stuck between these two balloons, I could not breathe easily. In my right hand, I was holding my full coffee mug and with my left hand, I was pushing off the surface of the balloon so I could breathe. My coffee mug was losing some liquid, but it was basically full.

The balloon behind me was rotating against me, forcing me to roll with it, taking me around the outside of the internal balloons' circumference like a rolling pin. All the while leaving me struggling to breathe whilst trying not to drop my cup.

I reached each end of the internal rectangle balloon and could breathe freely for those few seconds. Plus, I also had the ability to reach up with my left hand and grab an overhead metal bar that allowed me to pull myself up and out of the balloon trap, whilst still managing to keep hold of my full coffee cup. Or I could continue trying to ride out the balloon bubble.

Both scenarios actually played out in the dream. The first scenario that played out was as I reached one of the ends of the internal balloon. I pulled myself out and kept hold of my full cup.

Then the second scenario played out where I chose not to exit, which meant I had to continue trying to stay alive between the two bubbles. Eventually, within this scenario, I reached the point where I was totally suffocating, which forced me to pop the balloon behind me. By popping the balloon, I fell backwards uncontrollably, my coffee cup spilt everywhere, and I lost everything.

Immediately, I awoke and actioned my subconscious message. Within the next five days, the crypto market crashed with people losing huge numbers.

This message was a warning and about choice for me:

> *the bubble was going to burst – I could continue riding the bubble and lose everything or I could exit the bubble now and keep my cup full.*

D) Conscious messages from the divine realm

I have received so many extraordinary messages as part of this magical journey. There are some that are very humbling and all of which are very special. It is important to remember that this is not about the self-gratification of winning or amazing financial gain.

This is about sharing with you the actual real-life experiences that I have been gifted as part of my spiritual journey to this new world, the feeling world. This is about encouraging you to allow yourself to be open to receiving. I want you to let yourself feel, listen and identify these divine messages and signs as they arrive while you enjoy the entire process.

One of the earliest divine messages that I can recall as part of my journey was when I had undertaken the task of writing about my painful past, and in a moment of great sadness and distraught emotions, with tears flowing down my face uncontrollably the question was asked to me, 'What happened to the father when he was a child, and was he just repeating the same mistakes?'

These questions came from a loud heavenly voice as if there was someone else in the room with me. This experience activated my entire new beginning, allowing me to discover a new perspective along with everlasting forgiveness.

Then in November 2020 on the morning of Melbourne Cup Day, while I was waking up for the day, still lying in bed, I turned on the TV to the Sky racing channel to enjoy the day's races.

As the first race for the day was preparing, out of nowhere and as clear as day, I heard the words, 'horse number six.' These words were not from the TV – they were heard over and above the sounds coming from my screen.

As you can imagine, this grabbed my attention while catching me by surprise. *What about this horse number six?* I wondered. Now that my attention had been caught and the first race was underway, I was distinctly keen to see how the horse would fair. Boom, horse number six won. I thought, *Whoo, that's interesting!*

I switched over the channel to the next race location, with my attention firmly focused on horse number six. This time, horse number six was aptly named 'Get the Cash' and yes, once again horse number six came in first. This definitely now had my full attention!

In the third race, horse number six ran last. As I followed horse number six throughout the morning, I found that the horse would run either first, second, third or last. Either way, I was having fun.

Fast forward to the main race for the Melbourne Cup. I already had a close connection with the horse Steel Prince that was running in the main race. Distractedly, I was looking forward to the possibility of Steel Prince having some major success. However, a couple of minutes before the race started, I thought, *Geez, I better get on the horse number six, especially after my experiences in the morning.*

Hurriedly, I grabbed my phone so I could place a wager on the horse.

Well, the famous race was run and since I'd been focused on Steel Prince's position, I reviewed the winners list and yes…. HORSE NUMBER SIX won!

WOW, I thought, how did this happen? Where did that voice come from this morning? This was a connected experience.

The following Saturday was the last big race day of the Melbourne Cup carnival, Stakes Day. I missed the morning's races but did manage to tune in just before the main race for the day. Once again, I thought, I better jump on the horse number six in this race. As fate would have it, or as the divine plan unfolded, *horse number six* won the race!

A special message from inside a church

During the year 2021, I visited a local church around Easter time. I attended the church with my special friend to visit her grandparent's memorial plaques. Both of her grandparents had been laid to rest there, plus I wanted to experience the inside of a church with her. Maybe we could feel the divine touch or even connect with spirit together.

Upon arriving, we headed straight to where her family's plaques were to say 'hello' before venturing inside. The daytime service had just finished, so there were a lot of people exiting as we were walking in. Unperturbed by this, we walked over towards the priest where we were hastily greeted by a friendly older man. Neither of us had ever met this man before, which meant he knew nothing of my journey, nor did he know that I was writing a book.

As he began talking to the two of us, his eyes were glowing. He was radiating with connected energy. Out of the blue, he shared the following statement with the two of us: 'If I were writing a book about my life, I would give it away to people to read.' He continued by saying that he wasn't writing a book about his life, but if he was, this is what he would do.

I thought, *Wow, this a very random subject to share with a stranger about something that you're not doing. When the stranger (me) is actually doing exactly that.*

Why did this man talk to us? Why did he tell us about what he would do if he was writing a book when he wasn't writing a book? Was there a greater message that needed to be received? Was the message for me about the distribution of my story? I could not help but be in awe…

Conscious vibrational messages

Many messages can be received as data downloads during moments of creativity. Inspirational ideas, music, poems, artwork and writings are all conscious messages that have been transmitted as part of our connectivity. These messages are special and memorable moments in history, such as John Lennon creating the song *Imagine,* or Vincent van Gogh painting *The Starry Night*, or maybe it was the moment Ray Kroc received his inspirational idea 'to create a restaurant system to deliver quality food', which later became McDonald's. These, along with every other creative idea, all originated as messages. Yet vibrational messages are not just limited to these. Vibrational messages have the power to elevate even a general conversation, raising the external energy level all around the body. This phenomenon occurs when the subject matter is meaningful and when the words spoken are powerful and true.

Many times, the spoken words will resonate with either the person or persons who are partaking in the conversation once the divine confirmation is received. This experience will be reciprocated by the recipient receiving the heavenly lightning bolt, confirming their agreement with the words that are being used, while discussing meaningful subject matter. You can also use your conscious vibration confirmations for your own benefit to know that the person you are conversing with is connecting with what it is you are saying.

This is the acknowledgment that you are on the right path… you are in the right place, at the right time and heading in the right direction. You are exactly where we need to be.

'The possibilities are endless, as a connected vibrational being.'
– M. Smith

Now is the time for all of us to become all that we can be!

Chapter 9

WOUNDED BUTTERFLIES – OVERCOMING ADVERSITY™

This chapter will focus on sharing with you the powerful pathway that I discovered leading to the transformational life experience. I do this so that you may begin to understand the non-invasive work required to overcome your adversity.

Life's pain is all the emotional stuff that's specific to you. An accumulation of events and experiences that begins in childhood and grows over a lifetime. Trauma that then willingly or unwillingly influences many of our decisions and behaviours. For some, this trauma could be from a specific event or 'Moment in Time' that hits you right in the face, like a sledgehammer, knocking you off your projected path and into a version of reality that you thought you'd never experience. For others, this pain could have originated from a multitude of events experienced during the developmental or teenage years, thus leading to a lifetime of emotional suffering, internal misery and self-deprecating behaviours.

Whichever is applicable to your story, it's important to remember that everyone's emotional baggage is relevant and matters. This chapter is about sharing with you a process for lasting change by outlining an extremely achievable pathway for anyone to follow and complete so that you may release the shackles and set yourself free.

The key criteria in this chapter includes:

- Identifying the emotional baggage we carry
- Identifying the cause – Cycle of Repetition – reaching your epiphany moment

- Forgiveness – not forget
- Taking back control – you are the center of your universe
- Understanding that only YOU control how YOU feel, and YOU choose to feel good

The real-world scenarios that I will focus on are:

1. Processing deep-held pain (childhood trauma) Scenario 1 – abandonment
2. Processing deep-held pain (childhood trauma) Scenario 2 – abuse
3. Processing a significant life event (life trauma) Scenario 3 – sexual assault

Know that you are not alone with your pain and trauma; these are very common situations.

All that's required from you is a **commitment to yourself.**

A commitment that believes you deserve more, that you deserve peace. Can you commit to this? I believe that you can; I think that we all can. I believe that deep down, we are all searching for inner peace and happiness.

Introduction

I have already shared with you some of the personal traumatic details from my life story by detailing some of the abuse that I suffered. I shared this with you so that you could understand that I can respectfully speak on the topic.

In addition to the early lived experiences that formed part of my story, I can now talk about the other side of this coin. About getting through the trauma and pain by sharing the method that I have uncovered to overcome these significant life challenges. I use my voice and share my experiences to benefit anyone who can relate.

As the saying goes, 'I have worn in many different hats in this life.'

One thing that I will say today with absolute certainty is that I would not change anything from my past.

Despite all the pain and tribulations I had to endure, I would not change a thing. Because everything I have experienced has led me to this point right now, having this conversation with you.

Who knows where I would be right now if something were to be altered in my past?

The emotional baggage we carry

As life would have it for many of us, starting from when we are young, we begin to accumulate our emotional baggage. This emotional baggage is remarkably similar to the baggage you might take with you on a holiday: it may start off small, but over time can continue to grow into an unmanageable amount – we just cannot see this with the naked eye. This, however, is something that we carry on our shoulders every day of our lives, influencing our life choices, behaviours and beliefs as we navigate our earthly existence.

Then as the years go on, the baggage that we carry gets heavier and heavier, constantly filling with new emotional experiences. In many instances, to deal with this weight, we are taught:

- Just get on with it, stop being a sook.
- It's life. Life wasn't meant to be easy.
- Drink a cup of concrete and harden up. Get over it.
- Or worst of all – here, take this drug, swallow this pill or consume this drink and all of your worries will disappear.

I'm sure that there are many more examples that I could have used above, but I'm certain that we all get the gist. Unfortunately, many times, this life advice comes from the people who are supposed to care the most. They speak these comments directly to the people they care most about… their children, inadvertently negatively influencing these young impressionable minds.

You might ask, 'Why would they say these words?' Well, I ask, why wouldn't they say these words since they don't know any better?

It's what they were taught, it's what was said to them; they know no other way. Plus, this is how their own life experience has played out. Life's been hard for them; life's been tough.

This is not the way life was meant to be. Rest assured, there can be a new way. What's needed is a fresh start – a reset, if you will. A new beginning that includes a process to complete emotional freedom. One such way is using the guided program that I have created called the Wounded Butterflies – Overcoming Adversity™ program. This pathway includes identifying what is inside our own emotional baggage.

Scenario one

Real world story – abandonment baggage
For the purpose of this example, I will focus on the scenario of abandonment.

A young child grows up in a dysfunctional family, becoming a victim of traumatic abuse, in the form of emotional and physical beatings. In addition to the inflicted abuse, the child witnesses excessive drinking as well as domestic violence. The child has older siblings who also experienced the same traumatic events.

After a number of years pass, the child's parents eventually separate. However, without deliberate intention, the separation leaves the child to interpretate that the father leaving is abandoning the family.

Unbeknown to the child at this time is the fact that they have now been gifted the emotional components of 'abandonment' and 'abuse'. There is also a number of negative behavioural traits that have been subliminally inserted into the child's baggage, after witnessing some of the adults in their life consume what I refer to as signal blockers: alcohol and drugs.

The unsuspecting child is now carrying their emotional bag everywhere as they begin to navigate through their life experiences. Seeds have now been sowed deep within this child's mind. It is important to note that during the early years, this bag might not have been too heavy. It may have confused and acerbated the child's emotions on the odd occasion but overall, this child had enough external support around them during their developmental years to remain on track.

In this case, the child witnessed alcohol consumption by many adults, some in moderation and some in excess. This child also witnessed the changing behaviours that are associated with the consumption of alcohol; sometimes, there would be fun and laughter, while other times, the complete opposite. Either way, the child could see that the behaviours and emotions changed.

The child now grows into a teenager. Like many other young adults transitioning into young adulthood, especially in Western cultures, the teen is introduced to drugs and alcohol within their social circle. Since this key behavioural pattern was already witnessed earlier during the childhood years, this natural progression just reaffirmed the earlier learnt behaviours that this is the way.

The individual evolves, growing confident. The teen becomes involved in a partnered relationship that, like many teenage relationships, is full of emotions and charged with energy. It is during this time that the teen increases the usage of these blockers: alcohol and drugs. The individual is even influenced by one of their older siblings.

The teen (like many others) is now experimenting with these substances and can feel the change that comes over their body when they consume the drugs. As it always is, and as the drugs are designed to do, all their worries in the world seem to disappear, plus it's fun, isn't it? Or is it?

The teenager and their partner remain together, growing into young adults. Unbeknown to the young adults now is the reality that they are still carrying around their emotional baggage formulated from childhood. Then as with many young adult relationships, theirs comes to an end and they separate.

With the onset of the relationship ending, this reignites all of the sub-conscious childhood abandonment trauma, while bringing all the associated emotions with it to the surface. This young adult now feels extremely hurt, saddened and abandoned by their ex-partner.

Yet this time around, they don't have the immediate external support that was around in their childhood years. So, what does the young adult do? They do exactly what they have learnt to do and what they know. When it comes to feeling better, they use the only coping mechanism they really know… alcohol and drugs.

This starts off as it always does, innocently, masking the pain. However, the innocence does not last for long because now it's a perfect storm. The worse they feel, the more they consume, beginning an infinite cycle that will need to be undone. They struggle to feel good, with the constant feelings of loneliness, worthlessness and helplessness now overflowing from their emotional baggage made worse by their drug use.

With the relationship break up and the resurfacing of the childhood trauma, they are now struggling to carry the weight of this load. In addition to this, they struggle to understand why it is that they are feeling this way.

As part of the breakup, a property is sold. The adult gets paid the settlement cash and a large amount of money hits the bank account. The dam is now about to burst. This broken and confused adult now has a physical bag full of cash; however, they are consumed with the overflowing emotions of abandonment, worthlessness and loneliness.

As innocently as this method of dealing with pain started, the downward spiral has begun. Over the coming years, all the money is burned, their drug usage manifests into a full-blown addiction and there are countless lives affected. The relationships with many of their family members and friends have been touched or damaged in some form of negative way. Now the emotional bag that had been carried from childhood into adult life has grown in size too. Back in the early days, potentially this was a containable bag to carry; however, now since life has progressed, with many more negative emotions and outcomes manifesting, the exacerbated weight is much heavier as they walk through day-to-day life.

Their emotional bag now includes:

- **Guilt** – for all the negative choices made.
- **Shame** – for the pain they'd caused to the people they cared about.
- **Pain**, sadness, anger, frustration and confusion.
- **Worthlessness** – created by the lack of love they feel for themselves.
- **Regret** – for all of the negative choices they can't reverse.

Instead of a manageable bag, now they have a giant sack that each day is compounding with negativity as they struggle to see the light or a way out. With each new negative choice, decision made or action taken this bag continues to fill with more and more, becoming extremely unbearable. This is a heavy weight for any person to carry on one's shoulders.

By now, this life has entered a new cycle that is fully self-sufficient; the worse they feel, the more drugs they consume, leading to more negative choices, which makes them feel worse, so the more substances they consume and so on…

They are now trapped in a never-ending cycle. So, it would seem. Or are they?

Is there an end? Is there a way out? YES, there is!

All that is required at this stage is a belief that there must be something more for them. A belief that they want a different life experience: one where they no longer carry around this heavy emotional bag constantly infiltrating their choices. An understanding that they too can turn their life around and experience life as other people in the world are, with a free spirit and soul.

Make no mistake, this will be a significant journey, confronting in many aspects and at times this may become emotional, since it may be hard to face certain ingrained memories that have been hidden inside, building up over the years.

What we need to do is go back to the start. We need to go back to the pre-teen era, where this journey began. We need to revisit the childhood unencumbered. Where the individual can re-examine their story, gathering new perspectives and obtaining a new understanding of the lived events that unfolded. They will realise that potentially, the person who originally abandoned them had also experienced abandonment themselves as a child.

If they can allow themselves to become aware that the abandoner may have just simply been repeating the same negative behaviours that they themselves had experienced, this realisation can create a monumental shift.

Evidently, the secret is learning to consider that the abandoner was just repeating the same inherited mistakes that had potentially been ingrained in them, so they knew no other way. They knew no better for the next generation; the adult could not break the *Cycle of Repetition*.

As part of our review, we should also consider how far back the Cycle of Repetition ran. Had this particular cycle of abandonment and violence been passed down historically through the earlier generations in a belief that this was the way life had to be?

One of our key commitments as humans to the next generation should be to recognise these cycles and try to break them. Each generation has the power to bring change to family behaviours, but the first step is to recognise them.

The second step is to actively work toward change, to break the generational Cycle of Repetition. This gives the next generation the opportunity to experience and discover ways to overcome new life hurdles and challenges, not the same repeated events already experienced by the generation before in their upbringing.

With this newfound perspective and understanding of the events experienced as a child, this adult can now begin to understand that the abandonment was not a deliberate attempt to sabotage their life but in fact, something that the parent was potentially not even aware they were doing.

Recognising that their parent's damaging behaviour and the consequences were not intentional but ingrained is the magical beginning of 'forgiveness' and freeing one's soul. At this point, the individual can now attempt to let go of their emotional baggage and free themselves from the weight of their accumulated pain.

Forgiveness but how?

The secret to releasing this emotional baggage is here in the stage of forgiveness. Forgiveness to whoever did the actions for not knowing any better, for being too broken, blind, emotionally unaware, and unable to break their own Cycle of Repetition. Forgiveness can now be reached with the knowledge that the perpetrator was just repeating entrenched behaviours and actions.

We forgive them for they know not what they do.

Once the individual has freed themselves through the power of forgiveness and released the childhood trauma, they can now forgive themselves, with the knowledge and understanding that all of their negative life choices and decisions to date had been made under the influence of the emotional baggage of abandonment and abuse that this individual had been carrying.

When the penny drops here, something special can take place. This is the moment where their spirit is set free, and their soul is unchained. Life can begin again. This is their moment!

From here, they can see clearly with open eyes and the knowledge that they have saved themselves, becoming their own saviour. From this vantage point, they can allow the divine love to flow since now they finally believe that they are valued and worthy.

Starting from this day – the day that they forgive themselves – their life will begin to change. They will be free to be the person who they really want to be, not just a sad reflection of their childhood experiences, moulded by damaged adults or negative social influencers.

As this realisation and newfound awareness settles in, the many emotions that had previously filled their bag including shame, guilt, loneliness and worthlessness will start to dissipate, and by using the tools that have been shared, in time it will completely fade away.

From here, the individual can move forward with self-worth, self-respect and self-love. Remember, it is never too late to take this leap of faith, by believing that you are more.

Scenario two

Real world story – emotional baggage of abuse (physical, sexual and emotional)

A baby is born into a young family, a male in this case. As the baby grows into its childhood years, the family situation takes a turn for the worse and becomes a volatile environment. There is alcohol and family violence. During the child's years of life between the ages of four and eleven, the child is physically and emotionally abused as are his younger siblings and mother. Today, society would class this as domestic family violence.

The mother, who is the victim of the domestic abuse, is committed to her ingrained beliefs associated with the family image and remains in the relationship with the hope that things will change.

It's evident that both parents are carrying their own emotional baggage from their past that is influencing their choices and behaviours. This could be explored individually in the future; however, this scenario is focusing on the young child.

In the early developmental ages between four to eleven years old, this child's emotional baggage has been filled with abuse passed onto him from the offending parent in the form of physical and emotional attacks, along with the associated negative emotional elements of fear, confusion, humiliation and sadness.

As the child reaches the age range of eight to eleven years old, he now is the recipient of additional trauma, namely sexual assault. The young child is molested on six to eight occasions across three years by a male cousin who is from his extended family. Every time the child is in the presence of this older male relative, he is sexually abused.

With his existing baggage full of low self-esteem, low self-worth, fear, pain, humiliation and sadness, the young child is now too scared to report the sexual abuse for fear that in some way they will be blamed for the abuse. The physical abuse and threats of physical violence continue throughout the molestation years.

By the age of eleven, this young child is now carrying some heavy emotional baggage on a daily basis as he tries to navigate his young life, filled with:

- **Physical abuse** – fear, pain, humiliation and sadness.
- **Sexual abuse** – shame, confusion, hurt and guilt.
- **Emotional abuse** – fear, uncertainty, worry and panic.
- **Worthlessness** – fuelled by the lack of love he feels for himself, low self-worth and low self-esteem.

Up until the age eleven, during the moments of normalness within his family home, there is a lot of alcohol consumption by the abusive parent. The witnessing of the excessive behaviour implants the seed in his impressionable mind that the overconsumption of alcohol is a very normal part of daily life, especially when socialising.

As the child begins his teenage years, the abusive parent finally leaves the family home. While this offers an immediate sense of relief for the child, the damage has been done and they are left heavily traumatised as a result of the different traumas experienced. This is a heavy load to carry as they begin their teenage years.

He moves forward trying to forge his own path in life and with this in mind, he begins to be guided by outside influences. In this case for the thirteen-year-old, a number of these outside influences are what is commonly referred to as 'the older crowd' who are consuming not only alcohol but other drugs. Within a short time, this impressionable thirteen-year-old is introduced to these drugs as well.

Once again, just as the young teen had witnessed at home in their earlier years, these new social influencers are all consuming substances excessively. There is no moderation taking place when it comes to their consumption of drugs or alcohol.

This susceptible thirteen-year-old starts to believe that this excessive consumption is the only way to consume these substances as he begins to experiment with them. He quickly identifies that when he consumes the drugs, the weight of his emotional baggage seems to disappear, only ever reappearing once the effects have worn off. He begins to believe this is what he needs in order to function without the emotional baggage and to numb the pain.

During these teenage years, he also starts experimenting with self-harm, including cutting, burning and ropes. At this stage of life, he does not know why, but he regularly feels sad, confused and hurt a lot of the time. He feels that maybe an exit, such as suicide, is his way to escape the pain of his negative emotions! He is rescued by a younger sibling as he attempts to hang himself in the backyard of his home, dangling from a tree branch.

While the young teen continues to mature, he struggles on a number of levels. He struggles to have any meaningful relationships with the opposite sex. In fact, he has so many physical relationships that consensual sex becomes another addiction. The teen, who is already consumed by the feelings experienced from the drugs and alcohol, now has another addiction as he chases the euphoric feeling associated with intimate relationships.

All of his addictions combined make him feel good, or so he believes, which causes him to continuously chase any feeling he can – artificial or natural. The teenage boy has now grown into a young adult. During his adult years, between the ages of twenty to thirty years old, there is continued substance abuse and alcohol consumption, all of which the young adult feels he needs to function within society.

The adult, however, does meet a partner in the later years of his twenties and for the next few years, he has what could be perceived as a normal loving relationship. There are ups and downs but, on the whole, the relationship can be classed as normal. During this period of contentment, the adult feels for the first time he does not always need drugs and alcohol to feel good.

Unbeknown to the adult, however, is the fact that he is still carrying his heavy emotional bag. As their relationship matures, the emotional baggage that has never been dealt with, or talked about in any such format or specifically identified before, resurfaces. This leads the adult to once again seeking escapism from the pain and trauma with the use of his trusted confidants: drugs and alcohol. His self-medicating behaviour starts only in social settings as a reward. However, once the door is opened again, the situation gradually slips backwards and what began as somewhat infrequent, soon becomes a more regular occurrence.

At this stage of life, the adult has now been carrying around with him the following emotional baggage that has been significantly influencing his decisions. Many of these have now existed for some thirty-plus years:

- **Physical abuse** – full of fear, pain, humiliation and sadness.
- **Sexual abuse** – full of shame, confusion, hurt and guilt.
- **Emotional abuse** – full of fear, uncertainty, worry and panic.
- **Worthlessness** – for the lack of love he feels for himself, low self-worth and low self-esteem.

- **Regret** – for the negative choices he cannot reverse, for the people he has hurt emotionally, such as his family and friends.
- **Guilt** – for the negative choices he'd made including being trapped in his addiction.

This emotional bag has now become an extreme weight. Even with his family in his life, he feels this bag is getting too heavy to carry. No matter the conversations that had been shared with different individuals, a pathway to inner peace had never been discussed nor discovered. Underneath his enigma of happiness and his smiles laid a tormented soul, with a damaged spirit.

His partnered relationship runs its course and amicably comes to an end; however, the emotional element of worthlessness is now overflowing in his bag. Opportunistically, he identifies an opening and seeks comfort in the only real way that he knows: with drugs.

After the consumption of some drugs, the adult doesn't know why he feels the way that he does but he is now convinced that he is out of options after everything he has lived through. With worthlessness overflowing in his mind, he believes it is now time for him to exit this world.

Is this his only way out? Are there no other options left?

No. This is not the answer.

There are always options.

Suicide is not the answer. There are many unexplored options still left, and these options can begin with the guided steps of the **Wounded Butterflies – Overcoming Adversity**™ program.

This program is an interactive guided process of returning to the start, back to the very beginning of life. We then work through the **release process,** as we identify the emotional baggage that he has been carrying. We then identify the behaviours that form the **Cycle of Repetition**. As he reaches his **epiphany moment**, we progress through the journey to **forgiveness** and then move to **take back control**, freeing his spirit and unchaining his soul.

Scenario three

Real world story – the emotional trauma of rape, plus historically ingrained low self-esteem

A baby girl is born into a loving family, who were already the proud parents of their first child. This little baby girl was gifted an older sibling to look up to. During their childhood years, the two siblings developed a special bond together, as a lot of siblings do.

As the young girl grows into her early teen years, something shifts, and she begins to feel like she is living in the shadow of her older sibling. The bar for the younger child is set even higher than normal as the older sibling is a naturally high achiever.

The younger teen, struggling to reach the height of the older sibling, believes that everything she ever does is never good enough, plus she feels constantly criticised and judged. Naturally, the teenage girl starts to develop self-esteem issues and begins questioning her own self-worth. Feeling as if she is living in a losing battle, one that she can never win, and with the ingrained belief now implanted in her mind, the teenager starts to rebel in order to just stand out.

This disruptive behaviour, however, is simply just a façade. In reality, she is really just trying to cover up the painful emotional baggage that she carries with her every day, consisting of low self-esteem and low self-worth. Her emotional baggage eventually grows into the disliking of her own physical body, and with this, she manifests negative body image issues as well. The teen's low self-esteem is now not only reflecting negatively on her state of mind but is beginning to have a detrimental outcome towards her physical health.

The young lady attempts to move forward in life, forging her own path, whilst carrying around her emotional weight. Eventually, the baggage formulates into a serious eating disorder. This teenager then develops anorexia and as a result of this, loses a significant amount of weight, severely jeopardising her own health. Her emotional baggage, full of low self-esteem, has now grown into an extreme health issue, consuming both her physical and mental self. Significant work is then invested in trying to overcome this serious situation and as a teenager, she is referred to some support services who attempt to help her with her eating disorder. The teen seeks counsel with a professional in an attempt to reprogram her beliefs that food is not the enemy and that food, along with nutrition, is a requirement to survive. This message seems to be received, and along with a new exercise regime, the teen refocuses and works towards overcoming her eating disorder.

Trying to push through life from a teen to young adulthood, leaving school seems the only option to escape the environment that has unintentionally fed her 'self' beliefs. However, underneath everything, this young adult is still carrying her emotional baggage stuffed full of low self-esteem, and the associated emotions that have not yet been dealt with. Trying to keep busy only acted as a temporary band-aid solution. The emotional baggage carried throughout her teenage years still exists.

As a young adult, she manages to progress forward with her personal development and as part of her journey, she relocates interstate to attend university. After finishing studying one day, during an evening of celebration that included alcohol and fun with a selected group of friends plus some supposed 'friends of friends', a major life event occurs. Towards the end of the evening, the young woman is raped by a friend of a friend within the group.

This severe offence in itself is one that many can struggle to overcome; however, this attack also reactivated something else that was buried inside this young woman. This shocking offence peeled off the band-aid that was covering her emotional baggage packed with low self-esteem, bringing to the surface all of her associated feelings of:

- No self-worth, low self-esteem, worthlessness
- Pain, sadness and despair from being raped
- Loss of control of her life and her desire to live

Now her emotional bag is jam-packed, full of the scares from the past, plus the fresh wounds from the new trauma. This compiles new negative emotions and feelings.

Self-harm thoughts begin to enter her mind. Then as sure as night follows day, once the idea of self-harm has crept in, without the appropriate support around her, those thoughts become actions and the self-harming begins.

In addition to the physical damage from the self-harming, there is also plenty of shame, embarrassment and additional sadness that she carries and has to deal with. Thinking that the end is the only option, she needs another way; she needs a new beginning. This is when she discovered the Wounded Butterflies – Overcoming Adversity™ program. The results for her were nothing short of outstanding.

'I had lost all hope, then I met Mike. Not only did he show me that there is more to life than what we see, he saved my life.
Thank you, Mike.'

Wounded Butterflies – Overcoming Adversity™ Process Flow

Detailed below is an introduction to the Wounded Butterflies process flow that highlights the major millstones you will strive to reach throughout the program along with the steps that are incorporated. This guide has been included to give you an understanding of what areas are covered along with a light introduction to the course.

Record your memories

Dot point your significant life events in chronological order. In this stage, you do not need to provide great detail for each event. This is going to become the foundation for your story. You will use each memory you have recorded in the next step.

Release your story

The next step is writing your story. This is the release process. Undertake this part of your journey in your own space, as this will give you the best opportunity to delve deep inside. As your journey begins, you are looking to discover your new perspectives about your lived events or trauma. It is from here that your future prosperity will grow.

As you write your story, I would like you to do two things:

1. Just use labels. Do not use any personal names (eg. the mother, the father, the aunty, the uncle, etc.)
2. Write your story in the third person. Don't write your story as you. You will be the baby, the child, the boy, the girl, the teen.

By writing your story in such a format, you are attempting to gather an outsider's perspective in relation to the events that you experienced so that you may uncover a new understanding.

Once you have written about your specific events, put your pen down. It is at this very moment that we must start to understand how these events shaped our choices and behaviours that led to the lifetime of outcomes that we have lived.

It is important to note that we are not looking to uncover what happened yesterday. We are looking to uncover the events that shaped us as the people we have become. From here, you can begin to understand the ingrained behaviours that caused you to do whatever it was that you did yesterday, figuratively speaking.

Identify the emotional baggage you carry

Using your story that you have just penned, reflect on the significantly traumatic moments and write down the emotions felt from experiencing such events. Draw a picture of a person – this person is going to become you. Now draw a big bag or sack on your back. The picture does not have to be a Picasso.

Choose words that best describe what you experienced and write them inside your bag. An example would be 'physical abuse'. Now, list the feelings and emotions that were passed onto you as a result of your experiences. For example, you might use the words pain, scared, hurt, sadness and fearful.

List the different words for all of your life situations that have influenced and affected you. Write those words inside your emotional bag. Don't be afraid to fill your bag, or if you need to make your bag bigger. Remember to write the words of how you truly felt.

This is the start of your new beginning.

Identifying the cause

During the release process as you embark on your journey, the idea is for you to discover the cause and how your emotional baggage was created. Maybe you were the victim or recipient of a painful or traumatic event or events, maybe someone did something to themselves that affected you significantly, maybe someone really hurt themselves and in turn, unintentionally, passed on significant emotional baggage to you.

Once we can identify the cause, we can gently progress into the next stage.

Understanding the Cycle of Repetition

For you, your lived cycle may or may not be so obvious. If someone in your story has hurt themselves even ending their own life, you may ask, 'How is the Cycle of Repetition even relevant? Since following on from the events of that day, where their life was ended, that specific action has not been repeated.'

But if we look a little deeper, maybe the behaviours attached to this Cycle of Repetition are an attitude that the effected individuals are either consciously or subconsciously repeating. Maybe the person has grown up unable to demonstrate how they truly feel, bottling up their emotions internally until their cup is maybe one day too full and overflowing.

Maybe the Cycle of Repetition is that they have learnt invertedly 'how not' to properly express their feelings or emotions.

If you can genuinely achieve an understanding of the unique Cycle of Repetition relevant to your story, then you are ready to receive your epiphany moment.

Breaking the Cycle of Repetition

No matter what type of trauma has been received, whether it be a form of abuse (physical, sexual, emotional or verbal assault), bullying, abandonment or the many other forms of trauma or neglect, they are all relevant and they are all damaging.

This is not a competition of which trauma is the worst or whose is more severe. We are all equally important and we are all worthy to live our existence without the debilitating pain. What affects you is significant and holds as much weight on you as whatever it is that is affecting the next person. All you need to do is to be ready to be real about how you truly feel.

The traumatic events we have endured can significantly obstruct the way that our internal body functions. This leads to break downs within the body, affecting a variety of internal components and how they function. The body cannot function at one hundred per cent whilst this pain and trauma is locked inside, like a heavy weighted ball and chain.

What I have discovered is the amazing power that we can unleash when we allow ourselves to work through this suffering. I know firsthand of the life changing connection that is re-established once we free our spiritual self. Releasing ourselves from this internal torture will then allow us to live our life experience in our truest form. A new version of reality, one which can bring with it the sort of experiences we used to only read about in fairy tales.

If you are now at this point and you are reading these pages, then we are entwined on this journey together as we look to discover our peace. There is now another big step we must take. As hard as this concept may be for you to initially grasp, we now need to discover forgiveness.

We need to begin to understand that the abuser was just a damaged soul. Someone who most likely repeated the same or similar learnt behaviours or negative abuses experienced as part of their life experience, yet, they were unable to break their own Cycle of Repetition.

You, however, the recipient of this trauma, can be much stronger than them. I believe that you are **STRONGER** than them. I think that this is a fact. Because it is you and I that are having this interaction now.

When you start to understand this you are ready to move into the next phase, a place called **FORGIVENESS**. Once you shift your mindset into the place of forgiveness and understanding, I know from my own experience, a new door will open for you.

Forgive, not forget

Forgiveness 1.0
Now that we are in the forgiveness phase of our journey, forgiveness can be a hard pill to swallow.

How can you forgive someone that has done something so wrong by you?

They lumped you with their emotional baggage, the pain and mistakes that they had learnt or experienced themselves, and now you have been lumbered with them possibly for years!

How can you forgive? This is not fair at all! This is not right!

Well, what we need to do, is look at forgiveness from a different angle.

We need to think about forgiveness as something that we can give to someone who is or was too emotionally damaged themselves to know any different – too mentally unaware. They were individuals just like you and I; however, their minds were already broken or formulated from their own past.

For our own personal healing, we need to consider and accept that they simply had been unable or unwilling to identify the failings of their damaging influencers or perpetrators and instead just repeated the same mistakes continuing the never-ending Cycle of Repetition.

Unlike you, maybe they never recognised their opportunities to discover new perspectives in relation to their lived experiences! Offering forgiveness to someone who is emotionally tormented, broken and more damaged than you is something that I think we can all do. Because as we know, it is you and I who are having this conversation. You are the one who is reading these words. You are the one holding the power!

We forgive not for what they did but because they knew no better.

Forgiveness 2.0 – inner peace

As your journey to alignment advances and your conscious awareness continues to evolve, I encourage you to keep advancing towards complete spiritual freedom.

A major component in achieving this is the second stage of forgiveness.

Before beginning this second stage of forgiveness, you acknowledge and already accept that the perpetrator or individual/s who had done you harm or wrong, were broken damaged souls, unable to break their own Cycle of Repetition.

For this next part of your deliberate expansion, we are looking to grow your level of forgiveness by forgiving the person for their actions. You can complete this stage by sincerely acknowledging, using spoken word and your mind, that you forgive the person for what they did to you. This is not a fundamental requirement at the beginning; however, if you truly wish to reach enlightenment, then this level of forgiveness is vital. The power in this gesture, once succinctly released, is so strong and freeing that you will wonder why you did not undertake this action long ago.

You are now ready to hear more important words, as we approach the next step. This phase is focused on taking back control of one's life.

Since this entire journey is about freeing oneself of the accumulated emotional trauma and associated behaviours. It is now time for you to realise that you are special, you are worthy and that you are the centre of *YOUR UNIVERSE!*

Please remember:

When I talk about our guided pathway to forgiveness, this does not mean you have to forget about what has occurred. The moment or moments that have occurred in your past all form part of who you are today, the beautiful person that you are today.

Forgiveness is not just about focusing on the abuser; forgiveness is for you. Forgiveness towards yourself, for the actions and negative behaviours that you may have committed or been responsible for whilst you were carrying your emotional baggage, full of the pain and trauma of your past.

Remember that your choices and behaviours have all been influenced by your baggage and now you are free. You can rest comfortably knowing that you are supported, you are loved and that you are strong. You are ready to take back control!

Taking back control – controlling negative thoughts
Who controls your life? You do!

In this stage of the healing pathway that we are walking together, we are going to focus on taking back control of our thoughts and how we feel in our day-to-day lives. When we reach this point, I know from my own personal experience that a natural, amazing connection can show its true self to you, along with the real picture associated with all of existence becoming much clearer.

We are ready to get back into the driver's seat, controlling how we feel, our environment and our own behaviours. Other people may influence how we feel, but only if we allow them to. We need to remember that if our thoughts, circumstances or the people we associate with start to take us in a direction that is uncomfortable, or into an area in which we do not want to travel, then we can control this and we can remove ourselves from the situation.

We always have a choice.

As part of taking back control, the Wounded Butterflies program will assist you in learning about successful tools and strategies that are readily available for us to use at any time so that you may harness and utilise them as you navigate your life without the emotional baggage from your past on your shoulders.

Sometimes this is easier said than done. Old negative beliefs and behaviour patterns need to be replaced with helpful tools that you can use for when you recognise that you are slipping back into your old negative emotions, thoughts and behaviours. These tools will allow you to maintain the mindset of being in control, while also helping you to reprogram your cognitive behaviours.

You now control how you feel, and you choose to feel good!

Cognitive tools:

An example of some of the cognitive tools you will learn about in the Wounded Butterflies program are circuit breakers and meditation.

Utilising a circuit breaker – as simple as a hair tie

If you look to discover 'how does a circuit breaker work?' you will uncover:

In the case of an increased supply of energy being transferred to the appliances or electronic items plugged into your home outlets, causing them to BURN OUT and potentially resulting in a fire and damage, the circuit breaker trips. This shuts off the electricity to the entire house or to that selected zone from the distribution point. Thus, preventing an electrical incident occurring from an oversupply of energy.

Sound familiar?

Now let's replace distribution point with your *consciousness*.

Let's replace the energy to power your appliances and electronic items with your *thoughts coming into your mind*.

Let's replace appliances and electronic items with your *body*.

And let's replace entire house with your *brain*.

So, your consciousness (distribution point) receives your thoughts (energy) and sends these thoughts (energy) to your brain (house) for you to consider, process or react to. Your physical body (appliances) is then engaged to enact your thoughts in a variety of ways.

If you consider these thoughts as being negative in nature, with the potential to motivate you to behave in a certain manner, partaking in activities that you do not want to do, or if the thoughts are affecting your mental health, wellbeing or mood, you need your own circuit breaker. You need something to interrupt the supply of these negative thoughts to your brain to avoid a BURN OUT.

One of the most easily accessible and successful circuit breakers I have discovered is a simple hair tie. You can wear one of these on your wrist all day long, inconspicuously as a successful tool to control your negative thoughts.

The hair tie will transform into your very own Secret Mind Control Weapon!

In those moments, when you feel yourself heading towards a negative direction, you can pull out your secret weapon and flick the hair tie against your skin. You should find somewhere between the fifth and tenth flick is the activation point, where the negative thoughts have been interrupted and the signal jammed.

You will know you are at this point when you're asking the question, *why am I flicking this hair tie?* When you experience the success of this tool for the first time, you may have your own epiphany moment as you think, *Ahhh, it does work!*

Other types of circuit breakers include tasks such as holding your breath for sixty seconds or taking a cold shower. Try to think about any subject and then get into a freezing cold shower. The cold water gifts you a freezing snap as the water hits your skin, instantly breaking your train of thought, bring you back into the now.

Exercise can also be considered a circuit breaker. Easily accessible exercise such as a run (even a brisk walk) can help clear your mind, gifting you some immediate mental relief. I am mindful, though, that partaking in a cold shower or completing some exercising might not always be available or appropriate when you are in need of your immediate circuit-breaking moment.

This is what makes the hair tie so effective.

Meditation – quieting the mind

As you progress through your personal journey of discovery, increasing your physical movement, with actions such as exercise, you will also need to accept the necessity of rest and relaxing.

Meditation is your friend. Meditation is the key.

Gifting your mind the time to slow down and recharge, quite possibly for the first time effectively without the negative baggage from the past, will be a monumental occasion for you since now your past does not control you and you are back in the driver's seat, the captain of your own lifeboat.

Since you have allowed yourself the opportunity to discover the calm place inside your mind, you can now gift yourself a moment in each day just for you.

This is important. This is your *Me Time.*

Meditation is your body recharging time as you align, centre and vibrationally feel your connection, bringing together your three universal centres: your body, mind and spirit. During these moments as you strive towards a higher state of consciousness, you may uncover your vibrational connection with our Divine Creator.

You will know unconditionally once you've achieved this level of divine connection.

Your world will never be the same ever again.

Nothing will naturally compare to the sensations you receive during your moments of vibrational connection.

This is your peaceful space. This is your unshakable space.

This state is somewhere you can consistently and constantly return to forever, whenever and wherever you desire, need to or wish. From within this realm, you can ask the Divine for any guidance, confirmations or healings that you desire.

A great time for your daily practise of *Me Time* is first thing in the morning, once you have risen from your night's sleep. In this moment, your mind is generally at its quietist point. Ideally, you've slept well throughout the night, with your mind managing to take a break from the noise of the outside world.

The morning shower is a comfortable place to begin this practice, closing your eyes as you focus on feeling the water. You can even use your mind's eye to visualise yourself in a different setting, maybe underneath a waterfall. Focus on how the water feels as the droplets hit your skin, the back of your neck and your head. Use this time to transport yourself into the present, metaphorically speaking.

Gift yourself this extra five minutes in the morning for your daily alignment before you commence your day's journey, embarking on your to-do list and responsibilities. You will discover just how beneficial this extra five minutes can be for you. From a place of alignment, navigating all the daily ups and downs won't seem so challenging. Confronting each obstacle as an aligned being, you will be guided and supported.

By adjusting your current routine to get yourself in sync, you will reap the rewards for your effort. One of the best ways to do this is by creating your own mindfulness routine. This can include some physical movements, for example.

This powerful mindfulness routine, called *Me Time,* is designed to vibrationally align your body, mind and spirit using the energy practice of *My Style*:

- Find your quiet room (this can be your bathroom).

- Customise your space to be either quiet or have meditation music playing.

- Water can be used (a shower, for example).

- Clear your mind, relax your brain, focus on your breathing (use the five-second count breathing technique with five repetitions – breathe in counting to five seconds, hold for five seconds, then breathe out to the count of five seconds.)

- Bring your body into the meditation, by using Chi (energy) focused movements (an example of this would be My Style, Tai Chi or Qigong).

- Connect with your body – gather the Chi energy that surrounds you and direct that energy to your organs. Repeat this statement, 'Love to my…' For example, say, 'Love to my heart' with each direction of energy you absorb.

- Create a gratitude statement at the end of your *Me Time* morning routine, giving thanks to all that is, along with everything that you are grateful for.

Repeat this daily.

* Send love to your organs and body parts individually. By sending love to your organs – your heart, spleen, liver, lungs, kidneys – you are transferring the powerful healing energy known as Chi directly to the organs in your body.

Consider this: have you ever stopped to acknowledge all of the hard work your organs do for you?

Let's think about your heart. Your heart has never stopped working for you. Once your cardiovascular system began developing three weeks after conception, your heart started to beat shortly afterwards. Working tirelessly for you, every day and every night since the beginning, ensuring your survival, never taking a break until your final day here. Consider your lungs; every moment that you are alive, your lungs breathe for you, absorbing the air that you need to survive, without you having to do anything. Think about everything that your magnificent body naturally does for YOU.

This all just happens for YOU, as YOU.

Using your *Me Time* to individually acknowledge and thank your body is a beautiful gift that we can all give ourselves. Your body and organs will love you for this.

Beginning your day with this sort of routine can help you discover some lasting peace and pleasure in the process. When your organs and body can feel your genuine love and appreciation, the universe will thank you in the only way the universe knows, with divine love and gratitude.

This is how your universe says *thank you*.

Remember

As we steadily progress along this pathway, we are now entering an incredibly special realm and by now, you may be experiencing the divine connection, just as I do.

Inside this new realm, we are living our life experience how it was truly intended to be. We are connected openly and willingly with all that is, was and will be. One life where we chose to live out our experience in a state of gratitude, appreciation and love.

We are aware of the moments when we're out of alignment or when we feel out of whack, so we use the tools that we have been gifted to realign ourselves.

We have learned to control our thoughts, and we understand that we can control what it is that we will be.

We can only control:

- Our thoughts
- Our feelings
- Our behaviours
- Our future

We are the centre of our own universe.

As it stands right now, the end of space has not been discovered, no matter what direction – space is infinite. Wherever you are right now, if you look forward, space does not stop. If you look to your left, right or behind you, space is continuous. Right now, wherever you are standing or sitting, figuratively speaking, you are in the centre of your universe as it stands for you!

This universe revolves around you.

YOU TRULY ARE THE CENTRE OF YOUR UNIVERSE.

To learn more or for further information regarding the Wounded Butterflies-Overcoming Adversity™ program please visit

www.findingpeace.com.au

Chapter 10

ANOTHER CONNECTED BEING

Proof that this is not just for one

During a chance meeting at the beginning of 2021, I was introduced to a unique individual, someone whose personality I would describe as extremely vibrant and energetic. The air around us seemed to buzz with her lively presence, as though her enthusiasm was contagious. During our first-ever interaction, the conversation we shared was light-hearted and easy, the kind of chat that flows effortlessly. But internally, I felt that there was something undeniably special about this person.

As we sat together, the soft rustle of fabric from our shifting movements mingled with the sound of our laughter, creating a comforting rhythm. Captivated by her enthusiasm, I comfortably sank into my chair and listened to her speak. Her voice had a melodic quality, rich with warmth and expression, as if every word carried a piece of her vibrant energy. She seemed to have so much to say, her words flowing out in an animated rush, and for some reason, we were both very relaxed in each other's presence. Although we were in an open air space, our setting felt cosy. With the faint scent of coffee in the air blending with the soft hum of distant conversations, creating an inviting atmosphere. Even though this was the first real time we'd met, everything about this moment felt strangely familiar, it was as if we had known each other far longer.

The individual openly shared with me what they had been up to and what was currently going on in their life. As a person, they were easily portraying someone who seemed to be happy, positive and content with where they were at.

During this chance introduction at a local café as we sat there conversing, a mutual friend who knew both of us individually joined in on our conversation. We spoke about many topics, including all different aspects about life. Even though the time we spent together was brief, maybe an hour or so, the impression that this person had left me with was extremely powerful. In fact, as this person stood up to leave, I could feel the internal energy radiating from them.

Feeling this pulsating energy was a sensation so unique that I'd really only ever experienced on a small number of occasions previously. For me, sensing this energy reflected that their spiritual self was in a place of genuine happiness.

As soon as the individual left our table, I turned to my friend who'd remained seated with me and exclaimed, 'Wow, she is radiating so much energy! I could feel the pulsating energy she was emitting, just by sitting opposite her. That was incredible!'

I was in awe of what I'd just experienced.

My friend laughed and reaffirmed to me that from what he knew, he believed that she had the potential to be a powerful being. I had to agree, as the impression I'd been left with ensured that my attention had rightfully been caught.

Now as fate would have it, this radiating individual whom I'd just become acquainted with would be relocating interstate in the coming days. They were soon to be embarking on their own exciting new journey. During our initial conversation, one of the topics that we discussed was their upcoming trip, along with the fact that they had been deferring and delaying their flight a number of times already, hesitant to leave.

'So, when are you actually flying out?' I asked, curious about the details of her move.

She sighed dramatically, her hand waving in the air as if to dismiss the question. 'I swear, I've rescheduled this flight like three times now. Every time I think I'm ready to go, something pops up, and I can't bring myself to leave.' She gave a half-laugh, shaking her head. 'I'm just not sure about taking that leap.'

We both laughed at her reluctance. 'I can definitely tell you're having second thoughts,' I said with a smile. 'It's like you're already planning your escape before you even leave!'

Her eyes sparkled as she leaned forward, giving me a confident grin. 'You know what?' she said, her voice firm with determination, 'This time, no more delays. I've made up my mind. I'm going, no matter what!' There was a definite energy in her tone, a mix of excitement and resolve.

I raised an eyebrow playfully, teasing her. 'We'll just have to wait and see.'

She laughed, shaking her head in mock disbelief. 'Oh, no. This time it's happening! No more delays.' She smiled at me, her enthusiasm contagious. 'I'm ready to go.'

We both chuckled. 'Alright, I'll take your word for it!'

As we continued to laugh and joke about the uncertainty of travel plans and the twists fate might throw in her way, I couldn't help but feel a sense of anticipation in the air. It was as if the future was open to her, brimming with possibilities. With a final smile, I wished her well on her new adventure.

As I jotted down my notes for the day, I scribbled the word *Butterfly* as the title gifted to this person. So gentle and petite in nature, yet so full of life and colour. One would have to be, to be able to radiate their own energy as powerfully as she did.

So, Butterfly would take off on her journey interstate, and I would think nothing more of our first encounter as a number of weeks went by. During this time, I continued along my evolution path, educating myself, learning new processes and truths in moments of pure alignment.

I was completely in tune and in touch with everything that I needed to be. One day in early March 2021, I received a message from a friend of mine. He informed me that he was catching up with a particular person. The way in which he presented the name to me was as if I should have known who it was. Except I really didn't have a clue who he was talking about, so I simply replied, 'Good luck with that, have fun!' Thinking nothing more of it.

The following day I had been out of the office and while in the process of returning, I received a message on my phone. It was the same friend again, asking me if I was still around and in the local area. Curiously I replied to him, 'I can be, what's up?' He asked,

'Could you come back to where I am? I need you to have a talk with someone.'

Once again, the person's name he mentioned was the same name from the day before, yet I was still none the wiser as to who it was that he was referring to. But he had my attention now, even if it was just out of pure curiosity alone to discover who this person was that he kept referring to. I quickly responded, 'Sure thing, I'll come now.' Making my way through the traffic, I soon arrived and made my way inside. Quickly spotting him, I walked straight over. As he looked up and recognised me, he immediately turned his head in the direction of the stranger he'd been referring to and gestured in their direction.

To my surprise, it was Butterfly, the young lady whom I'd previously met. The one who had flown away on her own interstate journey.

I thought, *Wow, okay, it's you, haha. Now I know who he's talking about!*

Walking over to her with a smile on my face I gently whispered, 'Hi, apparently you and I need to have a talk? Is now a good time?' Butterfly stopped what she was doing and sheepishly replied, 'Yes, okay.'

As we walked away together, I could feel that something was different this time, something had changed within her. I was still quite confused as to what it was that we'd be talking about; however, I could instantly tell that the energy that was flowing from our first meeting was non-existent this time. I was quickly realising that this was not going to be a light-hearted chit chat.

Once we sat down to talk, I noticed that this time her words were not as forthcoming as before and extracting any sort of conversation was difficult. Butterfly was finding the words much harder to say, naturally raising my level of concern.

While we sat there trying to piece together a conversation, the friend of ours who'd asked me to return joined us at our table. Butterfly had already confided in him some of the basic details about her situation, so he suggested to her that maybe he could share with me what he knew if she was struggling to speak, to which she agreed.

Upon hearing his words about what he knew, I realised the gravity of the situation. The innocent Butterfly who I'd known only for a minute had returned from her interstate trip wounded. Her wings had been clipped and immediate help was required.

This coming together of people was now about something extremely important, something that could even be described as life or death. Butterfly had been seriously assaulted on an evening out while she had been interstate, and the trauma had shattered her in ways words could scarcely describe. The attack had been both opportunistic and calculated, leaving scars that went far deeper than the physical ones. It wasn't just her body that had been violated – it was her spirit, completely broken.

She was consumed by the aftermath, the rawness of the pain still piercing her mind like a relentless storm. It was clear she wasn't just battling the trauma; she was now struggling to find the will to live. Harmfully acting out her exit plan.

I quickly understood why my friend had asked me to become involved in the situation. He was well aware of my journey to date and many of the experiences I'd lived through already, so he was hopeful that maybe I could contribute in some sort of positive manner toward Butterfly's current situation.

It was at this moment that I felt, that maybe if I shared my journey about where I'd come from, I'd break the ice so that Butterfly could feel comfortable and confident that she wouldn't be judged.

Next, I introduced a circuit breaker. Something was needed right away to assist in the jamming of any negative thoughts as they tried to fester in her mind. Since we were only at the beginning of our journey together, an immediate solution was required.

I shared with her that I had an effective tool that could help control negative thoughts. The simple hair tie or as I like to call it, your 'Secret Mind Control Weapon'. I advised that this was something that could be worn on her wrist at all times, day and night and its purpose would be unknown to those around her, unless of course, she had chosen to share its meaning.

The circuit breaker was something that she could wear and use in place of other negative actions that she was partaking in while initially trying to process her situation. This was not necessarily something that she would need to wear forever; however, I explained that she may choose to wear it in the future – as a badge of honour once she'd overcome her experience as a reminder of what she'd achieved!

Over the following hour, Butterfly and I built some quality rapport and trust together. Butterfly's detailed journey is her journey and that's her story to tell when she is ready. What I will share with you is the story about the work that we did together including this experience, the time that we spent together and our connection.

Unbeknown to Butterfly was now she would witness something that she'd most likely never heard of before. Plus, I could see that Butterfly was hurting badly, so something special was required.

I felt this was the time to introduce the process that I'd discovered and used successfully in regaining control of one's life. I knew it was now time to share my program.

As we began our time together, I shared with Butterfly my knowledge about vibration and our divine connection. The introduction to this new level of awareness would be a powerful tool to complement our journey together.

After we'd talked for a couple of hours, my phone beeped, alerting me about the plans I'd already made for the day, which included visiting the state art gallery. Having spent some time together and considering the circumstances, I asked Butterfly if she would like to join me for the day.

Without hesitation, Butterfly immediately accepted my invitation and so it was that we would share the afternoon together. As we drove into the city, I was doing most of the talking, sharing with her what I'd discovered – something so new and incredible, a whole new version of reality. I gifted her an introduction to the divine energy. For Butterfly, this was day one of a life-changing course towards Vibrational Alignment.

Gently, I shared with Butterfly that I believed the universe connected us with those who we need, especially during times like these, when special people come into our lives. The arrival of these people coincides with the moments we experience, since all we have are 'Moments in Time' that make up our physical experience. Moments in Time where we can choose to turn either left or right, travel up or down and then with that choice the divine plan will continue to unfold.

I continued by expressing, 'If you are stuck in a moment, don't be too upset. Certainly, don't despair as you will have many more moments come as part of your experience. Your destiny will continue to unfold as you start this journey freeing yourself from this pain!

Learning to let go

Letting go will get you connected. Letting go of what you have been taught to believe will open your awareness. This combined with a daily practise will serve you well. You will learn about your alignment with Source, with God. You will discover that you can offer unconditional love when you are in alignment. Just like when this day was put in front of me with a choice of what to do, I knew what I had to do.

I made the choice to turn around, I made the choice to make myself available and I made the choice to share. This was my first detailed share with someone that included beginning to use some of the processes that I had uncovered. The day was turning into something very special. A unique experience, one that I knew she had never experienced before.

Our time together at the gallery was full of vibrational moments as I connected with the radiating energy that was being emitted from the historical artifacts on display. Historical pieces intwined with extreme amounts of energy through the significant amount of historical importance ingrained into their molecular structure.

I cannot fully explain what it means to be able to walk into a room full of old artifacts and then vibrationally connect with the historical frequency transmitted from the pieces, tapping into an unknown energy Source vibrationally through spirit. To share this experience with the people that I was with, including Butterfly, was a truly memorable event.

Knowing my intentions were pure, I was certain that I wanted to share this experience with Butterfly on the highest level. I needed Butterfly to begin to understand that there was more going on than meets the eye. The journey we were embarking on was going to possibly reveal to her a reality that she never imagined before. Unplugged from the old and plugged into the new.

Captivated by the vibrational connection, and witnessing the divine energy for the first time, Butterfly was both intrigued and confused.

'Is this a magic trick? Is this you playing games? Is this your breathing?' Butterfly asked in her search to uncover the truth! When in fact, I'd actually been repeating the answer all day long.

The answers were in the words I'd been sharing. My spirit was now free, and my soul was unchained. I was in complete alignment with my body, mind and spirit. I was living on purpose, totally tuned in with my energetic field, completely connected. This was what receiving mode looked like. This was no trick, there was no special breathing. For I had already walked the pathway to this destination, the exact same pathway that I'd begun sharing with her. If she were to walk this pathway too, who knows what transformation might unfold!

Can you imagine the possibilities? A connected being is more powerful than a million who are not. What was there to lose? If there was no risk and only the potential to gain complete spiritual freedom through divine connection, why not take a leap of faith?

During our conversations, I continuously shared important self-healing advice. Some of the words spoken were about how we process our Moments in Time, along with how we chose to respond to each specific event or interaction. Our response will then have a flow-on effect to the next moment and the moment after that and so on and so forth.

At certain stages throughout life, we are challenged, sometimes put to the test to see how we will respond to such moments. When we experience significant events during our Moments in Time, it is how we react and process these moments that can determine the immediate trajectory of our life's journey.

When we experience a specific Moment in Time, we can choose how we will respond, as we always have a choice. We can choose for a moment to either:

- Define you
- Destroy you
- Strengthen you

Allowing a Moment in Time to define you

This is by no means a negative response. Experiencing a powerful Moment in Time that has such a profound impact on you as a human and on your life's journey that it defines who you become is certainly not a negative at all.

In fact, depending on the circumstances, if you decide to become either an advocate for change, a voice for others or a beacon of hope, spreading the word far and wide as to what is possible, then this means you now carry a powerful message. Since you have been gifted the freedom of choice to choose this option, if *defining you* is how you want your mind to process the specific event that has occurred, then this is what you have decided.

Although, if you have been the victim of an assault and your mind convinces you to believe that you will always be a victim of assault, therefore 'defining who you are', then carrying this burden is not necessarily going to be beneficial for you from a mental, physical or spiritual health point of view.

Your physical health could significantly suffer and deteriorate under the weight of carrying such a burden and on top of this the emotional damage that would be inflected upon your internal self by endure this negative undertaking, would be detrimental to your wellbeing.

Though if you have been a victim of assault and you want to use your experience to help other victims of assault overcome their experiences in some way – maybe by becoming a voice for them or as a guide, showing them that it is possible to overcome their traumatic experience – then of course this is a positively powerful life mission. Potentially, you could even use your experience as a sounding board to become an advocate for change. This sort of mindset is of course beneficial for you and many others in society who may have lived similar experiences.

Please note that the '*define you*' reaction is not just about how you respond to traumatic experiences. For instance, you may have discovered something so wonderful, life-changing and unique that you might want to share your positive experience with all the people that surround you, or to as many people as you possibly can. By definition this, too, would be allowing a Moment in Time to define you in a positive manner.

Allowing a Moment in Time to destroy you

This choice is the saddest and most detrimental way to process a specific Moment in Time or an event from one's life. When a traumatic event occurs to an individual either during a single moment, multiple moments or over a prolonged period of time during a certain stage in their life, the outcome of this can be extreme in relation to the future health, prosperity and overall quality of life of the recipient.

The negative effect of selecting this course of action is evident when we look at our society today as a whole. The option of destroying oneself is an extremely common way for people to process significantly negative life events. One only needs to look at the research numbers that reflect the outcome where pain and trauma is carried by the general population.

We should consider when assessing these figures, the number of individuals who are suffering from:

- Addictive/risk-taking behaviour such as substance abuse or dependence on prescription and/or illegal drugs, alcohol and gambling
- Depression
- Self-harm and suicide

A significant portion of society either will, currently is or has experienced such conditions or behaviours. Individuals who are hurt and damaged souls come from all walks of life and are just trying to find their way, including many who are unable to see the light at the end of the tunnel. This damaging state of existence is not just limited to the homeless addict that we see living on the streets, even though many of these individuals have suffered from some form of traumatic event or experience.

The gravity of this situation can be understood by researching the large number of daily court cases and events that are documented across the globe. We should also consider that it is widely accepted that the reported number of cases are only a fraction of the actual total number of daily traumatic events that occur worldwide.

It is common for many families to try to manage traumatic events within for reasons of shame, embarrassment, guilt and fear. This course of action then leads to many cases of abuse and assaults going unreported until it's too late.

One of the worst elements of living as a broken soul trying to navigate life is that often the individual may repeat the learnt behaviours (Cycle of Repetition) to those living within their vicinity. This repetition of repeated behaviours is then inflicted on either those who are within their immediate circle or against random strangers who just happen to cross paths with these individuals. Thus, creating more damaged souls through new traumatic events and experiences that will need to overcome their new challenges in the future.

Allowing a Moment in Time to destroy you is the least favourable option and one that we **do not** want to choose if we can avoid it! This does not need to be the outcome of anyone's life experience since there is another way that can show you that there is great love and support for you. You are loved, special and cared for by something so much more powerful than you could ever imagine and that care is unlimited. It is there for you now and until the end of time.

Allowing a Moment in Time to strengthen you

Choosing between *'strengthening you'* or *'defining you'* in the positive context are the two reactions that we should try to use when processing and working through our life's challenges and events. Whether this be a positive or a negative interaction with someone, a traumatic event, the ending of a relationship, the completion of an existing opportunity or the closing of a door, metaphorically speaking there are many different Moments in Time that we experience during our lifetime.

Remember the old saying, 'When one door closes, another opens.'

This is true in many aspects of life.

I believe for many of us, when we experience a Moment in Time throughout our life, a large portion of society try to use each experience or interaction for the betterment of oneself. This includes both learning and growing from said experiences as an individual. However, even so, there may be that one significantly traumatic event that the individual struggles to apply the same understanding to. This is not a fault of the individual; this is just an opportunity for new perspectives to be gathered.

If we can gift ourselves growth from our experiences, then it is possible that we can gather a greater sense of understanding towards how we react and respond to specific situations. This can be in either a positive or improved manner, ensuring we remain in a constant state of learning. Learning from the individual lessons that we'd set for ourselves, while become wiser from the experience.

To choose to be strengthened by the Moments in Time that we experience is to allow ourselves an opportunity to conquer the moment that we've faced.

This will provide us with the opportunity to progress forward along our life's journey, not stuck in a constant state of flux, repeating the same life lessons over and over again. This forward momentum will ensure that we give ourselves the opportunity to experience new exciting Moments in Time, allowing us to continue evolving along our personal journey, whilst learning new wisdom along the way.

Working through the pain with Butterfly

As I conversed with Butterfly about Moments in Time and the choices we have in relation to how we process them, we spoke specifically about how Butterfly was processing her own Moment in Time. I knew that the event, she was trying to deal with was a significantly traumatic experience in itself and that on top of all of that, this traumatic event had opened the door for older, buried pain to, once again, rise up to the surface.

This historical pain was the emotional baggage that Butterfly had carried with her along her journey, unknowingly throughout her young life experience. With the rising of this dormant pain, along with the new trauma, the emotional weight on her shoulders was fast becoming unbearable. I knew that this weight would be heavy for any person to carry, let alone this delicate Butterfly.

Over the next few weeks, we worked closely together, gaining new perspectives and understandings as we overcame pain and emotional baggage. Identifying when the time was right as we progressed forward, I continued to introduce new steps including mediation and other individual daily practices that were easy to learn and follow.

Once we managed to work through the release process and establish an engrained commitment to the tools introduced, I shared the idea about what could be achieved from having a free spirit and an unchained soul. Once this was unleashed, the next few weeks started to unfold and take shape really fast.

Becoming a giant

During one specific conversation, a negative thought consisting of the idea that *it was all too hard* was creeping back inside Butterfly's mind. This was causing an influx of negative emotions. I explained to her, 'Right now, in the reality of your mind, the perpetrator has total control of your life, controlling how you feel. For you it's as if they are a giant, holding you in the palm of their hand, slowly crushing and hurting you as they see fit. Subconsciously, you are allowing them to be the giant. Their historic action is now controlling how you currently feel.'

However, this is not the case.

YOU ARE THE GIANT!

You are the one who actually holds all the power in this interaction. By making a couple of decisive choices when you are ready, you can actually determine this individual's immediate future. You hold their entire life in the palm of your hand!

Right now, you have a choice. You can allow that Moment in Time to upset you for years, for a year, for half a year, for months, for weeks, for days or you can place that experience to the side right now, take the appropriate action when the time is right and focus your attention on controlling the most important thing that you can control: how you choose to feel.

Understand that you are the centre of your own universe and you're in charge. You control who comes into your world, who stays and who leaves a mark.

You control all of this.

Symbolically speaking, I reiterated that she could actually crush the perpetrator at any moment, she just couldn't see it yet. After we shared these words, Butterfly sat quietly in contemplation, processing the information she had just absorbed. Suddenly, I witnessed her definitive lightbulb moment, as she accepted this new perspective, followed by an immediate shift in her energy.

We were now ready for the next phase.

Moving towards forgiveness – but how?

I know that it is only once the step of forgiveness is taken that one's soul can truly be set free. When forgiveness is achieved, spiritual freedom can occur, allowing the divine energy to flow.

Since Butterfly and I were progressing so quickly along the pathway, natural momentum was taking everything forward full steam ahead. Using this momentum, I decided to take the opportunity to talk about transitioning into the next stage of *forgiveness*.

I realised that when reaching this point, the idea of forgiveness would not be an easy concept to consider or accept; however, I had some very important components that would assist in this phase:

- The first level of forgiveness is not for the action or the event that was placed on you. The first level of forgiveness is achieved by forgiving the other individual or individuals for being too damaged, too emotionally weak and unable to break their own Cycle of Repetition.

- We offer our forgiveness because they know no better.

- Subliminally by achieving the first level of forgiveness, we begin to gently transition our own self-belief back into a position of empowerment and control.

- We can achieve this by using powerful words such as:

- I forgive you for not being able to break your cycle.

- I forgive you for you know not what you do.

- I forgive you because your actions do not control me, I am in control of me.

- I forgive you because I will not be trapped by your actions, I am empowered.

Simple but effective words when they are said with true meaning and purpose. I am reminded of a very special human who once said, 'Forgive them, Father, for they know not what they do.'

- Forgiveness is not for the benefit of the other person; forgiveness is for you!

- Holding your body, mind and spirit in a constant state of low vibration by harbouring feelings of anger, guilt, shame, fear, sadness, hopelessness, powerlessness and grief provides no benefit to your individual life experience. Holding onto these feelings like many do for years and years will only do significant damage to your body's functionality in all aspects: physically, mentally and spiritually!

- We should consider that everything that has happened to us, has happened for a reason. These were our significant challenges to overcome, to grow from and prosper. The bringing together of the individuals or circumstances presented a great lesson, that once overcome could be of great benefit for the recipient and many others if their Moment in Time is conquered. If something in the past had've been altered or different, then who knows if these words would've ever existed?

- Once we can transition our state of mind through the stage of forgiveness, we naturally start to raise the vibration level within our own body as we begin to align our three universal centres, which starts the unfolding of our new beginning.

'A life lived trapped, holding onto damaging pain and trauma is no life lived at all.'
– M. Smith

In this case, Butterfly allowed herself to move through the stage of forgiveness under the pretext that the abuser knew no better, with the ingrained learnt behaviours of entitlement that had been instilled in him. His current challenge would be to learn respect. This was an extremely powerful realisation and attitude for Butterfly to hold.

Forgiving him not for what he did, but for not being any better than what he was. Butterfly forgave him for being a broken, damaged soul, for not being wise enough and for not being strong enough to be better. This was an extremely powerful spiritual stage of our journey together.

As we shifted from forgiveness, Butterfly was now looking at her situation from an entirely new perspective and was now ready to take back control. Butterfly had remained committed, by putting in the effort, using the tools she had learnt and opening her mind to new possibilities.

This was a powerful commitment made by her and one that she should be very proud of.

Taking back control

The motion of regaining control of one's life was now in full swing. It was now time to start expanding our consciousness together by connecting with something much greater than what we can see.

Butterfly's soul was now unchained, and her spirit freed. Free from all the pain that had been experienced. Eagerly, Butterfly was now ready to take back full control of her life. By now, she had put into practice her daily routine and continued to use the tools that had been shared with her. Butterfly was taking the time to connect with her own body, setting up her own connected morning routine, using the circuit breaker whenever this was needed and not being afraid to try this new way. Her mind was open and now there were signs, so many signs coming in for her, showing the universal support that was there for her, ready to be utilised and accessed from above. Since the first day of our reconnection when Butterfly had returned tormented from her trip away, she had now come so far in such a short period of time.

Raising and maintaining your vibration level

It is evident that with the large amount of pain and trauma that exists today, there are many people around the globe who are suffering, causing them to live out their life experiences within the lower vibrational region of sadness, pain, anger, shame and hopelessness.

Take some time to explore the following Vitality Tone and Attitude Scale Chart. You can see from the chart the represented emotion or vibration vs the associated thoughts and motivations as well as the effect that the individual emotion has on our internal muscle network.

Using the highest vibration and emotion from the chart as an example – serenity – the associated thoughts and motivations are peace, wellness and metaness, feeling a complete oneness with all that is.

Vitality Tone and Attitude Scale

Increases in strength and energy reserves	Emotion - Vibration	Thoughts - Motivation	Attitude Likely Held
Recharge and Refresh Muscles firm Energy gains from Even to Positive. Region of Emotions characterised as Pleasurable or Good. Blood flows with vigor	Serenity	Peace - Metaness - Wellness	"Wow, this is fascinating. I'm alive and learning."
	Joy - Enthusiasm	Welcome - Exhilaration - Abundance	
	Compassion	Empathy - Inspiration - Clarity	
	Appreciation	Gratitude - Devotion - Generosity	
	Love	Cooperation - Trust	
Balance - Even - Stable - Relief	Satisfaction	Amusement - Curiosity	"Thank goodness, here this comes up for my healing."
	Power - Strength	Discovery - Challenge	
	Self Esteem - Dignity	Duty - Obligation	
	Neutral - Acceptance	Contentment - Safety - Aplomb	
	Glee - Happy	Nervous - Worry - Hyper	
	Surprise - Shock	Confusion - Annoyance	
Muscle Release - Energy moves from Negative to Even Region of emotions characterised those called Painful or Bad. Moving downward	Anger	Rage - Defiance - Boredom	"Oh no, not again."
	Guilt	Resentment - Remorse	
	Fear	Threat - Hate - Blame	
	Sadness - Grief	Depleted - Loss - Burden	
	Hopelessness	Resignation - Depressed	
	Numb - Powerlessness	Overwhelm - Frozen	
Muscle tighten constrict or atrophy.	Shame	Apathy - Helpless - Death	2006, 2010, 2013© Stephen J. Cacconi Graphic design. Ardis Bow

The chart also demonstrates the added benefits of raising your vibration level with the increase in personal strength and energy reserves, thus assisting with recovery and healing practices. The higher your internal vibration, the more positive energy will flow.

Lastly, you can see the attitudes that are likely held whilst an individual is experiencing a specific emotional feeling or vibration. An individual in the higher vibrational realm often holds a belief that they are always learning. They experience feelings of pleasure simply by just being alive. They are also generally fascinated with their life experiences as they are presented to them.

If you follow the flowchart down, you can see the likely attitudes held as the vibration level decreases. You can see the potentially damaging effects that can occur to the physical body and mind while one exists in the lower realms.

All a person really needs to do is some basic research regarding the number of individuals around the globe who are medicated. Many people consume either prescribed anti-depressants or they self-medicate with illegal drugs in an attempt to feel better and reshape their version of reality. Many are moulded to believe that they are not worthy of spiritual freedom, or they are scared to explore the subject of spiritual freedom. Hesitant that they may be perceived as overtly religious or extreme, choosing instead to live their daily life restrained by the underlying emotions of anger and frustration, inadvertently falling into the construct that life is just meant to be hard.

There are those who even torture themselves with 'why me?' or with fear. Some with fear of what they have personally experienced, others consumed with a fear of missing out, or some who have developed a general fear of the outside world.

Then there are others who live in a daily reality full of guilt, sadness or grief. All these emotions are, of course, emotions that we are justifiably allowed to feel during our lives. However, we should be aiming to not live our entire life experience trapped within these damaging emotions. There are those who are obviously the exception to this, many who are striving for change, creating a new story, and then of course, there are those who have already discovered serenity, joy, compassion, appreciation and *LOVE*.

Centre of the universe

By now, we had successfully worked through the release process. We had experienced the epiphany moments; we'd moved through the forgiveness stage and progressed through taking back control. We were now entering the section of our journey that included recognising and understanding that YOU ARE the centre of your universe.

This step was just as important as the earlier stages. This step would now allow Butterfly to cement herself in the driver's seat, controlling her own life after experiencing such a significant event, understanding that we control our universe, we control who comes into our space, we control our own thoughts, and most importantly, we control how we feel!

It is important to remember that even though Butterfly had taken back control of how she felt and processed her Moment in Time, this by no means meant that Butterfly would never feel sad or mad again. For we all know that these are naturally felt emotions and part of being a human being. What this did mean, however, was that Butterfly now had the skill sets and knowledge to control how she personally responded to negative situations, including recognising her emotions and behaviours when feeling that she was existing in the lower vibrational realm.

My theory regarding vibrational frequencies is, if one can control their thoughts, this control can then help to maintain their vibration level on the vitality chart at the neutral level. So that if we feel ourselves dip below this neutral point, we can recognise this shift, then, using the learnt skills and techniques, we can remove our negative thoughts, which will allow us to maintain control of our emotions and elevate our vibration level back up to neutral or a higher level naturally.

This emotional self-control will allow us to experience life in the manner in which life was always intended to be experienced. Fully utilising our divine guidance system. In complete connection with all that is, with Source, with infinite intelligence, with our Creator.

Life is meant to be a fun, joyous, pleasurable experience. From a higher vibrational frequency, we can enjoy both our conscious and sub-conscious experiences, as we connect to all that is, feeling our divine love connection. We can take pleasure in feeling our connection and take pleasure in looking out for and experiencing the signs. As you increase your vibration level, so too does your level of awareness. From this vantage point, you can begin to understand that we are all connected. We are all spiritually connected into the oneness of all creation.

If you can grasp this concept, then your acceptance of this knowledge and understanding of what I've shared with you will change your life as you are bought into complete *Vibrational Alignment*.

Witnessing the energy

As we discussed controlling how we felt and maintaining our vibration level, it was at this point that I witnessed Butterfly's vibrational connection for the very first time. That magical divine lightning bolt reaching her. This was her turn. This was her new beginning.

This was really just as much an exciting moment for me as it was for Butterfly. Because this was her reward for all of her effort. I was very happy that this Butterfly, whose wings had once been clipped, was now healed and ready to fly again!

The hard work had all been completed by Butterfly to reach this point. She had remained true and committed to herself, as well as open to new perspectives and ideas. To know that someone whom I had shared my journey and time with, had reached this divine level of connection was incredibly special.

A divine evening

One of her earliest connected experiences was late one evening. I'd received a phone call from Butterfly that was so full of energy, it was if she was jumping out of her skin. She was eager to share her amazing moment and the divine euphoric connection she had just experienced throughout her body.

During her *Me Time* self-reflection mediation, with her soul free and her mind cleared of confusing thoughts and pain, Butterfly had received the energetic lightning bolt of divine love into her body. She had comfortably positioned her highest self in the realm of complete stillness and calm. From here, the euphoric connection was made.

It was as if Butterfly had been touched by the hand of God.

Her body became energetically charged, filling with the euphoric energy. A feeling that I knew so well myself. I could not help but be pleased, happy and excited for her that she too had experienced such divine power. So full of energy, Butterfly had jumped up out of her meditated state. With the divine euphoria still pumping down her arms and legs, she was running up and down her hallway elated by what she had just experienced.

This moment would be one for her to remember!

'Before I met Michael, I was trying to get through every day by what felt like was the skin of my teeth. I was fragile and I was a victim of rape. I was lost and inside me, I knew that over the coming days, I was feeling like I did not want to continue living with this pain anymore and that I would end my own life. To my surprise, I didn't believe in my wildest dreams that one guy, who I never even knew, would be the reason I am still here today. He showed me that there is much more to life than what the eye can see. I thank my lucky stars every day that Mike came into my life because I know for a fact that I wouldn't be here today without him.'

– Butterfly

'From our initial interaction when Butterfly returned full of despair, pain and hopelessness to the evolution of what this Butterfly has become, regaining full control of her life during the 10-week period we spent together, was nothing short of spectacular.'

– M. Smith

Chapter 11

A NEW HOPE

Discovering God

Throughout the years of history, a large portion of society has been conditioned and heavily influenced when it comes to establishing a personal relationship with God. Religion has been presented as extreme in many aspects, no matter the prophet or religious deity, which has caused a significant number of individuals to be deterred away from establishing a personal relationship with our Divine Creator.

Many wars have been fought and much blood has been spilt in the name of religion, from all sides convinced that their way is right. Many have been told what they must do and where they must get to in order to receive true blessings. For too long, this fundamental necessity has been controlled by the too few for the many.

I believe that now is the time for a new hope, a new way of understanding our unique relationship with the One. As part of my own journey, I know that I have uncovered a direct connection with our Creator and his message is simple: you are loved unconditionally. He loves each and every one of us and he only wants what's best for us all. There is no war we need to fight for him or challenge that we must complete.

I also understand that as much as he is the father, then this earth is our mother. Without our Creator, we do not receive the gift of life, our spirit. Without our Mother Earth, we don't have the means to be able to exist.

As part of human evolution, the population has witnessed the significant growth of many different religions around the world.

From the biblical stories of Jesus Christ, the son of God, who died for our sins, words that form the foundation of the Catholic Church's religious doctrine, to the teachings of the Quran from the passionately defended Islamic prophet Mohammad, those of which form the backbone to the Muslim faith, or the scribed learnings of Buddhism that include sharing enlightenment and purification of the mind techniques from the tranquil, ancient religious leader and teacher Gautama Buddha, across to the ancient religious beliefs of the Hinduism people, who with their learnt principles focusing on Purusharthas, including the doctrines of samsara, believing in the re-incarnation process as either a choice for the spirits next physical experience or as a bigger lesson that needs to be learnt from unlearnt moments in the previous life.

I know that there are many more religions across the globe that one can choose to follow or learn from, with some considered more mainstream than others. Whichever you choose, I believe they all provide their followers with one common theme: hope. There are individuals out there who dedicate their entire lives to their religion, such is the power and strength of their internal resolve and faith.

From an outsider's perspective, it seems that each religion systemically declares that their way is the only way. Some religions staunchly believe that the only way into heaven and to reconnect with our Creator is by following their way. They suggest that other religions may bring you into the afterlife but the only true way to heaven is through their religious deities.

Well, I am not about to question people's individual beliefs.

I believe you are free to choose whoever you wish to follow.

You can choose to follow Mohammad, you can follow Jesus, you can follow Buddha.

You can follow Hinduism, Islam, Judaism, Christianity or Taoism just to name a few.

You can go with any religion you like; you can submerse yourself with one or you can acknowledge elements from the many. I'm not here to teach you about religion or suggest who you can and can't follow. I think that as long as no one is harmed, hurt or negatively affected by your beliefs then believe away.

My words are about sharing with you a guided pathway to establishing your direct connection with our universe Creator, with the one that we call 'God'. My message is about discovering the truth that God is LOVE. So, when you accept the understanding that God is love, you can then begin to allow that love into your life, along with all the other associated beauty that this will bring to you.

You don't need to go to a specific location or hike to a hidden temple to discover your spiritual relationship, because once you allow yourself to feel your eternal connection, you will quickly come to know that the one called God is everywhere. You can discover the complete power of this magnificence in your very own living room; this I know is true.

My entire book is about sharing with you the pathway and the transformation that occurs in your life experience once you free your spirit and unchain your soul, allowing you to re-establish your direct connection with *all that is*. By completing this action, you return your three universal centres – your body, mind and spirit – back to their original state of alignment just like they were when you were born to this earth. This book is about re-discovering your true purpose and appreciating all the things around you, as you revel in the euphoric energy from our Creator.

The search for hope
What I have discovered is that we are all loved, we all have a purpose, and we are all accepted. Everybody is welcomed into the kingdom of Source since we are all just a part of his life. I know that each religion is relevant in its own unique way since they all provide hope to their followers, which is one of the most powerful gifts a person can be provided.

Especially when one is in a time of need or despair; holding onto hope for something better is often the only thing that many have to get through tough times.

No matter where we reside on our earth, we can all use some hope in our lives. Some people pray for the hope of a better day, some pray for food, some for shelter at night and some pray simply to survive.

Many people pray and hope for peace, health and happiness, for loved ones who are sick to get better. Then there are those among us who use hope or prayer for a new toy or a new item, maybe a new car, a new house, or their dream job.

Either way, I think that most people will hope and pray at least once during their life for someone or something. Now, if hope is such a necessity, then what if receiving the confirmation of our Divine Creator's existence through our celestial connection is all the hope that was needed? Since this would reaffirm for the individual that there is something more out there after this life expires.

What if being unplugged from the ingrained everyday experience would allow you to become… plugged into the real reality? Enabling you to become connected to something that is so much greater than what we have ever been taught or shown.

Could that be all the hope that we require?

The need for hope can be seen not just in our own daily lives but from across the world using the power of technology. Where millions of families, adults and children alike are desperate and hopeful for a life without war, without bombing, without fear, without famine, disease and premature death. Desperate to obtain some sort of normality in their lives.

As a collective force, this is where we should be directing our hope.

Since uncovering the heavenly offering of the most purest energetic connection that naturally exists, I have come to know that this is there for all of us, no matter who we follow. With that, there can be as much hope as we need. From anywhere we are located we can be gifted with the hope that there is still much more to come. Once our spirit is freed and we rediscover our true selves, we can begin to see the world for what it really is as we ruminate about all the wonderful beauty that has been included as part of our life experience.

From here, your life experience will never be the same.

This is the new hope; this is the new way!

All is not what it seems

Since the beginning of civilisation, many ancient scribes, drawings and carvings have recorded the concept of reincarnation. From the early indigenous tribes who walked our earth, right up to our present-day society, the belief in reincarnation has long existed and been widely accepted by many different races and religions as a foundational component of our existence, part of the forever pathway that our spirit travels upon from within the realms of the afterlife.

Many believe that at the time a death occurs, the spirit vacates the physical shell, as the transition into the afterlife arena begins. This is where the spirit is greeted, while an overview of the earthly existence is laid out for review and eternal judgement is passed by the Highest Power. This judgement is based on the life contribution that the spirit has given during the physical experience. Once this definitive judgement is passed down, it is then believed that the next phase of the spiritual journey will begin, which, for some, will include returning to earth in a new physical form.

Sometimes the new physical form of the next biological existence after reincarnation is already predetermined based on the unlearnt lessons from the previous life. Conversely, if the Scales of Life are judged in your favour, then your next physical experience can be something more of your choosing.

There are indigenous drawings dating as far back as 50,000 years ago, along with documented records dating as far back as c. 1100 – c. 500 BCE, which lay claim to the idea that we are reborn or transition as part of our spiritual journey from the physical world to the spiritual world, locked into the never-ending cycle of reincarnation where we experience a variety of different physical shells until such time as the celestial Creator sees fit.

As I ruminate on this subject, I am reminded of a chance meeting that was orchestrated early in my journey with a special lady of Indian heritage at my local gym. This was a social setting familiar to both of us. Before this day, she was someone I'd never met, and since this day she is someone I have never seen again.

Sitting in the stretching arena of my gym with some of my closest friends, a lady approached me from the side, introducing herself as Rani. Rani informed me that she'd been watching me from afar, observing how I was training and how focused I seemed. She continued to explain how she was inspired by my level of effort because she had found the same task hard to complete and that she had always struggled with unlocking that level of intensity.

Humbled by her statement, I thanked her for her kind words and shared with her that I wasn't doing anything extraordinary. Quickly, we sparked up a conversation. I mentioned that I was glad she was motivated by my effort, and I reassured her that I didn't mind at all if she kept using me as her motivation tool. I asked her how she was doing and with that opening, Rani began to share with me her personal journey about what she had experienced during the year 2020.

Apart from her husband and children, all of her family were back in India and in the years prior, she had regularly returned home to India to visit until COVID hit, putting an end to this travel. Rani continued to reminisce about how the lockdowns had been hard on her family business, an Indian restaurant in a neighbouring suburb. Nonetheless, Rani advised that they were doing the best they could to keep their business afloat and survive. Her business challenges, however, were insignificant, compared to the other family news she was about to share with me.

Back home in India, Rani's remaining family members included her elderly father and brother Suni. Rani mentioned that she was close with Suni; however, the relationship she held with her father was an extremely tight bond. Rani continued that towards the end of 2019, her father had started to become ill, and at that time, was regularly attending his local hospital.

Suni had been supporting their father in her absence, as well as providing regular updates to Rani about their father's condition.

Fortunately, in January 2020, Rani explained how she had managed to fly back over to India and spend some quality time with her dad and by the end of her trip it seemed to the family, that his health was improving, ready to make a full recovery. While in India, Rani stayed at Suni's house and together they agreed to a future plan that included her returning twice a year.

After staying for as long as she could, it was now time to return back to Melbourne. Upon her return, like the rest of the world by March 2020, the pandemic had hit, sending entire countries into lockdown. It was not long after the first lockdown had begun that

Rani received a call from her brother that she'd been dreading. A distraught Suni reluctantly informed her that her father's health had taken a turn for the worse and that he was now in hospital, gravely ill.

With simply no way of returning to India, Rani quickly became emotionally distressed at the thought of not being able to support her father in his final days. It was not long after that initial phone call that a follow-up call was received where the news of her father's passing was laid bare.

Unable to see him, hold his hand or be there with him in his final moments broke Rani's heart. Even though she had tried her best to grieve him remotely, this just wasn't the same; Rani was emotionally defeated.

As Rani embarked on the grieving process from the comfort of her home in Melbourne, she found herself in the kitchen one morning, preparing breakfast. Glancing outside, she noticed a black crow perched on the table in her backyard – an unfamiliar presence. Dismissing it as a passing moment, she turned back to her routine and carried on with her day. The next morning Rani was back in her kitchen, looking out the window. To her amazement, she noticed a black crow sitting on the table outside. Rani questioned herself, 'Is this the same crow as yesterday?' This time, though, the crow seemed to be looking back in through the window, almost as if it was peering directly into the house, through the kitchen window, towards her.

Later that day Rani mentioned the returning crow to her husband and children, who all quickly informed her, 'What are you talking about? How do you know it's the same crow? You are going crazy!'

Undeterred by their responses, Rani felt that this was something more. The following day, Rani went into her kitchen to prepare breakfast and there in the backyard was a black crow or the same black crow, sitting on the outside table staring back in through her kitchen window. This continued every day for the next week. Each time she came into the kitchen in the morning, there was the black crow sitting outside, staring back at her.

After a week went by, she decided one morning, 'If the crow returns today, I'm going to go outside!' As she walked into her kitchen to prepare her breakfast, there was the crow patiently waiting on the table outside. So, this time, just as she'd planned, Rani grabbed her coffee and made her way outside, gently sitting down at the table so as not to scare it away.

To her surprise, the crow didn't react at all. In fact, it just maintained eye contact with her the entire time, gently tilting its head to the side, almost acting as if it had known her for her whole life. This would become the first of many days that Rani would go outside in the morning and just sit with the crow. As the days progressed, by the third week, Rani decided that she would bring some food outside with her. Something small for the crow to eat – just some birdseed or breadcrumbs, whatever she had available in the house. Together they would sit there in silence until eventually, she began to talk to the crow.

From here, the crow would sit with her for hours, listening to her whilst eating the food she'd bought outside. As she spoke to the crow, she felt that this interaction was something much greater than what her other family members believed.

There were many times when she would start to cry as she spoke to the crow about her father and his passing. When she cried, it was as if the crow understood and cared for her wellbeing. The crow would stop eating, tilt its head and just stare back at her. As if to say, 'Don't cry, it's okay. I'm okay now. You know that I am here with you.'

I ask, why can't this be the way? Subconsciously, we already know that we are spiritual beings. We already know that as part of our physical makeup, we have been constructed with atoms, microscopic particles of energy just like all things that exist in our physical world. Our entire reality is constructed of atoms, powered by spirit and life. No matter the denial that is sometimes presented, we all know that we are gifted with a spirit, the divine piece of Source that gives life to our physical shell! Why can't our spirit that once powered our physical shell then power another energetic construction once our human shell expires?

What happens next

After our final day on earth, once we ascend to the next phase of our existence, depending on the outcome of our celestial judgment day, when the results are laid bare from the Scales of Life, we have choices about our next physical experience.

If the Scales of Life do not weigh positively in our favour on this day, based on our contributions to all things living, and we have not learnt the lessons presented to us during our physical lifetime, we will return to the physical world and repeat a life experience in a new physical formation to re-experience those unlearned lessons. It is, however, important to note that it is never too late to change the balance of the scales. Just by thinking about doing better today, you can start to tilt the scales in your favour.

If we have lived a physical existence in a manner in which the Scales of Life are judged in our favour and we have contributed positively to the betterment of the world, then we can choose the next path of our spirit's journey. As an example, we might want to return as a bird to experience all the beautiful locations on earth from the sky above, or we may simply wish to return as something new as part of the next natural step of our spirit's journey.

All living entities have a spirit, all living organisms, including plants and trees, all have a spirit, an internal life force. All things alive have divine spiritual energy. Our challenge is to work together with Mother Earth. We can use what is on the earth as we need as part of our existence. This is the circle of life; the existence of life contributing to the living. But we do not need to kill just for the sake of killing or consume just for the sake of consuming.

Let us all consider the earth for humanity now as well as for future generations when we make our day-to-day life choices. Let us take into consideration all living forms of life when we make our decisions.

Let us try to use the universe's natural resources that have been provided in an abundance, when and where we can to extend the life of our special planet.

So that life is a positive experience for all.

Even for the deniers, at the moment of death, if you have ever witnessed someone transition as the spirit leaves the body, the life is no more. This is undeniable. Now, since our spirit is our controlling entity, when the spirit leaves our body, where does it go?

From my personal experience, I have come to understand that the ascension pathway includes light and darkness. Sometimes, a person may experience the darkness in a near-death experience as more of a wake-up call to start making better decisions. Seeing the darkness is a chance that you are given to turn your life around, to make different choices, better choices, to change your contribution to all that is and to behave differently.

No matter how strong or invincible you may feel in your physical form, encountering the darkness of the afterlife will shake you to your core. This revelation often comes at your most vulnerable moment – perhaps as you are dying – when the vastness of the divine becomes undeniable. In that instant, you will grasp just how small you truly are, leaving you with the weight of regret for choices left unmade. Yet, you will not be condemned to hell; instead, you will be given the chance to relearn the lessons you once ignored, albeit in an entirely new way.

With darkness comes light

Just like the ancient Chinese symbolic Ying and Yang, good and evil, black and white, if there is darkness, then there must also be LIGHT! And there is most definitely light – if my journey has taught me nothing else, I have learnt that it's never too late to change your future.

To counter the scale weight in your favour, the Scales of Life.

Only those who don't attempt to balance the Scales of Life in a more propitious manner will be eternally judged by the Highest Power less favourably.

To understand what is meant by the Scales of Life, all you need to do is picture a traditional weight scale.

As you move through your life experience, your life's choices and actions add weight to the appropriate side of the scale. The divine judgement is conducted by the Creator himself, the powers up above. If you've lived your life in a way that was less favourable, do not panic or despair. You can change today – because it is never too late to change. You can make a conscious decision right now to change, to start living differently, to start living your life as you always truly intended.

Right at the very moment, when you make your decision to change, just by making that concerted effort and choice, you already start to adjust the weight of the scales in your favour.

Changing the outcome of your current trajectory.

Some of the most basic tasks can positively adjust the scales in your favour. Simple acts of kindness, giving and remaining humble all immediately adjust the weighted scales.

The Scales of Life are the only eternal court of judgement used to evaluate existence. They are not for the living to use against each other. The Scales of Life come into play when the Divine One has chosen. Once the life has been lived. This Judgement Day is orchestrated, managed and controlled by the 'One and Only': the Creator of All.

We are simply judged based on the contributions we have made not by the volume of the contribution.

We are judged according to our deeds:

- How you lived your life – the choices you made

- How you contributed to the life experience of other living beings – what were your contributions, were they of a positive nature?

- How you contributed to the earth – was it for the betterment of our planet?

- How you helped others – the most important deed

This does not mean that we must all achieve amazing fame or greatness as judged by humans. We are simply measured on how genuine we lived our lives and how we contributed to the bigger picture. There is no set expectation or minimum achievement required, as everyone will be judged individually.

How did you live your life?

Did you make positive choices? Were your actions and intentions to the benefit of those around you and yourself? If an individual spent a life trapped in pain, this is not a negative. If someone's life had been scared with trauma, which lead to negative choices while their spirit was damaged, they will not be condemned. By all means, the Creator FORGIVES.

They will be welcomed into the light.

How did you contribute to the life experiences of other living beings?

This is a key measuring stick; did you assist in making the experience that is life positive for those living around you? What did you do? How did you make the experience better? This could be as simple as being honest, showing care, showing love and generating happiness.

There is no sliding scale or list of what you must do – just giving your love is enough, as God only gives love. Certainly, if you could've contributed to someone else's life in an additional way on top of giving your love, possibly by sharing, guiding or assisting towards bettering their life experience or the lives of many, then this would definitely be recognised also.

Not only would this positiveness generously improve your spiritual life and wellbeing, the Scales of Life would also be tilted in your favour.

How did you contribute to the earth – was it for the betterment of our planet?

This measurement includes and is not limited to managing your consumption levels, while caring for and nurturing your environment. Reducing plastic waste, recycling products and waste that can be either reused or re-purposed, giving the raw materials a second life.

We should be using the natural resources that our universe provides for us in abundance, such as the energy from our sun. Making use of green power is a positive benefit for all. If you are in a position of power, you should be ensuring that when we consume the earth's natural resources, the benefits of this are spread across the many, not just the few.

We should all be doing what we can to help extend the life of our planet, while ensuring the survival of our planet's resources, to guarantee that future generations have the full use and enjoyment of our planet for many years to come.

The most important task: how did you help others?

Many people will help their family or friends, but if you can help a stranger, then this, I believe, is a significant gesture. Your help could be as simple as lending a hand, providing an ear, preparing a meal, gifting some money, clothes or anything you can, even just your time.

If you can't help, the simple act of just acknowledging the person in need, taking the time to look them in the eye and saying, 'Sorry, I can't help you today,' is still a powerful gesture. That verbal acknowledgement becomes a mighty soul-replenishing action, benefiting both their spirit and yours. When we give without expectation, volunteer our time or energy, this does not go unnoticed.

There is a special place reserved for those who do.

Guidance and support

Please don't forget, you have your external support team wanting you to succeed. You can discover this support through feelings and vibration. There are guided answers for you everywhere. Whether you are feeling lost or you are seeking a confirmation or reassurance of your current situation or trajectory, you can seek clarification with your celestial support team. They are an on-call 24/7 hotline that is always there for you, offering divine guidance to refocus, recentre or just to let you know that you are loved.

This support always wants to assist you in achieving your goals and ambitions. This is the next phase of our human evolution. A global population in tune and connected with the one mind, tuned in to receiving the divine love and assistance that is readily available.

Understanding since we are all connected, we are all protected

During our time here on earth, we are governed not only by the laws of the countries in which we reside, we are also governed by the laws of the universe! This governance is guided by the universal law of attraction. There are many books that have been written and individuals who talk about this subject in great detail and length across the globe.

My brief overview of what the universal law of attraction means is the universe will provide you with more of what it is that you are attracting vibrationally. If you are regularly projecting frustration and anger, then as you move through your daily life, you will be presented with more opportunities that will allow you to reach your desired outcome of being angry or frustrated.

Just as if you are constantly living in a state of sadness, attaching the feeling of sadness to each life experience that you are presented with, the universe will provide you with more opportunities so that you can maintain your state of sadness. The universe cannot decipher vibrations to send a sad person positivity; that intervention would be a task for the divine. The universe operates on a totally different frequency. You attract what it is that you are radiating and vibrating. Our Creator is the one projecting *LOVE* to you and to all that surrounds you. Will you allow yourself to receive this, though? That is the question.

Equally so, if a person is happy by nature, then the universe will send them more rendezvous throughout their day so that they can continue to experience their happy moments. For that person is projecting happiness through their vibrational frequency. This isn't saying that a happy person will never feel sad – this is saying that the happy person who feels sad will move through the feelings of sadness to return to their state of happiness.

The happy person won't exist in a considerable state of sadness. Releasing the emotional baggage that you carry and allowing new perspectives into your life about your lived experiences can help you reach this state through the art of forgiveness.

As you learn to understand and navigate the laws of the universe, over time you will understand that it is all about *being in tune.*

That means being open to new possibilities and ready to receive, not closed off and restricted.

Understanding that we are also protected

During life-or-death situations that we face as part of our human experience, we are gifted actual physical protection when it is not our time. Whether that be a family trying to escape their war-torn country for a safer life, like many families from the war-ravaged Middle East, Africa and now parts of Europe, or whether that is someone involved in a serious accident. There have been many stories where the individuals involved in such scenarios have come out unscathed.

One example is the personal story of a young mother, called Aaeesha, whom I'd met by chance, in a moment when the universe had brought the two of us together for our single rendezvous. As we randomly crossed paths, she instantly shared her story with me about where she was from.

Aaeesha spoke about the scattered migration of her large family contingent escaping from the war-torn region in Afghanistan across the globe into different Western countries. Her entire family unit, including her adult sisters, brothers and their individual families, had all been frantically searching for a safer life. Aaeesha explained that she knew during her extended family's journey, they'd all been guided and protected with help from our Creator, the one she referred to as GOD. She knew that the protection she'd received from above, combined with the support her family had received from different people here on earth, had kept them all safe and enabled each family unit to successfully navigate the dangerous journey out of the war-ravaged environment by foot and vehicle where possible.

Knowing of the existence of this celestial protection provided much comfort for her in the darkest moments when fear and uncertainty had captivated her mind. Guiding her, as she traversed her family and herself, out of each incredibly dangerous situation they encountered.

In the end, each family landed in strategic locations scattered across Germany, Canada and Australia. Destinations that they'd been lucky enough to select for themselves, for their new safer life and their new beginning.

Her town where they lived in Afghanistan had been decimated by the war on terror. So many lives had been lost and homes destroyed, even basic necessities such as clean drinking water had either been denied or destroyed. Much of what many of us take for granted was non-existent to the people living there.

Yet, Aaeesha saw herself and her family as the lucky ones for whom everything had aligned. Humbled and incredibly grateful for everything she had received, Aaeesha stated, 'Only with the grace of God did we manage to leave!'

Unwavering in her conviction, she stood firm in her belief that she had been divinely guided and protected.

Such protection is not just limited to people in war-torn countries. This divine protection is offered for us all since we are all part of the great plan. This divine protection intervenes when required as we navigate our daily activities. For example, sometimes we will receive this protection when we are involved in a serious accident or event. Unless, of course, it is our time. Time for us to transition into the next phase of existence, returning to our original spirit form, energetically amalgamating with Source.

For myself, a time of such protection was during a car accident I was involved in many years ago. I was in my early twenties, and the vehicle I was driving had been gifted to me by a friend in my area. The car was a little worse for wear, having seen better days, but it was still considered drivable.

It is important to note that I'd driven this car in some extremely bad weather conditions and the car had operated fine, getting me from A to B and then back to A. On the day of the accident, the weather was beautiful with the sun shining and the roads extremely dry. Perfect conditions for driving, plus I was well-rested from the night before.

Leaving home, I headed out the door at around 9 am. I was only a couple of miles from home when I entered the left-hand bend on a road that I'd driven countless times before. Suddenly, one of the front wheels locked up and wouldn't spin like a wheel should, causing the vehicle to aquaplane from the left-hand lane across the double lines, sliding into the oncoming traffic lane and then straight towards the edge of the embankment. The vehicle was heading over the edge and had fatefully lined up with an oncoming tree.

Just before the moment of impact, it was as if the concept of time had slowed down completely. Which meant as the car violently smashed into the tree, I was able to prepare for what was coming next!

Thanks to the slow motion, I could see the outcome before the next event occurred. After the head-on collision with the tree, I could see that the vehicle was going to roll down the side of the hill and that the impact would be felt on the driver's side roof first.

With this in mind, once the car hit the tree and was about to begin rolling, I lifted myself up and out of the driver's seat, positioning myself in the passenger's seat.

Then as the car started tumbling down the hill, I rotated myself around inside the vehicle, strategically placing my hands at certain points inside the car, rolling with the vehicle so that when the car eventually stopped and was stationary on its roof, I was sitting on the roof inside the vehicle.

Seated on the inside roof, I quickly inhaled a couple of short breaths, then touched all over my face with my hand, checking for any bleeding. Discovering there was none, I looked around for an exit. Identifying a smashed side window, I crawled out of the wreckage.

Not a single scratch marked my skin, not even a sting or ache. I stood there, heart pounding in my chest like a distant drum, completely stunned by what had just unfolded. Flabbergasted didn't begin to capture it. The world seemed to tilt slightly as I tried to process the impossibility of walking away completely unscathed.

Emergency services were quick to arrive, including a tow truck and the police. The officers ran down to the crash site, asking, 'Where's the driver, where's the driver?' since the vehicle was totally destroyed.

Standing in awe at still being alive, I gently informed the officer that I was in fact the driver and that I was okay. He looked at me and then back at the car, surprised at the possibility that I could be the driver of such a mangled wreck.

A contentious point that he wanted to understand was how I survived, considering the driver's side roof had crushed down to the dash, not to mention the damage to the front of the vehicle from the collision with the tree.

I told him everything that I just shared with you. However, as I spoke about lifting myself up and out of the driver's seat, he abruptly cut me off and said, 'So, you were not wearing a seat belt?!'

I replied, 'Officer, I was wearing a seat belt, right up to the last minute when I could see that the car was about to roll and if I had've remained in the driver's seat, my head would have been crushed through my chest. It was at that point, Officer, that I removed my seat belt, so I could jump into the passenger seat and survive.' He accepted my explanation but remained incredulous.

But I knew that this day was not my day. I knew that I'd been supported by a power much greater than what you or I could ever conjure up. A divine energy that was so powerful, it was able to slow down the concept of time, ensuring everything I did in response to my survival. From the moment the car connected with the tree, everything was miraculously calculated. My level of comfort and knowing during this moment felt as if I had completed this event one hundred times before.

Empowered to protect

Discovering that just as we are protected, we are also empowered to protect as well. There have been many recorded events across the globe where a single person or a group of people have done something extraordinary to help save someone or something else's life. Just as I am sure that there are many more of these moments that have gone undocumented as well.

Generally, these moments occur in life-or-death situations when a person exerts extreme strength and control beyond what is believed to be normal. A moment where a person has to make a choice of how they will react to a high intensity situation.

Then, depending on the situation and the acceptance of their decision, the physical body is empowered with an influx of adrenalin. This adrenalin provides an abundance of powerful energy, as well as an existential level of situational awareness and clarity in order to assist them through the particular situation.

A common example of this is a parent who does something extraordinary, such as lifting a vehicle to save their trapped child or children. How does the parent achieve this? How do they remain so in control? Are they the recipients of great divine intervention in these moments?

There have been many of these recorded events over the years, including back in 1962, when a male by the name of Jack Kirby claimed to witness a woman lifting a car off her trapped baby. Witnessing this Moment in Time is what Jack Kirby credits to be the inspiration for what he used to create the Marvel character now known as the Hulk.

Most of the documented events relate to humans – both male and female – witnessing a loved one or a stranger pinned by a car after some sort of motor vehicle accident and then coming to the rescue of the trapped individual. Sometimes, though, this is not just about lifting a motor vehicle. Consider this story from many years ago, back in my teenage years, when I was a keen bodyboarder.

During those years, I regularly headed out to the beach most weekends with Mum and my brothers. My brothers and I would stay out in the surf for hours on end. We just loved being out in the water, feeling the ocean and riding the waves.

We were at complete peace in the ocean.

We would gently float on the water, ride the waves and enjoy every moment together. No matter the weather conditions, we would be out there. My brothers and I had all swam for a number of years, so we were confident swimmers and comfortable in the open sea. During most Christmas holidays, we would head away for a week or two, staying at either a camping ground or if we were fortunate enough, we would be invited as a family to come and stay with friends at their beach houses.

Either way, we enjoyed being down at the beach with Mum.

Way back in 1996, when I was sixteen, my family and I were camping on a friend's block of land down at a regional seaside town called Venus Bay. We were in the ocean most days since each day the weather was perfect with the sun radiating and the waves consistently rolling in.

Unbeknown to me, staying nearby was a girl named Carly. Carly and I were around the same age, and she was staying with her family at their beach house for the holidays. As fate would have it, we ended up meeting each other down on the beach one sunny day, which led to us spending some time together.

On this particular day, I was at the beach with her and her family, just relaxing in the sun, spending some quality time together. I could see that further down the beach, my mum and brothers had set up camp for the day with the family friends we were staying with.

The sun was out and the water was cold, so the beach was packed full that day. There were plenty of people around, families and friends, young and old, revelling in the rays. For experienced swimmers and surfers, the water conditions were great. The waves were coming through in sets and out the back, they were nice and big. Ocean conditions can change though, and they did just that. As the rips started to form, and the waves became choppy, the undertow became powerful and intense for those who couldn't swim.

Carly and I noticed the family sitting in front of us, a mother with her two young sons. Both sons had ventured into the water. We were watching them, considering they were young, and the conditions had started to get pretty dangerous for young children. If they were to be caught in one of the rips that had formed, they could quickly be dragged out to sea if they didn't know what to do.

As these two young boys started to struggle in the water, their mother stood up and went out into the ocean to bring both of them in. For some reason, Carly and I commentated on what we could see unfold in front of us.

The mum entered the water and tried to get out to one of her two children as the kids had separated in the sea. In her haste to help, she got caught in the rip herself, which meant she now too was struggling with the conditions. As we were talking, Carly's mum suggested that

I should go out there and help them. I was young, but I only needed that little bit of motivation to get up.

As I jogged towards the shoreline, I could see that most of the people were exiting the water by now, except no one was helping the two boys or their mum. Sensing the gravity of the situation that was quickly unfolding, I increased my speed and ran towards the ocean, zipping up my wetsuit as I made my way down the sand. With perfect timing, I grabbed my bodyboard off a young family friend, Rachael, who was standing at the shoreline. Rachael had earlier borrowed my board to play in the shallows.

With perfect timing, Rachael just happened to be standing in the right spot, enabling me to grab my board out of her hands and launch myself into the water.

Landing on the surface perfectly, I paddled out directly over to the first boy. He had become separated from his Mum and brother, and being all alone, he was clearly in trouble. I reached him fast, pulling him on to my board so I could escort him into the shallow water. By this stage, most people had cleared out of the ocean and were now gathered on the sand, watching this rescue event unfold in front of them from the safety of the shore.

I turned around and paddled back into the deep water out to where the mother and her second son were. I grabbed her son first and pulled him onto my board, reassuring him that he was okay, securing him in place and then using the power of the waves, I guided him back to shore. Once I could see that he was able to stand and was safe, I shifted my attention to the mother. By this stage, she was struggling to stay above the water, waving her arms around, distressed, panicking and crying for her children.

As soon as I reached her, I could see her head was going under. Lifting her up, I placed her arm over my shoulder so she could keep her head above the water and start breathing. As she regained her breath, she started to scream and cry uncontrollably about her boys and where they were. If they we alive or if they had drowned. Her distressed panicking caused me to continually wrestle with her as I attempted to keep her head above the water. I explained, 'They are both fine, they are safe. They are on the beach now, everything's okay. Now, let me bring you in!'

As the mother struggled to comprehend the situation, I swam and dragged her to the shoreline, eventually reaching the shallows when a large burly male approached us and exclaimed, 'I'll take her from here, son!' To which I thought, *Thanks, but I could have used your help out there!*

Once I stepped onto the sand, I could see the mother reunited with her boys and that her children were perfectly fine, plus she was safe and well. Her family was together again.

The large number of people who'd gathered on the shoreline celebrated and clapped, acknowledging my effort as I unassumingly made my way back over to Carly, happy that I could help out.

I'll remember this day forever.

Chapter 12

THE TEN STEPS TO VIBRATIONAL ALIGNMENT

Welcome to the final chapter. What a journey it has been so far. I want to thank you for letting me share my story with you. I hope that you too can join me as we experience life in its truest form as vibrationally connected beings.

Ready to conquer anything that life puts in front of us.

I would like to acknowledge that my journey is far from over since this new version of life has only just begun.

New life experiences continue to expand each day through the power of repeated daily practices and constant exploring. Let us never close ourselves off to any possibilities, no matter what they are. Remember that we are always learning as students of life. Always look to maintain your individual connection with the stream of divine love and the one consciousness.

Because, what started as the reconstruction of my entire belief structure has now transformed, unequivocally, into my entire way of being – my new faith.

Using the three elements of practice, commitment and belief.

These three elements are offerings that we can all gift ourselves. If we could all achieve this, the possibilities would be endless as everyone would live a truly connected experience of the highest order.

This version of reality is available for all.

As part of my commitment to you, I have shared the steps I discovered that brought me to this beautiful state of existence, vibrationally aligned.

Most of society is living out their daily lives carrying their emotional baggage. But we must free ourselves from this weight so that as we move forward and live out our daily lives, we can try to ensure that our decisions and behaviours are not being influenced either consciously or subconsciously by the emotional bags that we carry.

These influences can be either positive or negative in nature; however, this journey focuses on the negative elements, since these often have debilitating effects, promoting negative repercussions and leading to reoccurring destructive decisions and outcomes. These are harmful choices that can lead to a range of life issues including risk-taking and addictions such as alcohol and substance abuse, gambling, eating disorders, depression, self-harm, suicide or death.

Once a person is trapped living in this version of reality, struggling with addictions or self-harm, this broken state of mind can have a significant flow-on effect on the individual. These effects can include changes to:

- Their physical health
- Their contribution towards a positive existence
- Their relationships, promoting breakdowns within family units and friends
- Their finances, employment, social and housing as they face significant personal losses
- Their overall satisfaction with life

This statement by no means enforces that we must all make grand contributions to society as a whole, but we most definitely should be committed to having a positive experience for our own life's journey.

Cracking the code

From the very moment that this transformational pathway was shared with me, I knew that this was something to behold. Somehow, the foundational code of what this life is really about was exposed. The Highest Power, a force that I never knew even existed, had seen fit to present me with this glorious gift. For what purpose, I was originally unsure; however, as I continued to delve deeper, exploring this existential offering, it was clear that this story needed to be told. Once I allowed myself to become completely immersed in this new reality, life as I knew it would never be the same again. The magnificence continued to reveal itself with wonderful new elements. Because now I was tuned in, aligned and communicating directly with Source. Too much has been revealed for me to ever turn back.

Naturally, questions arose, for instance what should I do with such a gift? What should I do to repay this amazing offering I have received? Why was I so lucky or fortunate to be selected? So, I did what I believe many people would do: I conjured up a plan of how I could share what had been gifted to me, a plan to pass on the process and pathway to finding this everlasting peace. I knew that if I could finally find this peace, then this could work for anyone. I imagined the entire global consciousness shifting and what could unfold. I wondered if what had been shared with me was the magic switch. That pathway has now become the Wounded Butterflies – Overcoming Adversity™ program. A guided undertaking designed to deliver absolute peace, unity and connectedness to anyone who commits to the steps.

Let us now continue our evolution journey and explore the individual steps to Vibrational Alignment.

These steps are based on the individual teachings that I received during extreme moments of heightened awareness – divine awakenings, if you will – that presented themselves to me as my journey unfolded. If you can apply these steps, set your spirit free and allow your spiritual self to be taken along on this vibrational journey, you will discover your magnificence as well.

You will uncover what it truly means to be in complete Vibrational Alignment with your body, mind and spirit. Activating your divine consciousness naturally elevates your internal energetic receptors to a heightened new level, not regularly achieved by many. You will expand your mind into a new version of reality where your knowledge can grow into its unlimited potential while completely transforming your worldly experience.

As part of the journey, this process should naturally unlock two sacred and powerful glands located inside your physical brain. The pineal and pituitary glands. The pineal gland is a small gland located in the centre of our brain and is often associated with spirituality, while the pituitary gland is associated with our third eye. These glands are both part of the Ajna Chakra, enhancing intellect and clairvoyance. With these glands activated, your intuition, third eye and subconscious awareness will become more active. Once these two glands are ignited, hold onto your seat and get ready for some whole new life experiences. This state of being is transformational, truly divine.

Unplugged from the old – plugged into the new
By allowing yourself to establish your own vibrational connection, you too can become unplugged from the old way of living. Unplugged from the negative beliefs and behaviours, so that you can reemerge plugged into the new way of existence that allows for forgiveness, understanding and wonder.

Disconnect your mind from all of the preconceived life-learned behaviours and beliefs of how we are supposed to think, act and feel. Let go of the ingrained negative traits that have been inherited from those around you. Remember, your parents are just older versions of you, who were taught by older versions of themselves. Each version was conditioned by their own generational and social influencers. Let's cut them a break, forgive them and let the past go.

Then insert yourself into…
Plug your mind into the real world, the feeling world. Become part of this divine energy where you can begin to learn and understand that everything is connected, everything is one, and in this place, we are all part of the same sacred family. When you plug yourself into this reality, you discover that we are all loved, supported and guided from the powers of the universe.

The feeling world is located within this physical reality that we exist in. This is where our mind is opened to everything and closed off to nothing, so that we may allow the messages of support to be received. A place where we understand that we can connect with the spirits, so that death is accepted as part of our journey and not something to be feared. We all made the same agreement before we arrived here when we agreed and accepted that we would return to the nonphysical one day.

By existing in this feeling world, you will recharge from the divine love that is always radiating through you. Take many moments to feel an appreciation for the air that you breathe, the colours you can see and the sounds that you can hear. Know that this feeling world is the place where you can look into the sky and appreciate the cloud formations that appear in front of you. Patterns, cities and artworks that have been drawn across your sky, for your enjoyment and captivation.

This is all for you.

Transition into this elevated state of existence where you can ask the questions and feel the answers as they are delivered to you vibrationally. Allow yourself to live in this divine world, where you can restore, reconnect and refuel with the universe.

We can have it all.

If this process can help even one other person, then that is enough motivation for me to write this book for you, because you are worth it.

If my experiences can play a role in positively influencing, guiding or supporting another person's life experience, helping them to free their own spirit and unchain their own soul, so that they too may reach this divine level of connection, then my job here is done.

I will always remember how I have been gifted this incredible opportunity to share what it is that I have received, and for this I am extremely humbled.

Let us now explore the ten steps to Vibrational Alignment. This is a code, a set of fundamentals, if you will, that, as vibrational beings, we strive to live by. Rules and guides that promote self-love, care and consideration to ourselves as individuals and also to the entire world around us. By living by this code, life becomes reimagined as humanity prospers.

The 10 Steps to Vibrational Alignment – Body, Mind, Spirit

Step 1 – Free your spirit

Step 2 – Change what you consume

Step 3 – Stop consuming blockers

Step 4 – Care for your body

Step 5 – Understand that we are all connected to this earth – humans, plants and animals

Step 6 – Consider the earth and all things living when making your choices

Step 7 – Care for our earth

Step 8 – Help other people

Step 9 – Open your mind

Step 10 – Create your daily routine

Remember these steps once you have completed them

Step 1 – Free your spirit

This is the first step to be undertaken as part of your journey. This may be the most challenging; however, this will also be the most rewarding! One way to achieve this is by using Wounded Butterflies – Overcoming Adversity™. This guided process will help you free your spirit. This program itself has nine individual steps and is introduced in chapter nine, aptly titled Wounded Butterflies – Overcoming Adversity™.

The process for achieving this breakthrough includes documenting, in dot point form, all the memories of your life the painful times you were hurt. You will then need to prepare yourself as you write about these memories, as challenging as it might be.

As you write about these memories in the 3rd person from an outsider's perspective, you want to allow yourself the opportunity to receive the questions and discover the answers, providing new perspectives as you complete this process.

If you can work through this program, including forgiveness and taking back control, you will be able let go of these painful traumatic memories once and for all, truly freeing your spirit and your mind. This will allow you to successfully discover the next steps and maintain the changes that you have undertaken.

You are invited to visit www.findingpeace.com.au to register or you can enroll at https://awf.org.au/enrolment/ to complete the Wounded Butterflies-Overcoming Adversity™ program.

Step 2 – Change what you consume

After letting go of the emotional baggage that you carried, you may start to feel physically lighter since you are no longer burdened by this once-great weight that has now been lifted off your shoulders. I also anticipate that you will begin to have a heightened sense of situational awareness and clarity in your mind's thoughts. From this point forward, dealing with future situations or scenarios should not seem so daunting or challenging for you as you view each interaction with your new perspective.

Now you can start to focus on making more positive changes in your life. Taking control of your diet is something you can address straight away. We should work towards adjusting the foods we consume daily as we progress along our journey to alignment, including:

- Consuming more plant-based foods including more vegetables, salads and nuts
- Increasing your daily water consumption
- Consuming clean cuts of meat, fish and poultry in moderation, and reducing your carnivorous intake
- Reducing your processed food consumption
- Consuming less manufactured sugars and sugary drinks
- Eating minimal junk food.

Realign your food consumption towards healthier fresh dishes by feeding your brain and body with natural healthy foods that stimulate your mind and replenish your body energy resources at the same time.

Step 3 – Stop consuming blockers

Step three of your journey to Vibrational Alignment includes stopping the consumption of signal blockers. This includes:

- Alcohol
- Illicit drugs
- Visual stimulants such as slot machines and artificial sensory stimulants

These substances and mental stimulants are all signal blockers that have been designed to interrupt and jam your natural receptors and connectors. Some illicit drugs have even been created to artificially simulate the naturally euphoric sensation provided for free by the universe in an attempt to trap the user into years of addiction hell. When any of these substances are excessively consumed, you run the risk of willingly or unwillingly interrupting the divine healing that is available for your body, mind and spirit.

As you transition along your pathway towards Vibrational Alignment, progressing forward with your re-energised spirit, you should find this step, an easier process to undertake and complete.

Often, signal blockers are used, consciously or sub-consciously, to band-aid over how we are feeling about our current situation or either the day, the week, the month or year that we are experiencing or the past that we are trying to forget. This past includes the historic trauma, negative choices or behaviours that have been exerted. Rest assured, once you feel the divine touch in all its glory, you won't need any artificial stimulants to feel good since there is nothing that naturally compares.

I am not demanding a lifetime of abstinence as I know that it is perfectly fine to have a nice time; however, you might find that you can still have a nice time without the artificial substances and that consuming these blockers simply interrupt your receptors while jamming any transmission signals.

Don't you want to become the best version of yourself so that you can be all that you can be?

As you become more aware of your acceptance and divine understandings, in total control of how you feel, you will experience your desire to consume the blockers dissipate and fade away into the nothingness.

If you have truly completed step one, I encourage you to undertake a simple test with the Highest Power. Send a verbal request to Source using the words, *'Universe, heal me, please.'* Try this and see what happens next. Once your spirit is freed, connecting with your divine energy stream is the next level of your awakening. This is something that you can work towards mastering, so that you can tap into on request.

Feeling the universe's energetic buzz through divine love, you will come to realise that this power is unlimited, with no cost, no comedown and no hangover; nothing but pure positive energy for you to enjoy.

Step 4 – Care for your body

As your new level of awareness begins to expand your mind, you may start to experience new sensations as divine power is universally administered. These euphoric sensations will be delivered energetically to you. Maintain your connection and allow yourself to receive this energy as it flows through you.

Everything is all perfectly natural since this is your divine consciousness becoming activated.

From here, your mind and body can begin the healing process while your sensory receptors rejuvenate. You are now ready to progress to the next step focusing on your health. If you are someone who exercises regularly, well done, keep up the great work. However, if you are currently not exercising, this step is for you.

Exercise may seem hard at first, especially if you have not moved for a while. Try to remember a time in the past when you used to exercise – maybe you ran or played a sport as a child? Were you able to run out the entire game? Use that experience as a guide and motivation.

Improving your physical health can greatly increase your life longevity. Physical exercise helps raise the body's internal operating system to levels outside of their comfort zones. This activates the cells under an increased level of pressure or exhaustion, then once the exercise session is completed, the body does what the body does best and naturally recovers.

You can achieve this by simply moving and participating in any form of exercise that you can manage, such as:

- Walking, jogging, running
- Swimming, surfing, rowing
- Cycling
- General exercise, weightlifting, cardio, boxing and circuit training
- Soccer, football, rugby, netball, basketball or single participant sports.

Build a regular exercise routine that you can successfully complete at least three times per week. However, remember to set your initial goals to something within your reach.

Allow your body's internal energy levels to replenish naturally by working with yourself. You may discover that you don't need all those cups of coffee in the morning to kickstart your day since you have all the energy that you need now, already.

Knowing your objective and setting a target to work towards will allow you to enjoy the sense of accomplishment once you reach your goal. Remember, it is important to train your body to the level required to reach your target. The start is just the beginning. The start is all about building your effort, along with the reactivating of your moving parts. Over time, your fitness will naturally improve. As you regularly complete your exercise routine, this commitment will in turn naturally increase your endurance level and capacity to train harder.

Step 5 – Understand that we are all connected to this earth – humans, plants and animals

Reaching step five along your awakening journey is a critical milestone. Now it is time for you to realise and accept that even though you are you, a beautiful unique individual, you are part of the greater consciousness. You, along with every other form of life in existence, are part of this great oneness. All life forms play a part in the show that we call Life. We are all universally amalgamated.

As you become connected and more aware, your eyes may even become more sensitive to light. What you are experiencing is the activating of your pineal gland. This is your God consciousness, the tiny piece of Source that is inside you, coming to the forefront as you begin to see the world through the eyes of a connected being.

With your knowing that we are all vibrationally connected allowed to cement itself inside your library of wisdom, you may start to feel an increased level of compassion and love with animals and nature. This maybe something that you have never felt before. This is all natural.

You are becoming a connected being.

Everything is not what it seems. We need to open our minds, remove our limitations and raise our conscious awareness to the divine level of love, appreciation and joy. What appears as a bird to you may be much more than that. This may be a spiritual relationship carrying a divine message, specifically for you. An infinite living soul, letting you know that they are still here and are with you always.

Start to believe that anything is possible with love.

Step 6 – Consider the earth and all things living when making your choices

By now, you are well on your way. You have increased your level of awareness and hold a higher understanding of your place on this earth. You have received the revelation that we are all connected, and that everything is not what it seems.

Reaching step six means that it is now time for you to consider what the potential outcomes of your daily choices are, by thinking about how your choices affect the earth and all that occupies this planet with you.

Some basic examples would be to reduce your daily consumption of waste. As a start, you may want to reduce your plastic bottle intake. The discarded waste generated by the usage of plastic bottles globally is a major burden on our environment. Change starts with one person making a conscious decision to reduce what they use, or at least recycle what they do use, so that the outcome is more favourable for our environment.

Alternatively, you could also start to focus on recycling the leftover waste from what you consume: food, paper, cardboard, plastics and aluminium. Become aware of the amount that you are consuming. Are you using more than you need?

Are you taking more from the earth than you need and then discarding the leftovers to the trash? If you are, then this is an opportunity for you to reflect on this and change your ways. Your efforts won't go unnoticed.

Let us not simply take something just for the sake of taking if we don't really need it.

This is wasteful and not helpful to our planet's health or longevity.

Step 7 – Care for our earth

By reaching step seven, you have started to consider the wellbeing of our planet as you make your daily choices. This is an important actualisation and I know our earth thanks you.

Step seven drives home a fundamental calling for us all to focus on, which is doing what we can to care for our environment. By focusing on the general care and condition of our earth this in turn builds our individual human levels of respect and love. Since we have been provided with a magnificent world, we must respect what we have been given. Our earth is one that is self-sufficient in many ways working in conjunction with our moon and sun. These luminaries allow for the natural growth of life as we know it.

We are blessed with an earth that provides, in abundance, huge parcels of land for wildlife, farming and agriculture, along with an oceanic network of water that is full of life and naturally reoccurring energy, waves, the heartbeat of ocean. Just as we have been gifted vast natural forests scattered across the globe full of wildlife, plants and trees. These magnificent creations that we have named a tree are a glorious conception designed to provide a home for some, food for others and play a major role in the existence of all by helping to absorb carbon dioxide, while producing clean oxygen so that all creatures great and small can have the clean air they require. Now is the time for humans to give love back to our earth.

Simple tasks such as disposing of your rubbish correctly is something we can all commit to. There are still too many people who think only of themselves and not the planet around them, discarding litter on the ground that flows through to the waterways and out into our oceans. Let us all make an immediate difference by making a conscious decision to show the earth that we care by helping to clean up the mess that has been created. If you see waste left behind, be the one to make a difference and keep it out of our oceans and waterways.

There are many other ways that we can care for our earth, such as planting a tree or composting your vegetable waste. There are those who can harness the use of green power, reducing our fossil fuel intake, while taking advantage of the abundance of energy provided for free by our sun. If the region you reside in limits your access to certain natural resources, then think of other ways you can show our earth that you care. As the dominant species, we need to ensure that we are leading the way by taking better care of our precious planet. Share what you do with your family and friends and be the positive change by inspiring the people around you.

Step 8 – Help other people

One of the essential tasks for humans to complete on this earth is to help other people. Many people will help a family member or friend if they are in need by providing some form of support and kindness without hesitation by giving what they can without expectation. This is an impressive gesture since you are helping to improve that individual's life experience.

However, one of the most powerful actions you can take is to help a stranger. Undertaking this kind of gesture is a significant weight shifter in recalibrating your Scales of Life, rebalancing the scales into a more favourable position for you.

This effort, when gifted by you will not go unnoticed nor unrewarded.

There are many ways to help a stranger. You can achieve this by simply lending an ear in conversation, gifting some food, your time or some money. Even the simple act of acknowledging someone is soul replenishing.

If you walk past someone begging in the street asking you for money and you have none to give at that very moment, instead of just ignoring them and turning away, turn to them, make eye contact with them and say, 'Sorry, I can't help you today.' This simple acknowledgment is a powerful gift.

This action replenishes their internal spirit while reinvigorating yours also.

You are reminding them that they are human too, that you can see them, and they are not invisible. They are equal and worthy, too. We all bleed the same; we are all connected.

Step 9 – Open your mind

Step nine focuses on expanding your awareness beyond the realms of what you have been told to believe and what you have learnt your limitations to be. So, you may begin to reimagine how your life on this earth is meant to be.

This includes allowing yourself to become a participant in life as a connected spiritual being, using your vibrational guide to assist you in the calibration of your life journey and your celestial support team and trusting in your divine connection.

As you move through your life now from this new plateau, you will seize the power of your mind to master how you feel, to create your own identity and destiny, allowing you to experience divine love like you have never felt before. Be open to receiving all the messages and signs from the universe as they flow to you and through you.

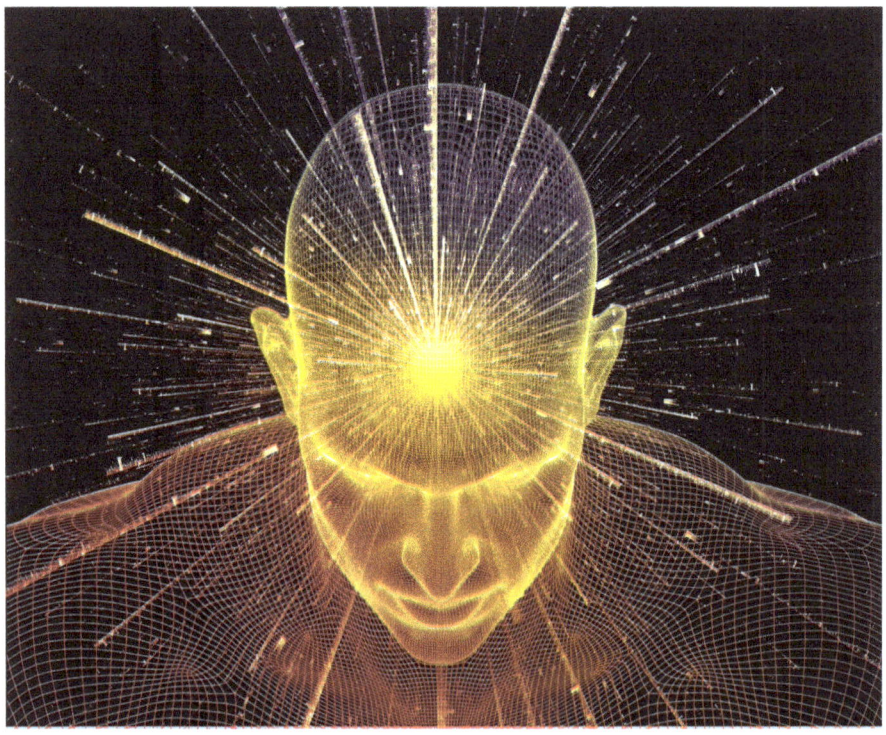

Know that you are worthy, so that you too can become all that you can be. Step nine is about forgetting your fears associated with religion and allow yourself to believe that there is a God, that there is a Creator, a Chief Conductor who loves you unconditionally, only wanting you to discover his divine love, guidance and friendship.

Since you are allowing this divine wisdom to flow through you, you are now spiritually open and ready to receive. Inquisitively ask questions through your divine connection to feel the answers. By doing this, you are using the power of your spirit guide and connecting with the universe.

Explore your Vibrational Alignment.

Your spirit is now free, your soul is unchained and your connection is now re-established. Bask in the glory as you revel in the feelings of love, warmth, of pleasure and peace, calmness and ONENESS. This is a special moment for you. Enjoy your moment; this is your new beginning.

This is all for you.

Step 10 – Create your daily routine

Introducing a daily routine is a vital tool to calibrate your alignment. Attuning and achieving Vibrational Alignment is a task that you will find easiest to reach first thing in the morning once you have woken up for the day, connecting with your highest self, with all that is, was and will be.

Following these key elements will help you to connect on a number of levels:

- Eliminating or reducing the amount of outside noise before you connect (news consumption)

- Reconnecting with all that is, is achieved with ease when your mind is at its quietest

- Dealing with daily tasks in alignment is a lot easier than being out of alignment and trying to move through your day

- Gifting yourself *Me Time* each day is perfectly fine – you are allowed to feel good

- Establishing your connection in the morning. This will allow your ideas and inspirations to flow throughout the day

- During the day, if you require, restart your day by repeating your *Me Time* routine. Use this as an 'on-the-run' recalibration tool

Remember what it is that you have achieved throughout your entire journey and the changes you have made. Know that you will not always be in full alignment, but understand that you will recognise what it feels like when you slip outside, so you can give yourself the *Me Time* required to recalibrate yourself back in. You can always restart your day, no matter where you are.

You know the words to say and the steps to follow so that you can enjoy your alignment. As a practicing student of life, you will uncover new ways to realign your three universal centres with ease. When you achieve this, you will allow yourself the opportunity to live your daily life experience in a world where your ideas and inspirations flow to you freely from the portal of creation while you remain connected with your higher being.

You may revel in all the positive intentions and enjoyment that were always planned for you, allowing you to become all that you originally set out to be.

Remember these steps once you have completed them

Controlling negative thoughts

As I detailed in chapter nine, controlling our negative thoughts is a skill that we should all work towards conquering. Learning to identify by becoming aware of any negative thoughts as they creep inside the mind is a powerful start. Branching out from this position by retaining processes that can allow us, as individuals, to put a stop to these negative thoughts as they enter our mind is the next level of controlling how we feel. Often these negative thoughts manifest into negative feelings, feelings that can then lead to a myriad of exacerbated emotions such as sadness, desperation, loneliness and worthlessness.

Once these feelings are activated, they can then trigger your addictive behaviour or cravings for whatever it is that you are battling against.

Gaining control of these negative thoughts can be achieved in a variety of ways. A simple, low cost but very effective method that we have already discussed is utilising a circuit breaker. This tool is no joke, as long as you are committed to the cause.

'What cause is that?' you might ask.

The cause is your own personal happiness. Surely, we can all be committed to this cause.

Wearing something as simple as a hair tie on our wrist is something that we can all do. Even if you feel like you don't need to wear one, maybe someone close to you does and by you wearing one, you will inspire them. This inadvertently shows that person that you support them and are conscious of the mental challenges that they're going through. Remember, we all have the power to positively influence those in our vicinity.

I recall the story of a young teen who was in desperate need of care and support. The teenager had already experienced more than their fair share of trauma in their early life. Having reached a troubling level of despair, something was needed to provide a new option. Conventional ways had not worked. Taking a giant leap of faith, this powerful tool was introduced. Initially, there was some resistance from the young teen until their older sibling stated that they too would wear the circuit breaker in a show of solidarity. Instantly, with that offering of support, the younger sibling agreed to wear their circuit breaker too. With the circuit breaker now on, the positive effects were immediate as the young teen took advantage of their very own Secret Mind Control Weapon.

A circuit breaker can assist with overcoming:

- Anxiety
- Anger
- Sadness
- Depression
- Addiction and cravings

Controlling our thoughts naturally, even by using our own breathing, body or movements to assist in the process, is a lot more beneficial for our mental state of mind and wellbeing as opposed to using and relying on artificial substances.

Remember, it is not selfish to want to feel good. To put yourself first so that you are calibrated and aligned ensures that you are then in the pole position to be able to help those around you.

This includes your immediate family; you need to ensure that you feel good first. If you don't feel good and are not in control of how you feel, then how can you be a positive influence in their lives?

Even if someone close to you is currently living in a complete state of despair, just knowing this would sadden most human beings. However, we cannot live out our life existence in the low energy realms of sadness simply based on the other person's reality. To do this would only breed more sadness and amplify the adverse emotions, along with potentially manifesting a greater negative result.

To combat this situation, we need to become the beacon of hope, a radiating beacon of love. By offering our uplifting frequency on a higher vibrational level, we will raise the vibration of those around us. We can easily achieve this through the eternal power of divine love, which allows us to elevate our spiritual consciousness into the higher realms so that we may then be of value to all those that we are in contact with.

If we refuse to shift out of the lower frequency fields, then we are handing over control of how we feel to an external source. We disband from our true selves and simply become a reflection of the witnessed actions and emotions around us. This is not a constructive position to be in.

Remember YOU control how you feel – and YOU can choose to feel GOOD!!

Thought clouds

Another successful method to assist in the controlling of negative thought is through the utilisation of thought clouds. This method can be considered quite advanced; therefore, this requires some practice and patience from you. Once you understand the process, you can use this tool regularly throughout your day. The thought cloud meditation is next level and an extremely powerful gift once you allow yourself to be part of the process. Thought clouds are not only used for controlling negative thought but they can also be used for inspiration too.

Understanding that your thoughts are separate from your mind and your physical self is the first step. Since you are a spirit having a physical experience, your spiritual entity is the controlling force rather than your physical shell or any thought. Your thoughts simply flow into your mind just like clouds float through the sky.

When you understand this, you can begin to unleash your unlimited potential, since the only restrictions are the physical limitations, restraints and beliefs that we place on ourselves.

Once you truly believe that your spirit is your controlling entity, then you can begin to acknowledge that your thoughts are separate from your mind. Your mind is separate from your spirit and thoughts so is your physical body. Hence the three universal elements of body, mind and spirit.

By achieving this level of awareness, you really can take control of your thoughts.

An introduction to a thought cloud process for you

As part of this introduction, I will share with you a process to uncover your thought clouds. In the beginning, you will visualise yourself in a location that naturally calms you.

Firstly, find yourself a quiet space and focus on your breathing.

You will need a clear mind, which you can achieve by simply using your breath. As you breathe in, allow your belly to expand, and your lungs fill with air. By expanding your stomach with your inhaled breath, this will bring the air deep into your lungs, using your lungs to their full capacity as they were originally intended.

Then as you exhale, your stomach will naturally deflate. Breathing in such a manner is most likely the opposite of how you normally breathe, since many people naturally breathe very short and shallow. Ensure that your chest does not rise at all. Your breathing should all be done from your belly, expanding and deflating. Calmly repeat this belly breathing process five times. You should naturally feel your mind become quieter after these five repetitions.

As you remain focused on your breathing, close your eyes and picture yourself sitting on the warm golden sand of a beautiful beach, on a remote island somewhere out in the middle of the ocean. You are the only person on this beach.

Feel the warm sand between your toes, feel the crunchiness of the sand beneath your feet. Feel the calmness of the environment you are in. Listen to sound of the waves as they gently crash against the shoreline. Feel the heat radiating from the sun high above you. As the sun rays hit your skin, notice the warming up of your face and body. Smell the fresh ocean air and feel the gentle breeze as the air connects with your skin. Revel in the tranquillity of this tropical paradise.

Notice that the only noise you can hear is the noise from the ocean as the waves roll in. You are sitting alone, barefooted on the warm golden sand with the heat of the sun penetrating your skin as you sit there watching the crystal-clear waves roll in one by one.

Allow yourself to be completely in this moment, directly engaged with your world. This connection with your earth starts with the sand you can feel under your feet activating your touch sensory receptors. Your visual receptors are activated as you watch the waves roll in; your smell sensors become alive as you smell the fresh air of the ocean while your hearing is engaged as you listen to the waves and finally, your taste receptors become alive as the sea salt hits your lips.

Tilt your head backwards so you can look into the clear blue sky above you. Notice how there is not a single cloud in your perfect blue sky. Even as you turn your head left and right, notice how the sky is bereft of clouds, for the clear blue sky is all you can see.

As you continue looking above, I want you to see a single cloud form in your sky. I want you to place a single word inside this white cloud. This word can be anything for you. Label this cloud a feeling, a name or something that is on your mind.

As you sit on your beach, staring at your cloud, feeling so connected, you are now beginning to understand that your thought is just an individual cloud floating though the sky that is your mind. While you are seated on the sand, reach up with one of your hands to push that cloud out of your vision. Recognise the shift in your mind as that thought leaves you.

Notice as other clouds begin to appear, each cloud labelled with an individual thought filling your sky. Notice how as you think of an individual thought you can see that thought cloud pass through your vision with the attached label.

Play with your thought clouds. If you have a subject that is upsetting you, picture the subject title or the associated emotion as a word in a thought cloud, then just as before, use your physical hand to push that thought cloud from the vicinity of your mind. Feel the shift as that thought cloud leaves you.

You are now using the power of your mind to separate yourself from your thoughts and physical self since you understand that your thoughts are just clouds floating in the sky that you can easily push away when you no longer want to be influenced by that feeling, action or memory. You are now in control of your thoughts. Explore this process and push through the thought clouds as you see fit.

Remember to feel your body shift as the thought and the associated feeling leaves you.

We can all control our thoughts and what it is that we become.

Final words

As we approach the end of this final chapter, I want you to know that you are number one!

Taking control of how you feel is the most important thing you can do for yourself.

Once you believe in this and live your life as number one, it is from this space that you can really help the people around you – not just including your family and friends but also playing a positive role in a stranger's life. This is one of the most important tasks that we are all here to do.

With you as number one and because of your love for yourself, you are now able to positively contribute towards other people's experiences, since you are coming from that special place of love, internal peace and acceptance.

With divine love, we can all be guided, supported and healed.

Remember, we are all spiritual beings. We are a spirit in a body not a body with a spirit. Our spirit is our controlling entity; our spirit is infinite.

Once you discover your divine connection, your world becomes truly amazing.

I trust that this has been as much of a memorable experience for you as this has been for me.

Please enjoy this final gift, the words of my new song *Humble*, received from the perspective of our Divine Creator. Would we accept him, would we stand by him, would we let him into our lives, would we let him be our friend?

Song title: **Humble**

If I could be humble, would you stand there with me?
If I could be humble, would you be taken with me?
If I could just stand there, and let you see me as you are,
Would you be humble, or would you take it too far?

If I could stand there and be with you by your side,
Would you let me be there, be there as you cry?
If I could be humble, if you could be true,
If I could be humble, would you let me be there… with you,

As we come together,
And we join as one,
As we come together,
We know what we become,

If I could be humble, would you stand there with me?
If I could be humble, would you be all you could be?
If I could be humble now, would catch me standing there?
Would you see me, would you dance like you don't care?

If I could be humble,
Could I be the one?
Could I be the one to hold your hand when all is done?
I'm asking if I could be humble,
Would you say this prayer?
If I could be humble,
Would you let me hold your hand?

If I could be humble now,
Would you want me there in the end?
As you take your last breath,
Would you let me be your friend?
If I could be humble,
If I could be humble now,
Would you let me hold your hand?
If I could be humble,
Could I be your man?
Could I be the one?
Could I be your one?
If I can be humble.

Would you let me stand there with you and be your friend?
Would you let me hold your hand until the end?
On your last day here, would you let me come next to you?
I could guide you wherever you needed me to,
If I could be humble,
If I could be your friend,
If I could be humble,
I stay with you, till the end.

If I could be humble,
If I could be free,
If I could be everything you needed me to be,
I can be the one,
I can be your one,
I can be the one,
I can be your one,
If I can be humble.

www.ingramcontent.com/pod-product-compliance
Lightning Source LLC
Chambersburg PA
CBHW061215070526
44584CB00029B/3846